ECONOMICS

A Self-Teaching Guide

Stephen L. Slavin

WILEY

John Wiley & Sons, Inc.

New York • Chichester • Brisbane • Toronto • Singapore

Publisher: Stephen Kippur
Editor: Katherine Schowalter
Managing Editor: Andrew Hoffer
Editing, Design, and Production: Publication Services

Library of Congress Cataloging-in-Publication Data

Slavin, Stephen L.
  Ecomonics: a self-teaching guide.
    1. Economics.   2. United States–Economic conditions.

I. Title
HB171.5.S6275   1988   330   87-29426
ISBN 0-471-62917-0

Printed in the United States of America

88 89 10 9 8 7 6 5 4 3 2

OTHER SELF-TEACHING GUIDES FROM WILEY

To the Reader

Like most other economics textbook authors, I will discuss both macroeconomics and microeconomics in this self-teaching guide. But this book differs from all those others in one very important way: It does not assume that you have a profound understanding of mathematics or of graphs. If you can add, subtract, multiply, and divide, that's all the background you're going to need. I'll take it from there. In fact, I'll even grant you permission to use a calculator, provided, of course, you feel at least some guilt.

This book is organized by chapter into numbered sections called frames, each one presents new material. There are also periodic self-tests throughout each chapter. Their purpose is to make sure you comprehend material before moving on. If you find that you have made an error, look back at the preceding material to make sure you understand the correct answer. Frames and self-tests are arranged so that they build on one another. To fully understand frames at the end of a section, you must first have completed all of the preceding frames.

In Part One I'll provide you with the tools you'll need to tackle economics. First, I'll place it in the historical context of the last seventy years. Then, together we will do the preliminary work in mathematics and graphical analysis.

In Part Two I'll introduce you to macroeconomics, which deals with huge aggregates like gross national product. I'll explain the four economic resources— land, labor, capital, and entrepreneurial ability—and the three key economic players—the consumer, the business firm, and the government. Then, we'll look at the two main problems that have beset our economy for generations: inflation and unemployment.

In Part Three we'll discuss various economic policies aimed at dealing with inflation and unemployment, particularly fiscal and monetary policy. I'll end this section by presenting the five main twentieth century schools of economic thought: classical, Keynesian, monetarist, supply-side, and rational expectations.

In Part Four and Part Five we'll look at our economy from the perspective of the individual consumer and the business firm. This is known as microeconomics, because it focuses on prices, costs, and output.

Demand and supply will be our primary concern in Part Four. When you finish this section you will be drawing graphs of supply and demand curves and deriving price and output for individual business firms and for entire industries.

Finally, in Part Five we'll discuss the four theoretical models of competition—perfect competition, monopoly, monopolistic competition, and oligopoly. We will find out, among other things, why some firms are more efficient, more profitable, or have less competition than others.

By the time you finish this book, you will have a basic understanding of how the American economy operates, and you can gain this understanding by yourself, if you wish, without taking a formal course in economics. You might even decide that economics isn't all that difficult and that you would like to continue in this field of study.

Contents

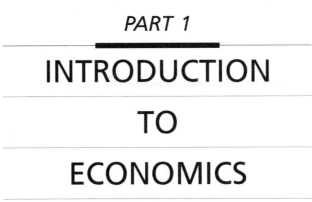

PART 1

INTRODUCTION
TO
ECONOMICS

CHAPTER 1

The American

Economy Since

World War I

To understand the principles of economics and how the American economy works, it is necessary to put things into their historical context. After reading this chapter you will be familiar with:

- The economic trends of the last seven decades.
- The major factors that contributed to America's rise to a preeminent position in the world economy after World War II.
- The factors contributing to our relative decline in the 1970s and 1980s.

As George Santayana said, "those who cannot remember the past are condemned to repeat it." It is not known today exactly what the great philosopher meant by this. The most common interpretation is that those who do not learn from the mistakes of the past will repeat those mistakes. Another interpretation is that those who do not learn enough history the first time around will be required to repeat History 101. Is history required to understand economics?

Obviously, it must be or I wouldn't have bothered writing this chapter. After all, economics does not occur in a vacuum. By placing the economic events of the last seven decades in a historical context, we will be able to make better sense of the economic theories and policies that have such a profound impact on our lives.

1 | THE 1920s THROUGH WORLD WAR II

The United States, believe it or not, is the world's number one economic power. In terms of total output of goods and services, we turn out more than Japan, the Soviet Union, China, and every other nation. True, the Japanese and the South Koreans are gaining on us. True, the United Arab Emirates, Kuwait, Switzerland, and possibly one or two other countries have a slightly higher standard of living (or output per person). But we are so far ahead in total output that we produce about double what Japan does, and they're number two.

What made us number one? There are a lot of explanations—an endowment of natural resources, a free enterprise economic system, American ingenuity, a huge nationwide market, geographic isolation, immigration, a class-free society, to mention a few of the more prominent theories. Which one is right? Perhaps all of them, as well as a few that weren't mentioned.

We became number one early in the twentieth century, we're not sure exactly when, because no one kept statistics in those early days. In the 1920s the era of mass consumption began. For example, in 1920 there were fewer than 100,000 cars on the road; by 1929 there were close to 25 million. Electricity, telephones, appliances, and indoor plumbing became commonplace during the 1920s. The outlook was one of almost unbridled optimism. Suddenly, all things were possible. Economic growth was rapid, unemployment low, and inflation nonexistent.

Of course, the optimism of the 1920s was reflected in, and in turn influenced, the soaring stock market. Although less than 10 percent of all Americans owned stock, it was possible for people to quickly become millionaires. When the crash finally came in late 1929, those fortunes were wiped out, and the entire financial structure of the country collapsed like a house of cards.

2   And so the prosperity of the 1920s gave way to a decade of economic depression. Between 1929 and 1933 both prices and national output were cut in half. (This decline, as well as the rest of our economic history since World War I can be seen on the graph in Figure 1.1.) By 1933 more than one-quarter of the U.S. labor force was unemployed. President Roosevelt's New Deal economic program got things moving again, but we didn't really recover from the depression until the early years of World War II.

The New Deal was an extremely important economic event though, because it set the precedent for federal government economic intervention. Never again

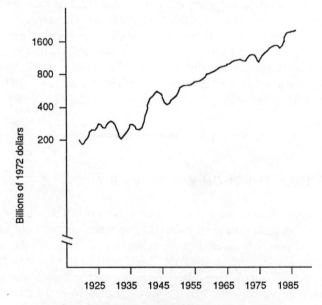

Figure 1.1 Real GNP of the United States, 1920–1986.
Sources: U.S. Department of Commerce, *The National Income and Product Accounts of the United States, 1929–1974; 1987 Economic Report of the President*

could the government ignore widespread unemployment, as the Hoover administration (1929–1933) did in the hopes that the economy would automatically bounce back. Also, during the Roosevelt years, a whole structure of safeguards was put in place to ensure that future economic downturns would not turn into depressions.

The New Deal is best summarized by the three Rs: relief, recovery, and reform. Relief was aimed at alleviating the suffering of a nation that was, in President Roosevelt's words, one-third "Ill-fed, ill-clothed, and ill-housed." These people needed work relief, a system similar to today's workfare (work for your welfare check) programs. An average of about six million people were put to work at various jobs ranging from raking leaves and repairing public buildings to maintaining national parks and building power dams. Robert B. Russell made this observation:

> The principal objects of work-relief were to help people preserve their self-respect by enabling them to stay off the dole and to maintain their work habits against the day when they could again find employment in private enterprises. It was also hoped that the programs, by putting some purchasing power into the hands of workers and suppliers of materials, would help prime the economic pump. (Robert R. Russell, *A History of the American Economic System* (New York: Appleton-Century-Crofts, 1964), page 547.)

The government hoped that all of this spending would bring about economic recovery, but the most lasting effect of the New Deal was reform. The Securities and Exchange Commission (SEC) was set up to regulate the stock market and avoid a repetition of the speculative excesses of the late 1920s, which had led to the great crash of 1929. After the reform, bank deposits were insured by the Federal Deposit Insurance Corporation (FDIC) to prevent future runs on the banks by depositors, like those experienced in the early 1930s. Also, an unemployment insurance benefit program was set up to provide temporarily unemployed people with some money to tide them over. The most important reform of all was the creation of Social Security. Although even today retired people need more than their Social Security benefits to get by, there is no question that this program has provided tens of millions of retired people with a substantial income and has largely removed the workers' fear of being destitute and dependent in their old age.

What was it that got us out of the depression? It was the massive government spending during World War II. That was exactly what the doctor, John Maynard Keynes, had ordered. Writing during the early years of the depression, Keynes had called for massive government spending to buy all the goods and services that the economy could produce. If there's no demand for a seller's product, reasoned Keynes, why would the seller produce anything? We'll discuss Keynesian economics more fully in Chapters 10 and 11.

You may ask, then, why the New Deal alone failed to get us completely out of the depression. After all, didn't all those alphabet agencies—the PWA (Public Works Administration), the WPA (Works Progress Administration), the CCC (Civilian Conservation Corps), and the like—spend a lot of money and put a lot of people to work? Yes, they did spend billions of dollars and put millions of people to work. But they didn't spend enough. Then, in 1937, before the economy was completely back on its feet, spending was cut back. And the

Federal Reserve picked that year to drastically slow the rate of growth of the money supply, which meant there was a lot less money available to business borrowers to finance new plant, equipment, and inventory.

Self-Test 1

1. What finally got us out of the depression?
   A. The New Deal.
   B. The Federal Reserve.
   C. It ended by itself.
   D. World War II.

2. The world's number one economic power, in terms of total output, is
   _____ .

3. In what decade did the era of mass consumption begin in the United States?

4. At the low point of the depression, about what fraction of the U.S. labor force was officially unemployed?

5. John Maynard Keynes believed that the way to cure depressions was for the government to _____ .

6. Which statement about the New Deal is true?
   A. It failed because it didn't spend enough.
   B. It failed because it spent too much.
   C. It succeeded in ending the depression.
   D. It made the depression worse.

Answers to Self-Test 1

1. D.
2. The United States.
3. The 1920s.
4. One-quarter.
5. Spend money.
6. A.

3 | THE POST-WAR PERIOD

The New Deal was the precursor of a succession of Keynesian spending programs. Until the 1930s, the federal government had generally played a relatively inconspicuous economic role—a policy known as *laissez-faire*. That's French for "leave alone" or "hands off." Under such a policy, the government does not interfere with private enterprise.

But when private enterprise fell apart in the early 1930s, the American people demanded that the government intervene, and this marked the end of the laissez-faire policy. Later on, Harry Truman, who succeeded Roosevelt, inaugurated the Fair Deal, which we'll discuss in a moment. This was followed, some eight years later, by John Kennedy's New Frontier and finally by Lyndon Johnson's Great Society program. Each of these programs—including the New Deal—spent a lot of money to try to solve the nation's social and economic problems.

Republican critics of these programs, particularly President Reagan and his supporters in recent years, have described them as nothing more than throwing money at problems.

In Table 1.1 we have summarized the main economic events since 1929. Of particular interest are the government programs, beginning with the New Deal, aimed at stimulating the economy and at solving such persistent problems as poverty and economic insecurity.

In April 1945 Franklin Roosevelt died suddenly, and Harry Truman became president. After concluding the war, Truman turned to domestic economic problems. At that time many Americans feared that the economy would sink back into depression, now that the economic stimulus of wartime spending was over. Truman's response was the Fair Deal.

The Fair Deal not only protected the basic New Deal programs, but extended them as well. Both Social Security and unemployment insurance were extended to cover millions of additional people. No new programs of this sort were enacted during Truman's nearly two terms in office; but by the time the Republicans took over in 1953, big government was a permanent part of American society.

Let's go back to 1945, when the war finally ended. Within a year, 12 million men were discharged and returned to their families. Since very few houses had been built during the war and the preceding depression, most veterans lived with their wives in overcrowded apartments, often sharing them with parents or in-laws. The first thing they wanted was new housing.

The federal government obligingly provided this housing by giving returning veterans VA (Veteran's Administration) mortgages at about 1 percent interest and often nothing down. The Federal Housing Administration (FHA) supplemented this program with FHA mortgages to millions of other Americans. Where were these houses built? In the suburbs. By 1945 there was little available land in the cities, so suburbanization was inevitable.

And how would these new suburbanites get to work? By car. But more highways were needed. Once again, the federal government stepped in. Before

Table 1.1. Summary of Main Economic Events Since 1929

Term of Office	President	Main Economic Events
1933-1945	Franklin Roosevelt	Great Depression (1929-1941), New Deal (1933-1941), World War II (1941-1945)
1945-1953	Harry Truman	Recessions (1945; 1948-1949), Fair Deal (1945-1953), Korean War (1950-1953)
1953-1961	Dwight Eisenhower	Recessions (1953-1954; 1957-1958; 1960-1961)
1961-1963	John Kennedy	New Frontier (1961-1963)
1963-1969	Lyndon Johnson	Great Society (1964-1968), Vietnamese War escalation (1965-1968)
1969-1974	Richard Nixon	Vietnamese War, Recessions (1969-1970; 1974-1975)
1974-1977	Gerald Ford	Recession (1974-1975)
1977-1981	Jimmy Carter	Recession (1980)
1981-1988	Ronald Reagan	Recession (1981-1982), Tax cut (1981-1983), Tax reform (1987, 1988)

President Eisenhower left office in January 1961, the interstate highway network was completed.

So, the late 1940s and the 1950s were one big construction boom. Highway building and home construction provided millions of jobs. The automobile industry, too, was prospering after a total shutdown during the war. In the postwar era, we not only supplied all the new suburbanites with cars, but we also became the world's leading auto exporter. The industrial plants of West Germany and Japan had been destroyed or damaged during the war; it wasn't until the mid-1960s that those nations reentered the world market, and it took them another decade to capture more than 10 percent of the American car market.

The returning veterans, like the nation, had a lot of catching up to do. Couples had been forced to put off having children, but after the war the birth rate shot up and stayed very high until the mid-1960s. This baby boom and low gasoline prices gave added impetus to the nation's suburbanization. Why continue to live in cramped quarters when a house in the suburbs was easily affordable?—as it was to most middle-class and working-class Americans.

The economy was further stimulated by the advent of television in the early 1950s, as well as by the Korean War, which broke out in mid-1950. It didn't really matter what individual consumers or the government spent their money on, as long as they spent it on something. That had been the message of John Maynard Keynes, and apparently America had learned it well.

Immediately after World War II, however, the problem of inflation appeared. The government had removed wartime price controls, and prices had risen by 35 percent in three years. Fueled by a rapidly expanding money supply and the pent-up purchasing power of consumers, who had been unable to buy many goods and services during the war, inflation was not brought under control until 1949. Then the outbreak of the Korean War brought with it another surge of inflation as people scrambled to buy television sets and other appliances that they thought might become scarce if the war widened. By the late 1950s, a mixture of tight federal budgets and low monetary growth brought inflation once again under control.

In 1960 John F. Kennedy was elected president. There was a New Frontier to be crossed, but, like Moses, Kennedy was permitted to glimpse this promised land only from afar. Although his administration did attain such memorable achievements as the Peace Corps, its most important contribution to the economy was to set the table for the Great Society program that would be carried forward by President Lyndon Johnson. In terms of money spent, three Great Society programs, all initiated in 1965 under Johnson, have had the most profound long-term effect on the economy: Medicare, Medicaid, and food stamps.

Nevertheless, during the terms of John Kennedy and Lyndon Johnson, the economic expansion continued. In fact, the 1960s was a time of almost uninterrupted economic expansion. A major tax cut in 1964 and our involvement in the Vietnamese War stimulated the economy and brought down the unemployment rate below 4 percent. But late in the decade we had another bout of inflation that would not be wrung out of the economy until the early 1980s.

Three important things affected the economy during the 1960s: (1) a high level of military spending in Vietnam, (2) the war on poverty, and (3) a slowing of suburbanization. The latter came about mainly because of the end of the baby boom in the mid-1960s. The first two are examples of the expanded economic role of the federal government since the time of President Franklin Roosevelt. Not until 1981, when Ronald Reagan took office, would any serious effort be made to reverse this trend.

Self-Test 2

1. What two main things did returning veterans want to buy after World War II?
   _____

2. The federal government facilitated suburbanization by providing _____ and _____ .

3. Japan did not lead the world in automobile production in the 1950s because _____ .

4. In the early 1950s the two new factors that stimulated our economy were _____ and _____ .

5. In the 1960s the two new factors that stimulated the economy were _____ and _____ .

6. When did the federal government abandon its laissez-faire policy? _____

Answers to Self-Test 2

1. Cars and houses.
2. Low-cost, easy-term mortgages; highways.
3. Japan's industrial plant had been destroyed during World War II.
4. The Korean War; the advent of television.
5. The Vietnamese War; the tax cut of 1964.
6. In the 1930s.

4 | THE 1970s AND THE 1980s

The 1970s brought Americans crashing back to economic reality. In 1974 we were hit by the worst recession in over thirty years. This came on the heels of an oil price shock: The Organization of Petroleum Exporting Countries (OPEC) had quadrupled oil prices in the fall of 1973, and by then, too, we were mired in double-digit inflation, an annual rate of increase in prices of at least 10 percent. About the only good thing during this period was that we were able to add a new word to our vocabularies—STAGFLATION. The first part of this word is derived from stagnation. Our rate of economic growth, which had been fairly rapid for twenty-five years after World War II, had slowed to a crawl. Usually when this happened, prices would stop rising, or at least would slow their rate of increase. But now the opposite had happened: we had a bad case of inflation, which gave us the second part of the word *stagflation*.

The 1970s and early 1980s were a period of economic stagflation. But President Nixon, who had other things to worry about, like being impeached, was unwilling or unable to get our economy back on course. His successor,

Gerald Ford, also seemed reluctant to make any bold economic moves, but he was at least able to point to a slowing inflation rate.

The president who seemed to have the worst economic luck of all was Jimmy Carter. The mounting budget deficits that he presided over, coupled with a rapid growth of the money supply, had pushed up the inflation rate to nearly double-digit levels. And then suddenly, in 1979, the Iranian revolution set off our second oil shock. Gasoline prices went through the ceiling, rising from about 70 cents a gallon to $1.25 in June and July of that year.

Alarmed at the inflation rate, which had nearly doubled in just three years, the Federal Reserve literally stopped the growth of the money supply in October 1979. By the following January we were in another recession, while the annual rate of inflation reached 18 percent. Talk about stagflation!

Still another disturbing development was a slowing of our nation's productivity growth, or output per hour worked. By the late 1970s it had slowed to only 1 percent, just about one-third its postwar rate. Until we found a way to boost our productivity, our economy would continue to stagnate.

Ronald Reagan, who overwhelmingly defeated President Carter in 1980, offered the answers to our most pressing economic problems. For too long, he declared, we had allowed the federal government to "tax, tax, tax, spend, spend, spend." Big government was not the answer to our problems. Only private enterprise could provide meaningful jobs and spur economic growth. If we cut tax rates, said Reagan, people would have more incentive to work, output would rise, and inflation would subside. After all, if inflation meant that too many dollars were chasing too few goods, why not produce more goods?

This brand of economics, supply-side economics, was really the flip side of Keynesian economics. Both had the same objective: to stimulate output, or supply. The Keynesians thought the way to do this was to have the government spend more money, which, in turn, would give business firms the incentive to produce more output. The supply-siders said that if tax rates were cut, people would have more of an incentive to work and would increase output.

In January 1981 it was Ronald Reagan's ball game to win or lose. At first he seemed to be losing. He presided over still another recession, which, by the time it ended, was the new postwar record-holder, at least in the length and depth categories. The second worst recession since World War II had been that of 1973–1975. But the 1981–1982 recession was a little longer and somewhat worse.

By the end of 1982 the unemployment rate reached nearly 11 percent, a rate that had not been seen since the end of the depression. But on the up side, inflation was finally brought under control. In fact, both the inflation and unemployment rates fell during the next four years, and stagflation, at least through the late 1980s, was a thing of the past.

Still, there were some very troubling economic problems during the period. The unemployment rate, which had come down substantially since the end of the 1981–1982 recession, seemed stuck at around 6 percent, a rate that most economists consider to be unacceptably high. A second cause for concern was the megadeficits being run by the federal government year after year. And finally, there were the foreign trade deficits, which were getting progressively larger in the mid-1980s.

These problems will be with us as we enter the last decade of the century. Inflation, recessions, unemployment, and budget and trade deficits are just not going to go away, no matter how much we want them to. Budget deficits occur when the government spends more money than it raises in taxes. We'll cover this more thoroughly in Chapter 9. And so, even as we look back at our past mistakes and try to avoid repeating them, we can also look forward to making new ones. And as we'll see, that is part of what economics is all about. In fact, economists are better than anyone else at giving cogent explanations as to why their predictions always seem to be wrong.

When you have completed this book, you will have had a guided tour of the economic mistakes of the past. You will also have a better idea of how to predict the economic future and avoid repeating these mistakes. Although you won't yet qualify for membership on the President's Council of Economic Advisors, you will definitely be a certifiable armchair economic quarterback.

Self-Test 3

1. In what year did the worst recession since World War II occur? _____
2. What is stagflation? _____
3. When was the inflation that started in the late 1960s finally brought under control? _____
4. What three major economic problems did we face in the late 1980s?
   _____
5. Ronald Reagan and the supply-siders had one key economic proposal in 1980, which was to _____ .
6. The Keynesians said the government could raise output by
   _____ .

Answers to Self-Test 3

1. 1981 (to 1982).
2. A combination of inflation and economic stagnation.
3. 1982 or 1983.
4. High unemployment, high federal budget deficits, and high trade deficits.
5. Cut taxes.
6. Increasing (government) spending.

CHAPTER 2

Understanding and

Manipulating

Numbers

You will need to do some simple arithmetic operations to get through any introductory economics text, but I'm not going to ask you to do anything harder than what you had in the eighth grade. In addition, you will need to understand figures in the millions, billions, and trillions, since numbers of these magnitudes are commonly used in economics.

After you have gone through this chapter, you will be able to:

- Deal with millions, billions, and trillions.
- Convert fractions into decimals.
- Calculate percentage changes.
- Work out percentage distributions.
- Deal with index numbers.
- Solve word problems.

---

1 | **WORKING WITH MILLIONS, BILLIONS, AND TRILLIONS**

Write out this number in words: 14,350,000,000,000.

Translate these words into a number with all the commas in their proper places: thirty-nine trillion, four hundred seventy-four billion.   *Go to frame 2.*

2   The answer to the first question is fourteen trillion, three hundred fifty billion. The answer to the second is 39,474,000,000,000.

If you answered these correctly, you may skip frame 3 and go directly to frame 4. But if you're not at ease with numbers of this magnitude, proceed to frame 3.

3   We'll start with millions. The number seven hundred ninety-two million is written as 792,000,000. The key thing to remember is that millions are followed by two sets of zeros, three zeros to a set. Now you try one: eight hundred fourteen million.

What did you come up with? It should be: 814,000,000.

Next we'll try billions. They have three sets of zeros. Write thirty-four billion.

It will look like this: 34,000,000,000. Now do five hundred sixty billion.

That would be 560,000,000,000.

Are you ready to add a new wrinkle? Write seven hundred nineteen billion, four hundred million.

The answer: 719,400,000,000.

Are you ready for trillions? Here you will need four sets of zeros. Ready or not, write six trillion.

What did you come up with? It should be 6,000,000,000,000. Six with four sets of zeros.

Now another one: nine hundred eighty-six trillion, five hundred billion.

The answer: 986,500,000,000,000.

Let's summarize:

- Fifty million: 50,000,000
- Fifty billion: 50,000,000,000
- Fifty trillion: 50,000,000,000,000

Remember that millions have two sets of zeros with three zeros in a set, billions have three sets of zeros, and trillions have four sets of zeros.

The prefixes can help you identify millions, billions, and trillions. The prefix *mil* or *mill* can mean one thousand or one million. *Bi,* as in bicycle, means two. *Tri,* as in tricycle, means three. In our lifetime, there probably won't be much use for the next two sets of numbers beyond trillions, but would you care to guess their names? Try quadrillions and quintillions.

I am assuming, by the way, that you are reading this book in the United States (or possibly in France). In Great Britain and Germany, one billion is one million millions (1,000,000,000,000), and one trillion is a 1 followed by eighteen zeros. This can be confusing, so be careful when doing business with the British and Germans.

Self-Test 1

Please express these numbers in words:

1. 4,378,500,000
2. 28,540,000,000,000
3. 735,000,000
4. 900,000,000,000,000
5. 1,375,000,000

Please translate these words into numbers:

6. Ninety-five trillion
7. Four hundred twenty-eight million
8. Eight trillion, two hundred billion
9. Five hundred fifty-two billion, three hundred four million
10. Sixteen trillion, seven hundred thirteen billion

Answers to Self-Test 1

1. Four billion, three hundred seventy-eight million, five hundred thousand
2. Twenty-eight trillion, five hundred and forty billion
3. Seven hundred thirty-five million
4. Nine-hundred trillion
5. One billion, three hundred seventy-five million
6. 95,000,000,000,000
7. 428,000,000
8. 8,200,000,000,000
9. 552,304,000,000
10. 16,713,000,000,000

4 | **CONVERTING FRACTIONS INTO DECIMALS**

We'll start with an easy one: 1/2. Go ahead and convert 1/2 into a decimal.
Go to frame 5 for the correct answer.

5   The answer is .5.
Now try this one on for size: Convert 2/3 into a decimal.
Go to frame 6 for the correct answer.

6   The answer is .667 or .67. You must round off your answer so that it ends in 7, since .6666666 ad infinitum (that's Latin for without limit, goes on forever.) is always more than what appears on the window of our calculators or on the top of our division problems. Correct answers would include .6666667, .666667, .66667, .6667, .667, .67, or .7. If you want to be accurate to two decimals, then .67 is the answer you're looking for.

If you got these last two problems right, either you know what you're doing and should go directly to frame 9 or you've just been lucky and should see if your luck holds through frame 9 and Self-Test 2.

Let's return to the first question: How did we get from the fraction 1/2 to the decimal .5 or .50? You can add any number of zeros to the right of a decimal without changing its value: .5 = .50 = .5000 = .50000. Think of this decimal, .50, as money. How many cents in a half-dollar? Fifty cents, or .50 of a dollar.

The problem in frame 5 requires a little more calculation. How can you get from 2/3 to .67? It's easy. You divide. Go ahead.

Did you get .67? If you did you are right. If you got 1.5, however, you made an understandable error: You divided the 2 into the 3. Now you'll have a chance to learn from your mistake.

Why did you divide 2 into 3? Because 2 is smaller than 3? Sounds reasonable. But you violated an important rule of arithmetic. Now don't feel too guilty. If you missed this one, you'll get lots of chances to make amends as you work through the rest of this section.

Always remember this simple rule: *When you convert a fraction into a decimal, always divide the bottom number into the top number.* Even if the top number is smaller? Yes, even if the top number is smaller.

Are you ready for the next problem? All right, then, here we go. Convert 2/5 into a decimal.   *Go to frame 7.*

7   You divide 5 into 2:

$$\frac{.40}{5\overline{)2.00}}$$

Let's do one more: convert 1/10 into a decimal.   *Go to frame 8.*

8   What did you get? How many times does ten cents go into a dollar? Ten times. How many times does a dollar go into ten cents?

$$1.00\overline{).1000} = \frac{.10}{100\overline{)10.00}}$$

When you divide decimals, you've got to be careful where you place those decimal points. When you're doing problems, you might find it helpful to estimate your answer before you do any calculations. We saw that 1/2 gave us .50. Now what about 1/10? Will that give us a bigger or a smaller answer?

$$1/2 = .50$$

$$1/10 = ?$$

Since we already worked it out and know the answer is .10, we can generalize: If you divide a number by larger and larger numbers, what happens to your answer, or quotient? It gets smaller! So, if you've already divided one by two and got .50, when you divide one by ten, you'll get a smaller number: .10.

As you work with decimals, you'll get used to them. Familiarity may breed contempt, but it also breeds more correct answers.

Self-Test 2

Please convert these fractions into decimals:

1. 2/7
2. 1/5
3. 3/8

Answers to Self-Test 2

1. $\dfrac{.29}{7\overline{)2.00}}$

2. $\dfrac{.20}{5\overline{)1.00}}$

3. $\dfrac{.375}{8\overline{)3.000}}$

9 | ## CONVERTING DECIMALS INTO PERCENTAGES

To convert a decimal into a percentage, move the decimal two places to the right and tack on a percentage sign.

Convert .50 into a percent.   *Go to frame 10.*

10 | The answer is 50 percent.

Let's add a new wrinkle: Convert .2 into a percent.   *Go to frame 11.*

11 | Remember that you are allowed to add zeros after a decimal. So you can make .2 into .20. From there we follow our rule of moving the decimal point two places to the right and tacking on a percentage sign: .2 = .20 = 20 percent (or 20%).

12 | ## CONVERTING FRACTIONS INTO PERCENTAGES

Let's put all of this together and convert fractions into percentages. Convert 1/4 into a percentage.   *Go to frame 13.*

13 | 1/4 = .25 = 25%

Let's try one more: Convert 3/5 into a percentage.   *Go to frame 14.*

14 | 3/5 = .60 = 60%

If you're having trouble converting fractions into percentages, go back to frame 4. It's very important in economics to be able to do these mathematical operations.

15 | ## THE NATURE OF PERCENTAGES

Take a look at the pie chart in Figure 2.1. Imagine that it is a silver dollar. How many cents in a dollar? One hundred. What is half of one hundred? Fifty.

Do you remember how to convert 1/2 into a percentage? Go ahead and do it.

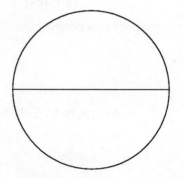

Figure 2.1

You should have gotten 50 percent. In other words, a half dollar is fifty cents. You may think of percentages as parts of a dollar.   *Go to frame 16.*

16   1/4 = .25 = 25%. This is shown in the pie chart in Figure 2.2.
A percentage is a part of 100 or 100 percent. Since the dollar is so familiar, we can think of any percentage as a part of a dollar.   *Go to frame 17.*

17   ## PERCENTAGE PROBLEMS

We're going to go over three types of percentage problems in the next eleven frames. First, what percentage of 50 is 10?   *Go to frame 18.*

18   Convert the problem into fraction form: 10/50, which can be reduced to 1/5 = .20 = 20 percent.
If you got this right, go to frame 2.21; otherwise, go to frame 19.

19   What percentage of 40 is 15?   *Go to frame 20.*

20   15/40 = 3/8 = .375 = 37.5%. If you are having trouble with division and other arithmetic operations, you would be helped by *Quick Arithmetic,* by Robert A. Carman and Marilyn J. Carmen (New York: John Wiley, 1984). *Go to frame 21.*

21   Now we're ready for the second type of percentage problem: What is 20 percent of 50?   *Go to frame 22.*

22   .20 × 50 = 10
If you got this right, go to frame 25; otherwise, go to frame 23.

23   What is 25 percent of 30?   *Go to frame 24.*

24   .25 × 30 = 7.5   *Go to frame 25.*

25   20 percent of what is 10?   *Go to frame 26.*

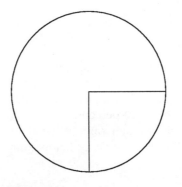

Figure 2.2

26 | 10/.20 = 50
If you got this right, go to frame 29; otherwise, go to frame 27.

27 | 40 percent of what is 20?   *Go to frame 28.*

28 | 20/.40 = 50   *Go to frame 29.*

29 | ## CALCULATING PERCENTAGE CHANGES

What is the percentage change when we go from 40 to 48?   *Go to frame 30.*

30 | The answer is 20 percent. If you got this right, the chances are that you won't need any more practice in calculating percentage changes, so you may go directly to frame 32. If you missed this one, go to frame 31.

31 | There is a three-step procedure for solving most mathematical problems: (1) write down a formula, (2) plug numbers into the formula, and (3) solve for the answer.

What we need, then, to calculate percentage changes is a formula:

$$\text{Percentage change} = \frac{\text{New number} - \text{Original number}}{\text{Original number}}$$

We'll apply the formula for this problem: Find the percentage change when we go from 40 to 48. Obviously, the original number is 40, and 48 is the new number. Plugging these numbers into the formula, we get:

$$\frac{48 - 40}{40} = \frac{8}{40}$$

Once we've gotten this far, we should find ourselves in familiar territory. Our next step is to convert our fraction into a decimal. You may want to reduce it from 8/40 to 1/5, or you may want to find the decimal using the original numbers. We'll do it both ways:

$$40\overline{)8.00} = .20$$

or

$$5\overline{)1.00} = .20$$

Either way, then, we get .20. One more step and we've got our percentage. We'll set up another rule: *To convert a decimal into a percentage, move the decimal point two places to the right and add a percentage sign.*

Therefore, .20 = 20 percent.

Now we'll do another one: What is the percentage change when we go from 50 to 53? Do it in the space below and then check your work.

$$\text{Percentage change} = \frac{\text{New number} - \text{Original number}}{\text{Original number}}$$

$$= \frac{53 - 50}{50} = \frac{3}{50}$$

$$50\overline{)3.00} = 6\%$$ with .06 above

Self-Test 3

$$\text{Percentage change} = \frac{\text{New number} - \text{Original}}{\text{Original number}}$$

1. Find the percentage change when we go from 35 to 29.
2. Find the percentage change when we go from 60 to 67.
3. Find the percentage change when we go from 23 to 21.

Answers to Self-Test 3

1. $\dfrac{29 - 35}{35} = \dfrac{-6}{35} = 35\overline{)6.000} = -17\%$ with .171 above

2. $\dfrac{67 - 60}{60} = \dfrac{7}{60} = 60\overline{)7.000} = 11.7\%$ with .117 above

3. $\dfrac{21 - 23}{23} = \dfrac{-2}{23} = 23\overline{)2.000} = -8.7\%$ with .087 above

32 | PERCENTAGE DISTRIBUTION

One of the favorite statistical presentations of economists is the percentage distribution, often done in the form of pie charts. Here we'll confine ourselves to figuring out percentage shares of the components of various totals.

GNP consists of the sum of four components: consumption ($3000 billion), investment ($800 billion), government expenditures ($1100 billion), and net exports ($100 billion). Find the percent distribution of these four components of GNP. As you know, GNP stands for Gross National Product, which is the nation's output of goods and services over the course of one year. It is the subject of Chapter 6.

Solution: GNP = $5000 billion.

$$\text{Consumption} = \frac{3000}{5000} = \frac{3}{5} = 5\overline{)3.00} = 60\%$$ with .60 above

$$\text{Investment} = \frac{800}{5000} = \frac{8}{50} = \frac{4}{25} = 25\overline{)4.00} = 16\%$$ with .16 above

$$\text{Government expenditures} = \frac{1100}{5000} = \frac{11}{50} = 50\overline{)11.00} = 22\%$$ with .22 above

$$\text{Net exports} = \frac{100}{5000} = \frac{1}{50} = 50\overline{)1.00} = \frac{2}{100}\%$$ with .02 above

Always check to be sure your percentages add up to 100. (Because of rounding, they may occasionally add up to 99.9 or 100.1.)

If you got this problem right, then after you finish taking your bows, go directly to frame 35. If not, then we have other plans for you: Go to frame 33.

33 Suppose that you spend $100 this week. If you spent $35 on durable goods, $25 on nondurable goods, and $40 on services, find the percentage distribution of your expenditures on these three components. To put this problem in simple English: What percentage of the $100 did you spend on services, what percentage did you spend on durable goods, and what percentage did you spend on nondurable goods?   *Go to frame 34.*

34 *Solution:* When the sum you're working with is 100 (or 1, 10, or 1000, for that matter), you don't have much work to do:

$$\text{Durable goods} = \frac{35}{100} = .35 \text{ or } 35\%$$

$$\text{Nondurable goods} = \frac{25}{100} = .25 \text{ or } 25\%$$

$$\text{Services} = \frac{40}{100} = .40 \text{ or } 40\%$$

Self-Test 4

1. National Income totals $3 trillion. Its components include: rent, $200 billion; profit, $300 billion; interest, $250 billion; and wages, $2 trillion, 250 billion. Find the percentage distribution of the components of National Income.

2. The U.S. government will spend $1.2 trillion this year. The main expenditures are: defense, $350 billion; Social Security and Medicare, $425 billion; interest on the national debt, $175 billion; aid to states and localities, $100 billion; and all other expenditures, $150 billion. Find the percentage distribution of the main expenditures in the U.S. government budget.

3. Of fifteen million business firms in the United States, twelve million are proprietorships, eight hundred thousand are partnerships, and the rest are corporations. Find the percentage share of total businesses held by each of these three types of business.

Answers to Self-Test 4

1. $\text{Rent} = \dfrac{200}{3000} = \dfrac{1}{15} = .067 = 6.7\%$ 6.7

    $\text{Profit} = \dfrac{300}{3000} = \dfrac{1}{10} = .10 = 10\%$ 10.0

                                                                                              8.3

    $\text{Interest} = \dfrac{250}{3000} = \dfrac{25}{300} = \dfrac{1}{12} = .083 = 8.3\%$ 75.0

                                                                                             100.0

    $\text{Wages} = \dfrac{2250}{3000} = \dfrac{225}{300} = \dfrac{9}{12} = \dfrac{3}{4} = .75 = 75\%$

2. Defense $= \dfrac{350}{1200} = \dfrac{35}{120} = \dfrac{7}{24} = .292 = 29.2\%$

   Social Security and Medicare $= \dfrac{425}{1200} = \dfrac{17}{48} = .354 = 35.4\%$

   Interest on the national debt $= \dfrac{175}{1200} = \dfrac{7}{48} = .146 = 14.6\%$

   Aid to states and localities $= \dfrac{100}{1200} = \dfrac{1}{12} = .083 = 8.3\%$

   All other expenditures $= \dfrac{150}{1200} = \dfrac{1}{8} = .125 = 12.5\%$

29.2
35.4
14.6
8.3
12.5
100.0

3. Proprietorships $= \dfrac{12}{15} = \dfrac{4}{5} = .80 = 80\%$

   Partnerships $= \dfrac{800}{15,000} = \dfrac{8}{150} = \dfrac{4}{75} = .053 = 5.3\%$

   Corporations $= \dfrac{2200}{15,000} = \dfrac{22}{150} = \dfrac{11}{75} = .147 = 14.7\%$

80.0
5.3
14.7
100.0

35 | DEALING WITH INDEX NUMBERS

Index numbers are used to make comparisons, usually from year to year or from month to month. The most popular index number of all time is the Consumer Price Index. When you get familiar with this index, you will be allowed to refer to it very casually as the CPI.

This index is so important that it is the basis of the cost-of-living increases paid to over forty million Social Security recipients, over twenty million food stamp recipients, and millions of additional workers covered by contracts with escalator clauses. In January 1987 the CPI stood at 333.1, with 1967 as its base year. What did this mean?

In the base year, an index is usually 100. (In this book, in virtually every other economics book you'll ever read, and in newspapers and magazines, the base year in every index will be 100.) This enables us to make instantaneous comparisons between the base year and right now. For example, how did the cost of living in January 1987 compare with that of 1967? You say it was higher? Can't you do any better than that? You say it was more than three times as high? Close, but no cigar. Try to figure out *exactly* how high prices were in January 1987 compared with prices in 1967. They were exactly 3.331 times as high.

Now how did we get that? We divided 333.1 by 100. When you divide any number by 100, all you do is move its decimal point two places to the left.

Next question: By what percentage did the cost of living rise between 1967 and January 1987? Careful—for nearly everybody, that first guess is wrong.

Remember how we worked out percentage changes earlier in the chapter? Just plug in the numbers into this formula:

$$\text{Percentage change} = \frac{\text{New number} - \text{Original number}}{\text{Original number}} = \frac{333.1 - 100}{100}$$

$$= \frac{233.1}{100} = 2.331 = 233.1\%$$

Incidentally, there's no need to go through the last two steps of the problem we just did. Any number that appears over 100 in a fraction may be read as a percentage:

$$\frac{233.1}{100} = 233.1\%$$

$$\frac{17}{100} = 17\%$$

$$\frac{156}{100} = 156\%$$

Ready for a couple of tricks with index numbers? Suppose that the base year is 1997 and in 1999 the index stands at 98.3. What happened to prices since the base year?

What's your answer? If the index went down, that means that prices have declined. By how much? Use this formula:

$$\text{Percentage change} = \frac{\text{New number} - \text{Original number}}{\text{Original number}} = \frac{98.3 - 100}{100}$$

$$= \frac{-1.7}{100} = -1.7\%$$

Just one more. What if the index goes from 261.4 to 288.5? What happened to prices over that period? Work it out in this space:

Solution:

$$\text{Percentage change} = \frac{\text{New number} - \text{Original number}}{\text{Original number}}$$

$$= \frac{288.5 - 261.4}{261.4} = \frac{27.1}{261.4} = 10.4\%$$

If you're comfortable with index numbers, you may skip Self-Test 5 and go directly to frame 36. If you feel you need more practice, take the self-test.

Self-Test 5

1. If the Index of Industrial Production was 100 in the base year, 1987, what has happened to industrial production since the base year if the index now stands at:
   A. 114.5?
   B. 96.3?
   C. 237.0?

2. If the Consumer Price Index went from 246.7 in 1988 to 239.4 in 1989, what is the percentage change in prices between 1988 and 1989?

3. If the CPI was 115.3 in 1984 and prices doubled by 1993, how much would the CPI be in 1993?

Answers to Self-Test 5

1. A. Went up 14.5 percent.
   B. Went down 3.7 percent.
   C. Went up 137 percent.

2. Percentage change $= \dfrac{\text{New number} - \text{Original number}}{\text{Original number}}$

$$= \frac{239.4 - 246.7}{246.7} = \frac{-7.3}{246.7} = -.03 = -3.0\%$$

3. 230.6

---

36 | **WORD PROBLEMS**

According to the cognoscente, every math problem can be reduced to one of five or six formulas. Your job is to decide which formula to use and then just plug in the numbers. In economics, as in mathematics, all word problems can be reduced to formulas, which can be easily solved.

We're going to work on a few word problems now. Remember, the trick is to recognize the *type* of problem it is. Then just follow three easy steps: (1) write down the formula, (2) substitute numbers for the words in the formula, and (3) solve the problem.

We'll start out with a hard one: Pick a number. Now triple it. By what percentage did your number increase?

Three hundred percent?

No, that's the wrong answer.

Let's pick, as an example, a nice round number. Let's try 100. Now let's triple it. We have 300. How much is the percentage increase when you go from 100 to 300? Whenever you go from 100 to a higher number, the percentage increase is the difference between 100 and the new number: $300 - 100 = 200$. Suppose you quadruple a number: $400 - 100 = 300$. Pretty easy, huh?

What we've really got here are index numbers. To find the percentage change from the base year (which is always 100, remember), we just subtract the base year from the current year. If we go from 100 to, say, 350, we just subtract the base year (100) from the current year (350): $350 - 100 = 250$ percent.

That's great if you have index numbers. But what if you start with a number other than 100? What if you were earning $40,000 and your income fell to $30,000? By what percentage did your income fall?

This is a typical percentage change problem (like the ones we did in frames 29–31). Work it out and go to frame 37 to check your work.

37 |

$$\text{Percentage change} = \frac{\text{New number} - \text{Original number}}{\text{Original number}}$$

$$= \frac{\$30,000 - \$40,000}{\$40,000} \quad \frac{-\$10,000}{\$40,000} = -25\%$$

Keep in mind that word problems are just another way of asking you to carry out a specific mathematical operation. In the final self-test of this chapter, you'll be applying the skills you've acquired in the previous sections. Then you'll be ready to make some sense out of the study of economics.

———————— ■ ————————

Self-Test 6

1. Suppose that the CPI rises from 200 (in 1984) to 250 (in 1988) and then to 300 (in 1993). Did the CPI rise by the same percentage from 1984 to 1988 as it did from 1988 to 1993?

2. If GNP rose from $3 trillion in 1983 to $6 trillion in 1988, and then fell to $3 trillion again in 1989, does that mean that GNP rose by the same percentage from 1983 to 1988 as it fell, from 1988 to 1989?

3. If your take-home pay doubles and if the CPI rises by 50 percent over the same period, how much better off will you be?

4. If your take-home pay triples and the CPI doubles, how much better off will you be?

Answers to Self-Test 6

1. Percentage change $= \dfrac{\text{New number} - \text{Original number}}{\text{Original number}}$

$$\frac{250 - 200}{200} = \frac{50}{200} = .25 = 25\%.$$

$$\frac{300 - 250}{250} = \frac{50}{250} = .20 = 20\%.$$

Since 25 percent and 20 percent are not equal, the answer is "no."

2. Percentage change $= \dfrac{\text{New number} - \text{Original number}}{\text{Original number}}$

$$\frac{6-3}{3} = \frac{3}{3} = 100\ \%;\quad \frac{3-6}{6} = \frac{-3}{6} = -50\%$$

Obviously, the percentage changes are different.

3. To solve this problem, let's first rephrase the question: How much more will you be able to buy after your pay doubles and prices rise by 50 percent? Let's say that you originally earned $100 and bought 100 units. Now you have $200, but each unit costs $1.50. You'll get 133.3. How much better off are you? 33.3 percent better off.

4. Use the same method: Your pay goes from $100 to $300. You used to buy 100 units for your $100, but prices have doubled, so now a unit costs you $2. Since you now have $300, you can afford 150 units. So you are 50 percent better off.

CHAPTER 3

Drawing Graphs

and

Reading Graphs

The word *graph* means diagram. People who are not familiar with graphs can easily get confused when suddenly confronted with very complex graphs. A person with no background in art asked to interpret some of the abstract paintings hanging in New York's Museum of Modern Art might suggest that they look like graphs in an economic text—in other words, they're indecipherable.

Well, your worries are over. When you've finished this chapter you will be able to:

- Understand graphs in economics textbooks.
- Read graphs in newspapers and news magazines.
- Understand how demand and supply determine price.
- Draw your own line graphs, bar graphs, and pie charts.

1 | LINE GRAPHS

Setting Up a Line Graph

We'll start out with an extremely simple line graph. How simple? So simple that it won't even have any lines on it, just a vertical axis and a horizontal axis. These axes are used to make measurements on the graph.

Are you ready? Okay, then, let's do graphs. The first thing we'll have to know is what the graph is measuring. We can find this out by reading the labels on the vertical and horizontal axes. In economics, by convention, price (or money) is always measured on the vertical axis—if there is money involved. Something else will be measured on that axis only if money is not being measured at all.

Also by convention, quantity appears on the horizontal axis. It could be, for example, quantity of goods sold, quantity of output produced, or quantity of workers employed. Sometimes time is measured on the horizontal axis, usually in years.

In Figure 3.1 price is on the vertical axis and quantity is on the horizontal axis. Notice the "0" where the two axes meet. That's the *origin* of the graph:

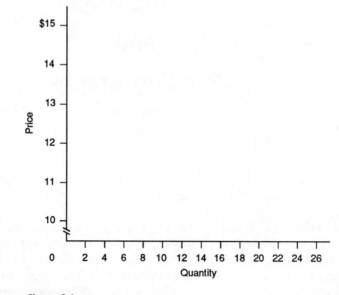

Figure 3.1

it shows you the lowest points of both axes. At that point in Figure 3.1, both price and quantity are zero.

As you move upward on the price axis, you'll see that the price rises. Notice that 11, 12, 13, and 14 are evenly spaced out on the axis. On the quantity axis, we move to the right to measure larger and larger quantities, which are also evenly spaced out.

2 | Drawing the Demand Curve

Now we're ready to read our first line graph. We'll start with the ever-popular demand curve. Notice that the demand curve shown in Figure 3.2 slopes downward to the right. Does that make any sense to you? It means that at a price of $15, people buy 4 compact discs; at a price of $14, they buy 6 discs; at $13, they buy 9 discs; and so forth. At lower and lower prices, in other words, they buy more and more discs.

Are you ready to draw a demand curve? Let's find out. Use the information from Table 3.1 to fill in Figure 3.3. I've gotten you started by placing the first dot (price: $7, quantity: 2). All you need to do is put in the rest of the dots and connect them by drawing a smooth curve. Go ahead and draw your demand curve and then check your work against the curve shown in Figure 3.4.

If your graph came out right, then go on to frame 5. But if you are still uncomfortable drawing demand curves, go to frame 3.

3 | Fill in Figure 3.5, using the data from Table 3.2. Then check your work against the curve shown in Figure 3.6.

4 | If you've had no major problems doing Figure 3.5, then you're ready to draw supply curves. Proceed directly to frame 5. If you still haven't gotten the hang of drawing demand curves, go back to frame 2.

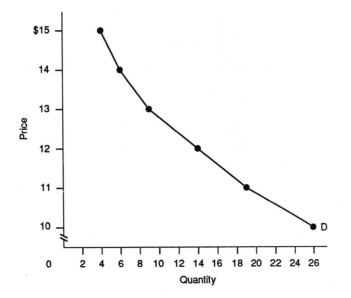

Figure 3.2

Table 3.1.

Price	Quantity Demanded
$7	2
6	3
5	5
4	7
3	10
2	14
1	20

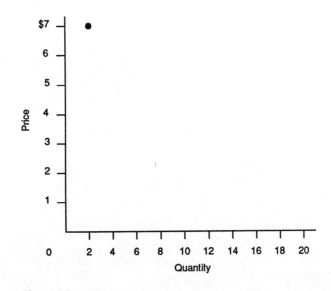

Figure 3.3

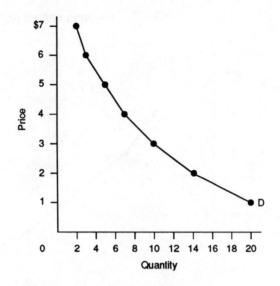

Figure 3.4

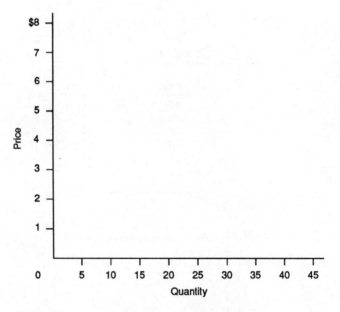

Figure 3.5

Table 3.2.	
Price	Quantity Demanded
$8	1
7	2
6	4
5	8
4	14
3	22
2	32
1	45

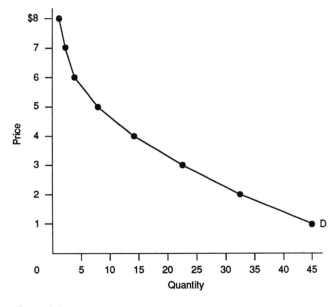

Figure 3.6

5 | Drawing the Supply Curve

The supply curve tells us how much of this product will be supplied by sellers at each price. As the price goes up, will the sellers supply more and more of the product? They sure will. Wouldn't you? (In Chapters 12 and 13 we will discuss why sellers are willing to sell greater quantities as the price rises.)

Draw a supply curve on the axes of Figure 3.7, using the data from Table 3.3. While you're at it, draw a demand curve as well. Then check your results with those in Figure 3.8. Next see if you can guess the equilibrium price and quantity (that's where the demand and supply curves cross).

6 | Finding Equilibrium Price and Quantity

Have you ever heard the saying, "You can never repeal the law of supply and demand?" Before anyone tries to repeal it, let's see if we can pass that law.

Are you ready for a little economic analysis? We need to find equilibrium price and equilibrium quantity. That's the point at which the demand curve and the supply curve cross each other. In Figure 3.8 a dotted line runs horizontally from the point where the curves intersect back to the price axis. What is the price? It looks like about $16.35 or $16.40. How about equilibrium quantity? If we run the dotted line down from the point where the curves cross (the equilibrium point) to the horizontal axis, the quantity looks like 13.2 or so. You'll be using this process in a problem in just a minute or two, and it will often help you understand graphs in newspapers and magazines.

You might have noticed a couple of things about the way these graphs are drawn. First of all, notice that we didn't bother to go all the way down to zero on the price axis in Figure 3.8 because the prices go down only as far as $10.

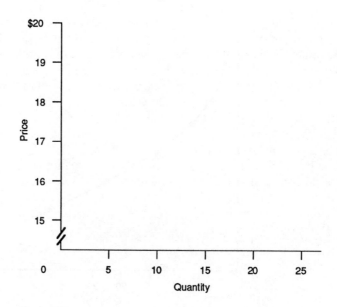

Figure 3.7

Table 3.3.

Price	Quantity Demanded	Quantity Supplied
$20	1	25
19	3	24
18	6	22
17	10	18
16	16	10
15	24	2

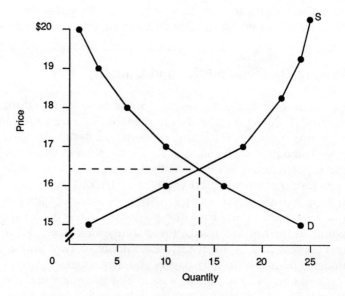

Figure 3.8

There is nothing wrong with coming all the way down to prices of $3, $2, and $1, but if you do, you waste a lot of space, and you also crowd your graph into the upper third or so of the page. This will make the graph much harder to read. When drawing graphs, bigger is definitely better.

Another thing you may have noticed is that we didn't bother to put in every single number on the quantity axis. For example, in Figure 3.8 we numbered quantity by fives. Why? Once again, because this makes the graph easier to read. Remember that you're the one who will have to read these graphs, so you'll want to make them easily readable.

One final thing: Notice in Figure 3.8, for example, that the demand curve is labeled D and the supply curve is labeled S. If you're more comfortable labeling these curves Demand and Supply, that's fine, too. But you must give every curve a name so as to make your graph that much easier to read.

Perhaps the best piece of advice I ever heard about drawing graphs was given by Dr. Lazare Teper, who for many years was the director of economic research for the International Ladies Garment Workers Union. He said that a person reading your graph should be able to understand what you're showing in less than a second. Of course, I don't know too many economists who could make that claim. But if you have to puzzle over a graph for even five or ten seconds, then either you don't know how to read graphs or someone else doesn't know how to draw them.

If you're still a little shaky on drawing graphs or finding the equilibrium price and quantity, use the data from Table 3.4 to fill in Figure 3.9. After you've done this, check your work against Figure 3.10. If you feel confident that you can find equilibrium price and quantity without further review, go on to frame 7. If not, go back to the beginning of this frame, work through the problems in Tables 3.3 and 3.4, and redraw the graphs.

7 | Graphing a Time Series

A line graph can convey information at a given instant in time. That's exactly what we've been doing so far. A time series shows us what has been happening to a particular variable over time: the unemployment rate, the rate of inflation, national output, interest rates, or whatever.

We'll start out with a simple time series showing the unemployment rate between 1964 and 1984. (See Figure 3.11.) As you can see, it certainly had its ups and downs. We might want to plot the unemployment rate to see what happened to it during recessions. These are marked with labels and arrows.

Next we'll try something a little more complex—a time series with two lines. In Figure 3.12 I've plotted the three-month Treasury bill rates and the Aaa corporate bond interest rates over the decade of the 1970s. You can tell at a glance that these two rates moved together, with the corporate bond rate generally a few points higher (because of the higher risk involved in lending to private corporations rather than to the U.S. government).

You may encounter some line graphs with four or five lines that will be harder to read. But the whole idea of drawing a graph is to give the reader a quick picture of certain relationships. We'll be moving on to pie charts and then bar graphs, which are alternate methods of pictorially presenting economic data.

Table 3.4.

Price	Quantity Demanded	Quantity Supplied
$15	1	27
14	4	25
13	9	21
12	16	12
11	22	6
10	26	2

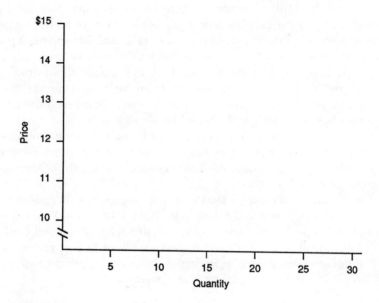

Figure 3.9

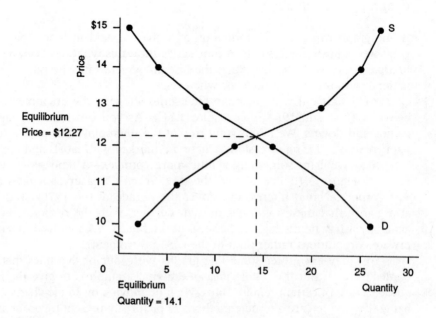

Figure 3.10

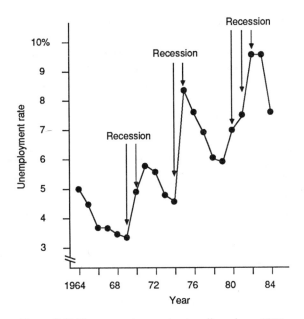

Figure 3.11 The unemployment rate, all workers, 1964–1984

Source: The Economic Report of the President, February 1986

8 | PIE CHARTS

Newspapers and magazines often use pie charts to show how a certain total is divided. The pie represents that total, and its slices must add up to that total.

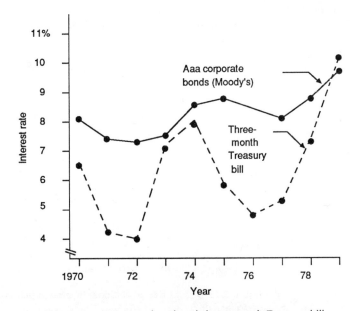

Figure 3.12 Aaa corporate bond and three-month Treasury bill interest rates, 1970–1979

Source: The Economic Report of the President, February 1986

Figures 2.1 and 2.2 in Chapter 2 are examples of pie charts. As I mentioned then, if an entire pie is equal to a dollar, then the percentage share of each slice may be thought of in terms of cents. For example, one-quarter of a pie (as in Figure 2.2), would be equal to 25 cents, or 25 percent of the pie.

The main advantage of pie charts is that they let us make a fast visual estimate of the size of each slice. You don't need to be an economist to realize, after a glance at Figure 3.13, that just under three-quarters of National Income is paid out in the form of wages, salaries, and fringe benefits.

This same information could be presented as a pie chart with each slice representing part of a dollar of National Income (see Figure 3.14). Using the data in Figure 3.13, calculate the percentage share of each piece of the whole pie if the pie is to add up to one dollar. Work it out to one-tenth of a cent.

If you got stuck, go back to frames 32–34 of Chapter 2, where we worked out percentage shares. If you're *still* stuck after that, you'll find this problem worked out below.

Solution:

$$\text{Wages, Salaries: } \frac{2372.7}{3215.6} = .738$$

$$\text{Profit: } \frac{541.4}{3215.6} = .168$$

$$\text{Interest: } \frac{287.7}{3215.6} = .089$$

$$\text{Rent: } \frac{14.0}{3215.6} = .004$$

Figure 3.15, which appeared in *The New York Times* in early 1987, illustrates the way pie charts are used in newspapers. Although they are particularly suited for showing percentage shares or distributions, they are not used as frequently as line graphs and bar graphs.

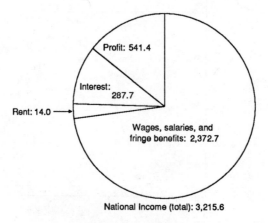

National Income (total): 3,215.6

Figure 3.13 Distribution of National Income in billions of dollars 1985

Source: 1985 *Economic Report of the President,* pp. 278, 279

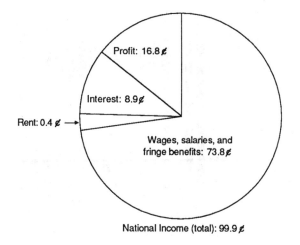

Figure 3.14 Distribution of National Income (1985) expressed as one dollar

Source: Economic Report of the President, pp. 278–279

9 | BAR GRAPHS

Bar graphs, which are often used in newspapers and magazines, lend themselves especially well to the presentation of monthly figures. Industrial production figures, shown in Figure 3.16, are a closely watched monthly series. Any trend in these figures becomes readily apparent from this graph.

Notice that the bars are cut off near the bottom of the graph. This device is used to save space, but, as we shall see, it can lead to either intentional or unintentional misrepresentation of the data. In the space provided in Figure 3.17, draw a bar graph of GNP ($3992.5 billion), Net National Product ($3554.3 billion), and National Income ($3215.6 billion) for 1985.

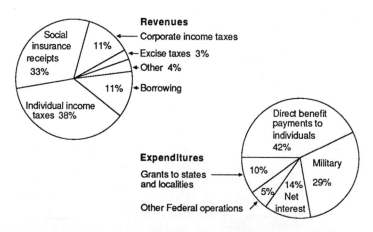

Figure 3.15 The Reagan budget; estimates for the fiscal year 1988.

Source: Office of Management and Budget, Jan. 6, 1987.

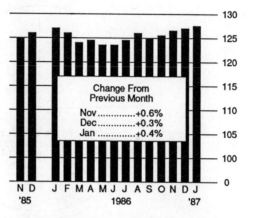

Figure 3.16 Index of industrial production,
1977 = 100, seasonally adjusted
Source: The New York Times, Feb. 14, 1987

Your graph should look like Figure 3.18. If you'd like a little more practice with bar graphs, try your hand at plotting the monthly data for the Consumer Price Index for 1984. Using the data from Table 3.5, draw your graph in Figure 3.19 and check your work against the graph in Figure 3.20. If you're sure that you understand bar graphs, go to frame 10.

10 | A WORD OF CAUTION

Graphs that appear in newspapers, magazines, and economics books are usually drawn by honest, competent people. These graphs accurately depict the data they represent. But a graph can be misleading if it is drawn by someone who is trying to pull a fast one or by someone who just doesn't know how to draw graphs.

Figure 3.17

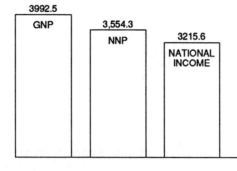

Figure 3.18 GNP, Net National Product (NNP), and National Income in billions of dollars

Source: 1986 Economic Report of the President, p. 276

Table 3.5. The Consumer Price Index, Monthly Data, 1984 (1967 = 100)

Month	CPI
January	305.2
February	306.6
March	307.3
April	308.8
May	309.7
June	310.7
July	311.7
August	313.0
September	314.5
October	315.3
November	315.3
December	315.5

Source: Economic Report of the President, February 1986

Figure 3.19

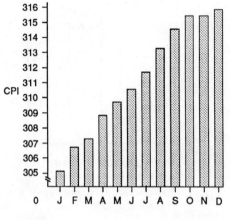

Figure 3.20

Let's look at some incompetent work. What impression do you get from Figure 3.21? Since the bars in this graph vary greatly in height, it appears that the industrial capacity utilization rate was all over the lot in 1985, doesn't it? Yet, if you study the figures on the vertical axis, you'll see that capacity utilization in 1985 was never lower than 79.8 percent and never higher than 81.1 percent. Really, now, do you call *that* wide fluctuation?

Why does the graph make it *look* like wide fluctuation? Is it because the vertical axis is cut between 0 and 80? Imagine what the graph would look like, however, if it weren't cut off at all. The bars would be extremely tall and the fluctuation wouldn't be apparent at all, so that would be going too far. Let's compromise. Figure 3.22 gives a more accurate picture of what happened to capacity utilization in 1985.

Now let's look at the work of someone who is purposely trying to mislead you by drawing a deceptive graph. For our tour de force, we'll show two tricks on one graph. Okay, hold on to your seat and look at Figure 3.23.

The person who drew the misleading graph in Figure 3.23 chose an extremely favorable starting point and, to a lesser degree, a favorable ending point. Notice that the graph begins with the unemployment rate at its high for the

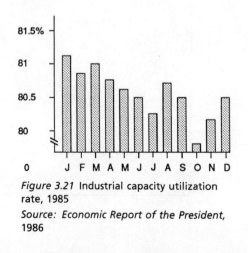

Figure 3.21 Industrial capacity utilization rate, 1985

Source: Economic Report of the President, 1986

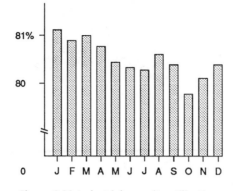

Figure 3.22 Industrial capacity utilization rate, 1985

period depicted by the graph and just happens to end with the unemployment rate at its lowest point. Now look at the clearer and fairer graph in Figure 3.24. By including all of 1982 and a little more of 1984, the person who drew this graph gives us a much better perspective on the unemployment rate during the period in question. The period from December 1982 to June 1984 *was* a time of rapidly falling unemployment, since we were recovering from the 1981–1982 recession, during which time the unemployment rate was rising. This is clearly shown in Figure 3.24.

A second offense of Figure 3.23, but not nearly as grievous, is the way it makes the unemployment rate look as if it's falling very sharply. While it is true that a decline of over 4 percent in a year and a half is quite rapid, it

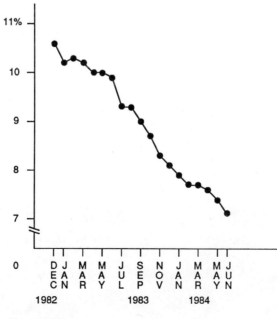

Figure 3.23

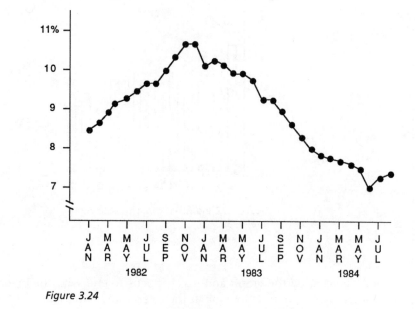

Figure 3.24

would be more reasonable to depict this decline as it is shown in Figure 3.24. Whenever you see a very marked trend in a graph, as you've seen in Figure 3.23, you would do well to ask yourself if the graph was drawn to get you to see things a certain way rather than the way they really are. If you are curious about how people perform all kinds of unspeakable acts with statistics, see Darrell Huff and Irving Geis, *How to Lie with Statistics* (New York: Norton, 1954).

PART 2

MACROECONOMICS:
THE
PROBLEMS

CHAPTER 4

Economic

Resources

Economics is about money, but as Adam Smith noted over two centuries ago in his classic, *The Wealth of Nations,* our real wealth is our resources and the goods and services we produce with them.

So, first we'll answer the three basic questions of economics: What goods shall we produce? How shall these goods be produced? For whom shall the goods be produced?

By the time you finish this chapter you will:

- Be able to answer the three questions of economics.
- Understand the definition of economics.
- Be familiar with the four economic resources.
- Be able to read and use production possibilities curves.
- Understand the basic reasons for economic growth.

1 | THE THREE QUESTIONS OF ECONOMICS

Every country must answer the three basic economic questions. Although there are no right answers and no wrong answers, the way in which these questions are answered will determine the type of economic system that a country will have.

2 | Question 1: What Goods Shall We Produce?

In the United States we put most of our effort into producing consumer goods and services. Japan, however, concentrates on the production of plant and equipment. And quite predictably, the Soviet Union expends a large part of its resources on the manufacture of military goods. Now, who makes these decisions?

In the Soviet Union the exact mix of military and consumer goods is decided by a government planning committee, while in Japan and the United States consumers and business firms make most of the basic decisions (albeit with some input from the government). For example, the United States devotes 8 percent of its national output to military goods, while the Japanese devote just 1 percent. Eventually, then, in these two countries the government takes its share of output—usually about 20 to 25 percent—and lets the private sector decide what to do with the rest. In other words, in the United States we all vote on what we shall produce, and the voting is very fair because it amounts to one dollar, one vote.

Question 2: How Shall These Goods Be Produced?

There are only two possible answers to this question: (1) the government or (2) privately owned business firms. In the United States, of course, nearly all goods and services are produced by private business firms. In socialist countries the government may produce most of the output. But even in the Soviet Union and China, there is a growing private sector.

Question 3: For Whom Shall the Goods Be Produced?

Every nation, no matter what its form of government, says that all production is for its people. But who gets what? And how much?

In Sweden the government provides all its citizens with the basic necessities of life and taxes away a large part of the income of the rich. Consequently, income is distributed fairly evenly. A few other socialist countries have similar income distribution patterns.

In many developing nations, a few very wealthy families, usually less than 1 percent of the population, receive most of the nation's output, while the rest of the people live at the subsistence level. Most of the industrialized nations—including the United States, West Germany, the Soviet Union, and France—have a few rich families, a very large middle class, and a minority of relatively poor people.

How the economic pie is divided, then, varies from country to country. In no country are the slices equal. But, to paraphrase George Orwell's *Animal Farm*, in some countries the slices are more equal than in others.

Self-Test 1

1. What are the three basic questions of economics?
2. Who decides what gets produced in
   A. The United States?
   B. Japan?
   C. The Soviet Union?
3. Goods and services may be produced by either _____ or _____ .
4. How does the distribution of income in the developing countries differ from that of the industrialized countries?

Answers to Self-Test 1

1. What goods shall we produce? How shall these goods be produced? For whom shall the goods be produced?
2. A. Individual consumers.
   B. Individual consumers.
   C. A government planning committee.
3. The government or business firms.
4. In developing countries a small minority of rich families receives most of the income, while most of the rest of the population lives at the subsistence level. In industrialized countries most of the people are in the middle class, so income is distributed much more evenly.

5 | THE CENTRAL FACT OF ECONOMICS: SCARCITY

We're going to start out by defining economics. Then we'll analyze the inferences that may be drawn from that definition. The word *scarcity* is so important in economics *that it is part of its definition: Economics is the study of the allocation of the scarce means of production toward the satisfaction of human wants.* What are the means of production and why are they scarce?

6 | RESOURCES

The scarce means of production are land, labor, capital, and entrepreneurial ability. Sometimes they're referred to as resources. We'll take up each in turn.

Land

Some land is so valuable that we price it by the square foot. What makes land valuable? Primarily its location and also its scarcity. For example, there is a very limited amount of land near the intersection of Fifth Avenue and Fifty-seventh Street in Manhattan, one of the most desirable locations in the world; as a result, that land is very expensive.

Land can also be expensive because oil or gold or another precious commodity is buried under it—or because people think it is. Rich farm land, too, particularly in the wheat and corn belts of the Midwest, is relatively expensive. In every case, the amount of land is limited, so it goes to the highest bidder. And in general, since there is a finite amount of land on this planet, the most desirable land is relatively scarce.

Labor

Economists consider virtually all paid work "labor." Farm workers, office and factory workers, and corporate executives are part of our labor force. Is labor scarce? Yes. Because only a certain number of people are physically, mentally, and emotionally capable of doing the work that needs to be done. We can tell just *how* scarce a resource is by how much we need to pay for it. Some kinds of labor—like a doctor's services or a plumber's—are so scarce that they can be very expensive indeed.

Capital

When we talk about capital, we mean essentially all the plant and equipment used to turn out the goods and services that we produce. Capital, then, includes factories, machinery, farm equipment, shopping malls, office buildings, computer systems, and all of the tools of production and distribution.

As you might well imagine, some businesses require a huge investment in capital. Imagine how much capital you would need to start your own airline or automobile assembly plant. And capital, like land and labor, is limited in quantity.

Entrepreneurial Ability

This last resource is sometimes called management ability, but it really goes a couple of steps beyond that. A manager runs a business enterprise, or at least a part of one. But an entrepreneur recognizes an opportunity to make a profit, raises the money to open a business, and eventually hires managers to run that business.

The entrepreneur is able to combine land, labor, and capital in a way that will make money. There is evidently no shortage of entrepreneurial talent in the United States., Japan, Taiwan, South Korea, and perhaps even in the Soviet Union and China as well. Nevertheless, entrepreneurial ability is a limited resource. Not everybody can set up a successful business. Proof of this lies in the fact that three out of every five new businesses in the United States fail within the first two years of operation.

7   UNLIMITED WANTS

The first half of our definition of economics had to do with scarce, or limited, resources. The second half deals with the satisfaction of human wants. Economists maintain that human wants are unlimited relative to the resources available.

On a macroeconomic level, we can look at our entire output of goods and services and ask if there are enough to go around. The answer is "no." Approximately 35 million Americans are officially classified by the U.S. government as poor, even after receiving welfare and Social Security benefits. What about the middle class? Are all of these people so completely satisfied with their living standards that they would refuse a new home, a Rolls-Royce, or a Mercedes-Benz?

And on a microeconomic level, how about you? If you hit the lottery, would you refuse to collect your millions because you couldn't think of anything to buy with them? In a word, then, we are still talking about *scarcity*. We just don't have enough resources to satisfy everyone's wants.

8 | OPPORTUNITY COST

Because there is scarcity, we have to make choices. Do we buy a VCR or take a vacation trip? Will you spend your bonus on new clothes or caps for your front teeth? The thing you give up (i.e., your second choice) is called the *opportunity cost* of your choice.

It would be great if we didn't have to make choices, if there were no scarcity, and if we could have everything we wanted. But until that day comes, we'll have to do the best we can with our limited resources, and we'll be forced to make choices, thereby incurring opportunity costs.

In the next section, we'll see that nations also must make choices. The production possibilities curve is a graphic description of those choices.

Self-Test 2

1. List the four economic resources.
2. What is the central fact of economics?
3. What is the difference between entrepreneurial ability and management ability?
4. Our resources are _____ , while human wants are relatively _____ .
5. What do we mean when we talk about the opportunity cost of buying a new car?

Answers to Self-Test 2

1. Land, labor, capital, and entrepreneurial ability.
2. Scarcity.
3. A manager simply has to be able to run a business firm, but an entrepreneur must recognize a business opportunity, raise the funds needed, and set up a going business concern.
4. Limited; unlimited.
5. Whatever your second choice was—say, new furniture.

9 | THE PRODUCTION POSSIBILITIES CURVE

How much output can one country produce? We've already talked about the limited resources—land, labor, capital, and entrepreneurial ability. A tiny country—say, Monaco or Luxembourg, with a very small land area, a very low population, a very low stock of capital, and only a small number of people with entrepreneurial ability—will never be able to match the industrial giants in total output of goods and services.

But remember that it's not just how big you are, but how you use your resources that counts. Does this little country operate at full capacity? Does it utilize the best available technology? Given its limited resources, is it producing at its full potential? If the answer is "yes" to all of the questions, then the country has reached a certain point on its production possibilities curve.

This curve is based on the assumption that the nation produces only two goods—cars and houses, for example, or consumer goods and capital goods, or guns (military goods) and butter (consumer goods). If it devotes all of its resources to producing butter, for example, it will produce no guns. The nation that is producing nothing except butter is at point A on Table 4.1. If guns represent military goods and butter represents consumer goods, what can you say about the military preparedness of this country? There *isn't* any. How about point B? One unit of guns represents *some* preparedness. But notice that consumer goods output has fallen to 14. So what is the opportunity cost of producing that first unit of guns? It's one unit of consumer goods.

When we go from point B to point C, what's the opportunity cost of that second gun? It's two units of consumer goods.

Figure out the opportunity costs of going from C to D, from D to E, and from E to F. Write your answers here:

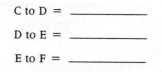

C to D = _____

D to E = _____

E to F = _____

Your answers should have been 3, 4, and 5.

The numbers in Table 4.1 can be easily graphed, as in Figure 4.1. If you don't remember how this is done, take another look at Chapter 3.

Where on this graph does the American economy operate? That depends on whether we are at full employment or less than full employment. It also depends on whether we are at war or at peace.

Exactly what is full employment? Does that mean that every person who is ready, willing, and able to work is currently holding a job? As wonderful as that would be, it would be quite impossible. Some people are always out of work for a multitude of reasons we'll discuss in Chapter 8. Even during World War II, when everybody was looking for help, the unemployment rate never fell below 1.2 percent. Economists can't agree on what unemployment rate represents full employment. Most liberal economists believe that we should be able to get the unemployment rate down to about 4 percent. The conservative economists feel that 6 percent is a more realistic rate. Let's split the difference and say that a 5 percent rate represents full employment.

If our economy were to operate at any point on the production possibilities curve (e.g., point D in Figure 4.1), it would be at full employment. Remember that when the economy operates at full employment, there is an unemployment rate of 5 percent. And finally, we'll assume that we are using the best available

Table 4.1. Hypothetical Production Schedule for a Two-Product Economy

Point	Units of Butter	Units of Guns
A	15	0
B	14	1
C	12	2
D	9	3
E	5	4
F	0	5

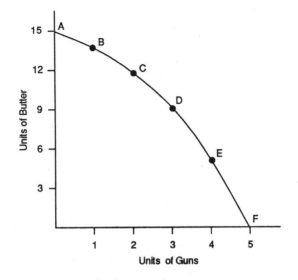

Figure 4.1 Graph of two-product economy

technology. (We'll do our typing on word processors, rather than on those big old fashioned office manual typewriters, for example).

We've already learned that point A represents zero military preparedness. Point B would give us some preparedness, C still more, and so forth. Would point F be a realistic mix of military and consumer goods? What do *you* think?

All guns and no butter would make for a very hungry society, wouldn't it? Not to mention other necessities and amenities like shelter, clothing, entertainment, gasoline, and medicine.

So where does all of this leave the United States? Somewhere between points A and F. Realistically, even a nation on a full wartime footing will have about a fifty-fifty mix of guns and butter.

Moving right along, let's apply some of these profound insights to Figure 4.2. Place a G on the graph to depict an economy that is at full employment, while on a wartime footing. Next, place an H at the point where an economy would be operating if there were full employment during peacetime. Check your results against those in Figure 4.3.

Point G shows about a fifty-fifty mix of military goods and consumer goods. At point H we have some military goods, but mostly consumer goods.

Now we'll look at three more points, this time plotted on Figure 4.4. Using what you've learned, place point I on the graph to indicate where the economy usually operates. Then mark point J to show production during a recession and, finally, point K to show a catastrophic depression. See if your answers match those in Figure 4.5.

Let's talk about point I. Are we generally on the production possibilities curve? When was the last time we saw an unemployment rate of 5 percent? It was back in 1973. On the other hand, is our economy usually in a recession? No? Then we're usually at point I. (As long as your point I is close to the production possibilities curve, your answer is correct because you've demonstrated that you're nearly at full employment. These possibilities could be 14 units of butter and 1 gun, 12 units of butter and 1.7 guns, or 9 units and 2.8 guns.)

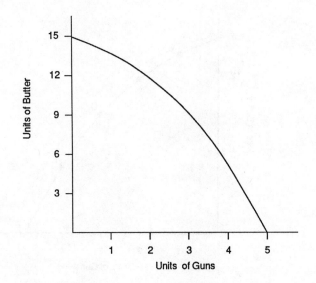

Figure 4.2

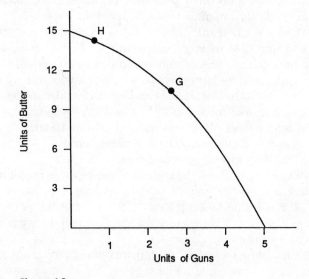

Figure 4.3

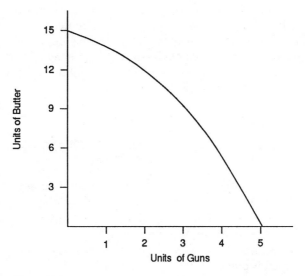

Figure 4.4

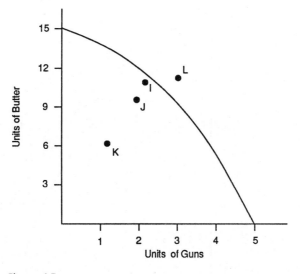

Figure 4.5

Now point J is a recession because we're somewhat further from the production possibilities curve. Even though J represents a severe recession, things could be a lot worse. Like at point K, a terrible depression. What's the difference between a recession and a depression? There is no clear dividing line. A popular view is that we're in a recession if your neighbor is out of work, and we're in a depression if *you* are out of work.

Self-Test 3

1. When a country is operating on its production possibilities curve, that country is operating at _____.

2. If a country were fighting an all-out war, about what percentage of its production should it devote to military goods?

3. If an economy is operating at full employment, can it increase its output of both guns and butter?

4. To operate on the production possibilities curve a country must fulfill two conditions with respect to its resources and technology. What are those conditions?

5. In the graph below, how much is the unemployment rate at points A and B?

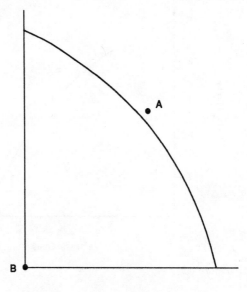

Answers to Self-Test 3

1. Full employment or full capacity.

2. 50 percent.

3. No. The more guns you produce, the less butter you can produce, and vice versa. This is easily demonstrated by moving along the production possibilities curve.

4. It must use all its resources, and it must use the best available technology.

5. A = 2 or 3 percent; B = 100 percent (nobody is working).

10 | ECONOMIC GROWTH

Can we go beyond the production possibilities curve, to, say, point L in Figure 4.5? What do you think? If the production possibilities curve depicts our economy at full employment, can we go beyond full employment? The answer is "yes."

After all, at full employment, we still have 5 percent of the labor force out of work. And during World War II we did reduce the unemployment rate to 1.2 percent. As late as 1969, near the peak of our involvement in the Vietnamese War, our unemployment rate fell to just over 3 percent. So from time to time, especially during wars, we have been able to go beyond the production possibilities curve.

That curve shows our economic potential at any given point in time. The real trick, then, is to push it outward over time. If the production possibilities curve represents our potential, then how do we increase that potential?

There are two ways. First, we can improve the available technology. In fact, our technology improves from year to year, as we discover new and better ways of doing things. Sometimes an invention will propel us forward, as did the steam engine, the telephone, the airplane, the assembly line, and the computer. Other, less spectacular technological improvements are always being made to enhance our productive capacity, thereby pushing our production possibilities curve outward (see Figure 4.6).

A second way to expand our potential is to increase our resources. Land, of course, is fixed in quantity, and, Harvard Business School notwithstanding, we'll assume that entrepreneurs are born, not made.

We can increase our labor force over time by increasing our birth rate, but since very few people begin working before they're 16 or 18, we can't do too much along these lines for at least a generation. Suppose, for example, that in 1990 a new baby boom began. We wouldn't see an increase in our labor force until 2010. We could, of course, make greater efforts to lower our unemployment rate and encourage more people (like housewives, students, and retired workers) to enter the labor force, but these workers are already counted as part of our potential.

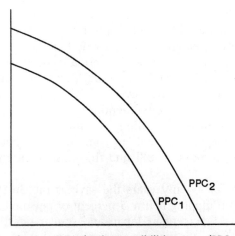

Figure 4.6 Production possibilities curve (PPC$_1$ and PPC$_2$)

The only other way to expand our potential is to increase our capital. By adding to our stock of plant and equipment, we can increase our potential output of goods and services. It is capital that makes the difference between an industrial society like our own and a subsistence-level society like many of the nations in Africa and Asia. One person working with one machine may be able to turn out more output than several hundred people working without machinery.

Where does capital come from? Let's consider an example. A farmer wants to buy a tractor so that he will then be able to grow twice as much wheat. But he has no savings, and no one will lend him money. This leaves him with two choices: either he can work more hours, or his family can cut back on its spending.

Let's assume that the farmer now works eight hours a day to produce eight bushels of wheat a day and that his family spends the entire proceeds of his sales. We'll assume that the farmer works seven days a week and that wheat sells for $5 a bushel.

Suppose that instead of working eight hours a day, he works ten hours. If a tractor costs $10,000 and wheat sells for $5 a bushel, he will have to work two thousand extra hours to save enough money to buy the tractor. It would take him one thousand working days to do that. On the other hand, if his family can cut back on its spending by $10 a day, it will take them one thousand days to save the money. Perhaps some combination of additional work and lowered consumption would enable the farmer and his family to save $10,000 in two years.

Once the farmer buys that tractor, his output doubles and his income doubles. Suppose that his family now goes back to living on the farmer's eight hours of labor a day, or $40 in earnings, and suppose the farmer goes back to working eight hours a day. How much money will the farmer now earn and how much will he be able to save?

Since his output has doubled, he is now earning $80 a day (16 bushels at $5 a bushel), so he can save $40 a day. In just 250 days he will be able to buy another tractor. With two tractors (and a son, daughter, or wife to drive the second tractor), how long will it be before the farmer can buy a third tractor? Just 125 days.

If it's so easy to raise capital, why don't all those poor farmers in India, Bangladesh, Ethiopia, Zaire, Mexico, and Peru just save up the money and invest in capital equipment like steel plows, tractors, and harvesters?

There are three good reasons why they don't. First, they may not be able to work longer hours because they are already working from sunrise to sunset. Second, they may be unable to cut back on their consumption because they are already living at subsistence level. And third, they can't just borrow the money, of course, because no one will lend it to them.

Capital is an elusive thing. The more of it you have, the more you can acquire, but you must be able to come up with that initial savings to invest in capital. If you're poor, you'll find that raising the initial capital is not an easy trick.

For the last twenty years the savings rate in the United States has been very low, often dipping below 5 percent of personal income. Compare this to a rate of 20 to 25 percent in Japan and similar rates in West Germany, Taiwan, and South Korea. No wonder those nations have been growing so much more quickly than we have.

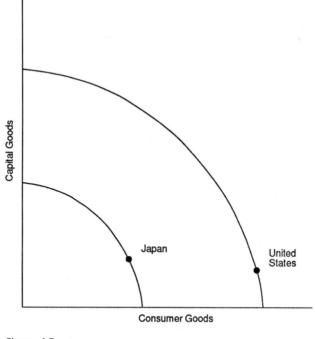

Figure 4.7

Figure 4.7 shows the relative positions of Japan and the United States on their respective curves. We're much bigger, but they're growing much faster. Will they catch us and, if so, when? The bet here is that Japan, a country with half our population and only a small fraction of our natural resources, will not catch us for at least one hundred years. And if you'd like to take that bet, I somehow doubt if either of us will be around to collect.

Self-Test 4

1. The production possibilities curve implies an unemployment rate of _____ percent.

2. In Figure A, put an M where the unemployment rate is 10 percent, an N where it is 5 percent, and an O where it is 2 percent.

3. In Figure A, draw in a second production possibilities curve illustrating economic growth.

4. There are two basic ways to bring about economic growth: (1) _____ _____ and (2) _____ .

5. There are two ways to build up capital: (1) _____ and (2) _____ .

6. Why do people in developing nations have so much difficulty raising capital?

7. What is capital?

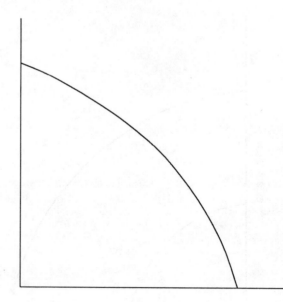

Figure A

Answers to Self-Test 4

1. 5 percent.
2. and 3.

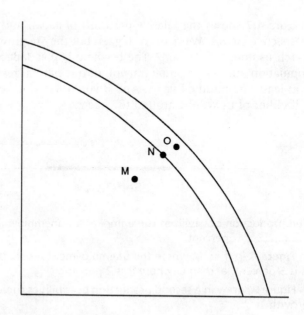

4. Improve technology; raise capital.
5. Save more; work more.
6. They are already working as hard as they can and they can't afford to cut back on consumption because they are already living at the subsistence level.
7. Plant and equipment.

CHAPTER 5

The Mixed

Economy

We'll be concentrating on one of the three basic questions of economics: How are goods produced? The answer to this question is the same for every economy: Some goods are produced by private enterprise and the rest by the government. The only question, then, is how much is produced by each.

Most of this chapter has to do with economic specialization. It is specialization that enables us to enjoy a high standard of living. As we end our discussion of specialization, we shall climb up on our soapbox to proclaim the virtues of free international trade.

By the end of this chapter you will:

- Be familiar with the invisible hand, the price mechanism, and perfect competition.
- Understand the role of government in the economy.
- Know the basic advantage and disadvantage of economic specialization.
- Be able to state the case for international specialization.
- Be familiar with absolute and comparative advantage.

1 | THE INVISIBLE HAND, THE PRICE MECHANISM, AND PERFECT COMPETITION

These three concepts are so closely connected that we will deal with all of them together. We'll discuss the price mechanism in greater detail in Chapter 12, and we'll deal with perfect competition again in Chapter 14.

2 | The Invisible Hand

What do you think the invisible hand is? Something that might grab you in a darkened movie theater? Not if you've read Adam Smith's *The Wealth of Nations* (a title economists frequently drop during conversations). When Smith coined the phrase, "the invisible hand," he was actually thinking about an economic guidance system that *always* makes everything come out all right.

Adam Smith believed that if people set out to promote the public interest, they would do less good than they would if they pursued their own selfish interests. That's right! If people are out for themselves, they will work harder, produce more, and grow richer. And that premise is the basis of the free enterprise system.

We can see how the invisible hand works by looking toward the Soviet Union, of all places. About one-third of that country's feod is produced on about 1 percent of the land under cultivation. That 1 percent happens to be made up of small privately owned plots; the other 99 percent is in the form of large collective farms. Obviously, then, Soviet farmers work much harder on their own land than on land owned by the government. As Adam Smith said, a man pursuing his own interest "frequently promotes that of society more effectively than when he really intends to promote it." (Adam Smith, *The Wealth of Nations*, Vol. 1, Book 4, Chapter 2. Edited by Edward Cannon. London: Methuen & Co., Ltd., 1961, pp. 477–78.)

The invisible hand that guides us, then, is the profit motive or, more broadly, economic self-interest. It gets us to do good by helping us to do well.

3 | The Price Mechanism

It is often said that everyone has his price. Which means that nearly all of us, for a certain sum of money, would do some pretty nasty things. The key variable here is price. Some of us would do these nasty things for just a hundred dollars, others would ask for a thousand, and the really principled among us would demand a million.

Not only does every*one* have his (or, for that matter, her) price, but every*thing* has *its* price as well. Think of prices as signals sent to buyers and sellers. When the price of something goes up, the signal to buyers is loud and clear: Do without or cut back, unless you're willing to pay the higher price.

Of course, buyers can also send a message to sellers. When they want more of a certain good or service, they drive up the price, which, in turn, signals producers to produce more. If the price rise is substantial and appears to be permanent, new firms will be attracted to the industry, thereby raising output still further.

4 | Competition

What is competition? Is it the rivalry between McDonald's and Burger King? GM and Ford? Most economists will tell you that in order to have real competition, you need many firms in an industry. How many? So many that no firm is large enough to have any influence over price.

If large sectors of American industry are not very competitive, the price system doesn't work all that well and the invisible hand becomes even more invisible. On the other hand (no pun intended), even without a perfectly competitive economic system, we can't just toss the price mechanism out the window. The forces of supply and demand, however distorted, are still operating. With all their price manipulation, even the largest corporations must be guided by the wishes of their consumers. Then, too, in recent years, foreign competition has become extremely important in many industries. In conclusion, then, let's just say that we have an imperfectly functioning price system in a less than competitive economy that is guided by a not too vigorous invisible hand.

Self-Test 1

1. What is the invisible hand and how does it work?
2. According to most economists, what provides people with their basic motivation?
3. Explain how prices send a signal to buyers and sellers.
4. In order for the price system to work well, what is needed in addition to the invisible hand and the price mechanism?

Answers to Self-Test 1

1. The invisible hand is the profit motive, which guides people, all of whom are acting in their own self-interest, to promote the general good.
2. Self-interest (or profits).
3. A price rise signals buyers that they'll have to pay more; at the same time, it signals sellers that they may want to increase production. A price decrease sends the opposite messages to buyers and sellers.
4. Some degree of competition.

5 | THE ROLE OF GOVERNMENT IN THE ECONOMY

Theoretically, there are three types of economic systems: (1) The government can produce almost all the goods and services (a command economy), (2) private enterprise can produce virtually everything (pure capitalism), or (3) there can be some government production and some private production (a mixed economy).

No economy is entirely privately owned. A few, mostly in Eastern Europe, are almost entirely government owned. Ours is clearly a mixed economy, but it leans heavily toward the private sector (about 90 percent). The British and Swedish systems are more or less in the middle, while the Chinese and Soviet are very heavily government owned and operated.

The U.S. government has three distinct tiers. At the top is the federal government, which I will generally refer to as "the government." At the middle and lower levels there are fifty state governments and tens of thousands of local governments, respectively.

Each unit of government has the power to collect taxes, provide services, and issue regulations that can have a profound effect on our economy. By taxing, spending, and regulating, a government is able to somewhat alter the answers to the three questions from Chapter 4: What will be produced? How? and For whom?

We produce some items in response to government demand: roads, schools, courthouses, stamp pads, paper clips, and missile systems, for instance. Government regulations *prevent* business firms from producing or selling other items: heroin, crack, alcoholic beverages (from 1920 until 1933), and prostitutes' services (except in the state of Nevada, where they are legal).

Production is also influenced by child labor laws, health and safety regulations, and antipollution legislation. And finally, the government, by taxing hundreds of billions of dollars away from wage earners and corporate shareholders, redistributes these funds to the old and the poor, thus strongly altering the outcome of the question: For whom? In Chapter 7 we'll further consider the government's role in the economy.

Self-Test 2

1. What are the three types of economic systems?
2. The U.S. economy is a _____ economy.
3. About 90 percent of U.S. goods and services are produced by
   _____ .
4. The government has three main powers that affect the economy. List them.

Answers to Self-Test 2

1. (1) Government ownership and production, (2) private ownership and production, and (3) mixed.
2. Mixed.
3. Private enterprise.
4. It can tax, it can spend, and it can regulate.

6 | SPECIALIZATION

You don't need to be an economist to notice that everyone is a specialist these days. You can't find a doctor anymore, but you're surrounded by endocrinologists, brain surgeons, cardiologists, opthalmologists, dermatologists, allergists, and urologists. Why? Why do *you* think? There's a lot more money in these specialties than there is in being a general practitioner.

Lawyers, too, are specialists—in corporate takeovers, patent law, real estate, or divorce. Secretaries, chefs, and assembly-line workers also specialize, as do the people in nearly every other line of work.

We're going to study three aspects of specialization: (1) the economic advantages of specialization, (2) the ways in which the proceeds of one specialty are exchanged for those of others, and (3) an unfortunate consequence of specialization—alienation.

7 | The Economic Advantage of Specialization

Are you ready for another Adam Smith story? This one's about a pin factory whose operation he had observed.

One workman, said Smith "could scarce, perhaps, with his utmost industry, make one pin in a day, and certainly could not make twenty." He then describes how pin-making has become specialized: "One man draws out the wire, another straightens it, a third cuts it, a fourth points it, a fifth grinds it at the top for receiving the head. . . ." (Adam Smith, *op. cit.* Vol. 1, Book 1, Chapter 1, pages 8 and 9.)

There are three distinct advantages to producing pins in this manner. First, the workmen get good at their jobs—better than they would be if they went from one function to another. Second, they don't waste time shifting from one task to another. Third, the factors can buy specialized and expensive equipment since it will be fully utilized. For example, the owner could purchase a special excrussion die to draw wire, since it will be used continually.

Smith estimated that ten people, working together in a factory, could produce 48,000 pins a day. That would be a lot more than these same ten people could produce while working alone.

8 Specialization and Exchange

If all of us got really good at something and concentrated on that one specialty, we could produce much more than we would if we tried to do everything ourselves. A family that tries to be self-sufficient will have a relatively low standard of living because it takes a lot of time to do the hundreds of things that need to be done—all on an individual basis. Imagine making your own pins, weaving your own cloth, growing all your food, and building your own means of transportation. Think how many hours it would take you to weave a yard of cloth, when you could buy the fabric in the store for a few dollars.

Specialization is useful, however, only if there is a demand for your specialty. If there is a demand for what you make or do, you can trade with someone who has what you want. This is called barter. Today, of course, we use money to facilitate exchange. Instead of finding someone to trade with, you can simply buy what you want and sell what you produce.

When you use money, you can pay for an item and be out of the store in a minute. Barter, however, can get pretty complicated. You could spend all day trying to think of something that you have that the storekeeper will accept as payment.

9 Specialization and Alienation

In spite of its advantages, however, specialization sometimes results in alienation. Some factory workers, for example, have become little better than cogs in a huge industrial wheel. There are workers whose sole function for eight hours a day is to tighten bolts or place front right fenders on auto bodies. Understandably, these people grow bored. Some express their unhappiness by frequent absences, while others (like the workers in a Chevy plant in Lordstown, Ohio) actually sabotage some of the products (e.g. cars) they are assembling.

Specialization leads to higher productivity, but only when not carried too far. Attempts have been made in Western Europe, particularly in Sweden, and in Japan, as well, to involve the worker in making a larger segment of the product.

Workers are frequently consulted and their suggestions solicited. Some degree of specialization is sacrificed in an effort to bolster employee morale. Although these new production modes have been successful, American factories have made only a few tentative efforts in this area.

Self-Test 3

1. What lesson can be learned from Adam Smith's story of the pin factory?
2. In order to have specialization, you also must have _____ .
3. An unfortunate consequence of specialization has been _____ .
4. Why would a self-sufficient family have a relatively low standard of living?

Answers to Self-Test 3

1. Specialization leads to increased output.
2. Exchange.
3. Alienation.
4. They would have to spend a great deal of time making things that they could easily have purchased for relatively little money.

10 | INTERNATIONAL TRADE: THE CASE FOR SPECIALIZATION

The basis for international trade is national specialization. Different nations specialize in the production of those goods and services for which their resources are best suited. Such an allocation of the world's resources lends itself to the efficient production of goods and services. If you look back at the definition of economics at the beginning of Chapter 4—the allocation of the scarce means of production towards the satisfaction of human wants—you'll see that international specialization and trade conform to that definition.

If we go from individual specialization and trade to national and international specialization and trade, we'll see that each induces an efficient allocation of resources. On a national basis, that's exactly what we do—specialize and trade. But we cannot do this unless there is a big enough market in which to buy and sell the goods and services we produce. Of course, the United States has long been the world's largest national market.

What makes sense on an individual basis also makes sense internationally. And so, just as it pays for individuals to specialize and trade, it also pays for nations to do the same.

Suppose that there were just two products in the world—photocopy machines and VCRs. Suppose also that the United States and all the other industrialized countries have resources and technology to produce both. The production possibilities curve shown in Figure 5.1A shows a hypothetical range of various combinations of outputs of photocopiers and VCRs in the United States.

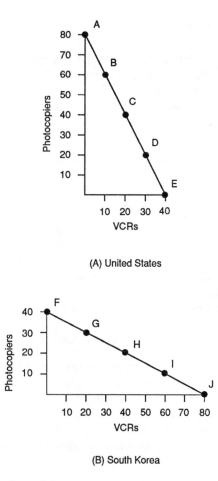

Figure 5.1

Let's make a couple of assumptions here as we did in Chapter 4: (1) that the nation is using all its resources to produce just these two products and (2) that the nation is utilizing the best available technology. Also, remember that if a nation is operating on its production possibilities curve, it is operating at full capacity and full employment. If you don't recall these things, reread the production possibility curve section of Chapter 4 (frame 4.9).

Notice that the production possibilities curves in Figure 5.1 are straight lines rather than rounded curves, as in Chapter 4. This reflects constant opportunity costs; in Chapter 4 we showed increasing opportunity costs. In the real world, every industry eventually faces increasing opportunity costs. But here we use constant opportunity costs because straight lines lend themselves much better than curved lines to our analysis.

One glance at Figure 5.1 will show you that the U.S. is better at making photocopiers and Korea is better at making VCRs. Before we conclude that we should specialize in photocopy machines and Korea in VCRs, let's consider what would happen if both nations produced both products and did not trade.

11 | Domestic Exchange Equations

If we examine a few points along the U.S. production possibilities curve (Figure 5.1A), we will find various combinations of photocopiers and VCRs that we could produce. At point A, with all of its resources devoted to photocopier production, the U.S. output is 80 copiers. At point B we make 60 copiers and 10 VCRs. At C it's 40 copiers and 20 VCRs, at D it's 20 copiers and 30 VCRs, and finally at E we make 40 VCRs.

From this information we can derive the equation:

$$2 \text{ photocopiers} = 1 \text{ VCR}$$

In other words, the opportunity cost of producing one more VCR is two photocopiers, or the cost of producing two more copiers would be one VCR.

Let's turn now to Figure 5.1B, which depicts the production possibilities curve of South Korea. At point F, that country would make 40 photocopy machines. At G, production would total 30 photocopiers and 20 VCRs. And so, the opportunity cost of 20 additional VCRs would be 10 copiers. Obviously, then, the Korean domestic exchange equation is:

$$1 \text{ photocopier} = 2 \text{ VCRs}$$

A comparison of the American and South Korean domestic exchange equations tells us that the Koreans are twice as efficient at VCR production as they are at making photocopy machines. And Americans have the exact opposite situation. Again, instinct would tell us that it would make economic sense for Korea to devote all its resources to VCR production and to trade its VCRs for American photocopiers, in whose production we would specialize.

12 | The Terms of Trade

We're finally ready to set up trading between South Korea and the United States. We know that Korea will trade its VCRs for our photocopiers, but what we don't know are the terms of trade: How many VCRs will Korea trade for each copier? Or, how many copiers will the U.S. trade for each VCR?

To help answer these questions, we will make a couple of simple observations. Let's look at the American domestic exchange equation again:

$$2 \text{ photocopiers} = 1 \text{ VCR}$$

Surely the United States would be unwilling to trade more than two photocopiers for one VCR. But what if Korea offered *more* than one VCR for two copiers? We would do better to accept this deal than to try to produce VCRs ourselves. Let's see why.

We have seen that we could produce either two copiers or one VCR, or we could devote our resources to producing two copiers and trading them for *more* than one VCR. By doing this we would be better off than we would if we used our resources to produce just one VCR.

The same logic applies to South Korea, whose domestic exchange equation is:

$$2 \text{ VCRs} = 1 \text{ photocopier}$$

Obviously, Korea would be unwilling to trade two VCRs for *less* than one photocopier. It Korea could trade two VCRs and get more than one photocopier in exchange, it would be better off concentrating on VCR production and trading some of its VCRs for copiers.

We can now make two general observations:

1. No nation will engage in trade with another nation unless it can gain by that trade.
2. The terms of trade will fall somewhere between the domestic exchange equations of the two trading nations.

The first observation is a truism, but the second might require further elaboration. We'll state the two domestic exchange equations sequentially and then derive the terms of trade.

$$\text{U.S: } 2 \text{ photocopiers} = 1 \text{ VCR}$$

$$\text{Korea: } 1 \text{ photocopier} = 2 \text{ VCRs}$$

Looking at these two equations, we ask ourselves if the United States and Korea can do business. The United States is willing to trade two photocopiers for more than one VCR; the Koreans are willing to trade two VCRs for more than one copier. Can a trade be worked out to the satisfaction of both parties? Try to work out such an exchange. How many copiers for how many VCRs?

Use trial and error. Would the United States accept one and a half VCRs for two copiers? Yes! Would Korea give up one and a half VCRs for two copiers? Yes! So that's one possibility.

Now, here's another. Would the United States accept two and a half VCRs for two copiers? Obviously. Would the Koreans give up two and a half VCRs for two copiers? Yes. So there's another possibility. In fact, we could easily demonstrate a very large number of possible terms of trade.

At this point you may well ask: So what *are* the terms of trade? The best we can do is say that the terms will definitely fall between the two domestic exchange equations. But where? That depends on the forces of supply and demand in the world market. Let's suppose that VCRs are selling for $200 each and that copiers are also selling for $200. What do you think the terms of trade for these two products would be?

I hope you said one copier for one VCR. Would these terms of trade satisfy both the United States and Korea? The answer is definitely "yes."

Over the last two centuries economists have insisted that both countries gain from a trade. Now we'll prove it. In Figure 5.2 we have once again depicted the production possibilities curves of the United States and South Korea, but this time we've added trade possibilities curves. These curves tell us that these countries are trading copiers for VCRs on a one-for-one basis.

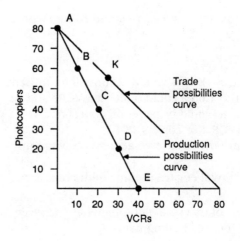

(A) United States

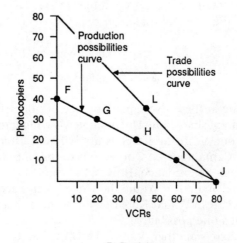

(B) South Korea

Figure 5.2

In effect, through international trade, both countries end up with more copiers *and* more VCRs. Suppose that the United States had been operating at point C of its production possibilities curve before discovering the benefits of international trade. At C we would have produced 40 copiers and 20 VCRs. But if we concentrated our resources on copier production, producing 80 copiers, and if we traded some of these copiers for VCRs, we would go to point K of our trade possibilities curve. At K we would have 50 copiers and 30 VCRs. What we've done, then, is produce 80 copiers and trade 30 of them for 30 VCRs.

It can easily be demonstrated that South Korea experiences similar gains from this trade. Start at point H of Korea's production possibilities curve and figure how much better off Korea is at point L of its trade possibilities curve. Do your calculations in this space:

Korea produces 80 VCRs and sells 30 of them to the U.S. in exchange for 30 copiers. So it now has 50 VCRs and 30 copiers. At point H it had only 40 VCRs and 20 copiers. Its gain is 10 VCRs and 10 copiers.

Self-Test 4

1. An efficient allocation of resources on an international basis calls for national _____ .

2. Brazil is better at producing _____ than at producing _____ .
   Argentina is better at producing _____ than at producing _____ .

3. State the domestic equations of exchange for Brazil and Argentina.
   _____ .

   _____ .

4. Is there a basis of trade between the two countries? If so, then Argentina would trade _____ for _____ , while Brazil would trade _____ for _____ .

5. Brazil would be willing to trade one ton of steel for more than _____ tons of wheat. Argentina would be willing to trade five tons of wheat for more than _____ ton(s) of steel.

6. State the terms of trade in steel and wheat:
   A. One ton of steel will be exchanged for more than _____ and less than _____ tons of wheat.
   B. One ton of wheat will be exchanged for more than _____ and less than _____ tons of steel.

Answers to Self-Test 4

1. Specialization.

2. Steel; wheat. Wheat; steel.

3. Brazil: 5 tons of steel = 2 tons of wheat.
   Argentina: 5 tons of wheat = 1 ton of steel.

4. Yes. Wheat for steel; steel for wheat.

5. 2/5; 1.

6. A. More than 2/5 ton of wheat and less than 5 tons of wheat.
    B. More than 1/5 ton of steel and less than 2 1/2 tons of steel.

13 | Absolute Advantage

From the trade example we have used you may have inferred that South Korea makes VCRs more efficiently (that is, at a lower cost per unit) than the United States does and that the United States is more efficient than Korea in photocopier production.

This may be true, but we don't have cost figures. If it *does* cost the United States as much to make a copier as it costs Korea to make a VCR, then clearly we're better at making copiers and they're better at making VCRs.

Let's assume that the U.S. *does* make copiers for exactly the same production costs that Korea expends on VCRs. Expressed somewhat differently, the United States must expend the same amount of resources to produce a copier as Korea does to make a VCR. Suppose it costs Korea $200 to make a VCR; it would follow that it would cost the United States $200 to make a copier.

Now try this one on for size. If the United States attempted to produce its own VCRs, how much would it cost to make them? If you're not sure, glance at Figure 5.2A. With the same amount of resources, we can produce 80 copiers (point A) or 40 VCRs (point E). So it would cost us twice as much to make a VCR as it would to make a copier, or $400.

The bottom line is that Americans can buy Korean VCRs for half the price that American manufacturers would charge. And so the Koreans have an *absolute advantage* in making VCRs. They're better than we are at making VCRs, so we would do well to take advantage of their low prices while we concentrate on making things we're good at making.

As we've seen, we are good at making copiers. In fact, we are so good that we enjoy an *absolute advantage* over Korea. And so, just as we find it advantageous to buy their VCRs, they buy American copiers rather than produce their own.

With absolute advantage, it is clear that each country sells what it produces most efficiently and buys what it produces least efficiently. But what about countries that do not enjoy an absolute advantage in producing anything? If a country can't make anything more efficiently than other countries, perhaps it can sell something more cheaply.

14 | Comparative Advantage

In the previous problem we saw that South Korea could turn out twice as many VCRs as copiers, using the same resources. We also saw that the United States could turn out twice as many copiers as VCRs.

We also found that there was a basis for trade in that example because both countries stood to gain. Now let's go a step further and ask if there would be any basis for trade if Korea were more efficient than the United States at making both VCRs *and* copiers? What do you think? No?

Guess again.

Imagine that there are only two countries in the world—the United States and Korea—and that they produce only two goods—VCRs and copiers. To keep things simple, we'll assume that the only resource used to make these goods is labor. We know that Korea must use twice as much labor to produce a copier as it uses to make a VCR.

Suppose it takes 10 hours to make a VCR in Korea and 20 hours to make a copier. Also, suppose it takes 30 hours to make a copier in the United States and 60 hours to make a VCR.

If the United States can make 1 copier in 30 hours, it can make 20 copiers in 600 hours. Similarly, the United States can make 10 VCRs in 600 hours, because it takes 60 hours to make 1 VCR.

If we used 300 hours of labor to build copiers and 300 hours to build VCRs, we would have 10 copiers and 5 VCRs. Similarly, Korea would produce 15 copiers and 30 VCRs. Together, then, the United States and Korea could turn out 25 copiers and 35 VCRs without trading. This is shown in Table 5.1.

Are you wondering where all of this is leading? It's all leading to Table 5.2, which demonstrates how a shift in VCR and copier production will lead to an increased output of both VCRs and copiers. That's right! Now, what you're going to try to figure out is this: Which country should raise VCR production and which should increase its production of copiers? Use the data in Table 5.1 as your starting point.

If you answered correctly, you may have reasoned that because Korea is relatively efficient at making VCRs, it will raise its VCR output while reducing its output of copiers, and the United States will do the opposite. If that's what you figured, then you figured right.

Table 5.2 shows that the United States has shifted all 600 hours of labor into copier production, so that we produce 20 copiers. Korea, on the other hand, has shifted 120 hours of its labor from copiers to VCRs. And so, in 420 hours it turns out 42 VCRs; in 180 hours it makes 9 copiers.

When we add up the total output of copiers and VCRs in both tables, we find that we have exceeded our Table 5.1 outputs in Table 5.2. There is a gain of 4 copiers (from 25 to 29) and 7 VCRs (from 35 to 42).

If South Korea and the United States are the only two countries in the world and if copiers and VCRs are their only products, then we are ready to trade. We will trade American copiers for Korean VCRs on a one-for-one basis.

A one-for-one trade will leave countries better off than they were before they began to specialize. Let's say that Korea trades 8 VCRs for 8 copiers. Korea now has 34 VCRs and 17 copiers, while the United States ends up with 8 VCRs and 12 copiers.

How does this compare with what each country would have had before specialization? For this comparison, look back at Table 5.1. Korea would have a net gain of 2 copiers and 4 VCRs, while the United States would have 3 more VCRs and 2 more copiers.

Table 5.1. Copiers and VCRs Produced by the United States and South Korea Using 600 Hours of Labor*

United States	10 copiers and 5 VCRs
South Korea	15 copiers and 30 VCRs
Total	25 copiers and 35 VCRs

*Each country devotes 300 hours to VCR and copier production, respectively.

Table 5.2. Copiers and VCRs Produced by the
United States and South Korea Using 600 Hours
of Labor*

United States	20 copiers and 0 VCRs
South Korea	9 copiers and 42 VCRs
Total	29 copiers and 42 VCRs

*The United States devotes 600 hours to
copier production; South Korea devotes 180 hours
to copier production and 420 to VCR production.

This is what is meant by a trade that helps both parties. So we see that even though one nation is better at producing both products, it still pays for each nation to specialize in the production of the product it is relatively good at making and to trade for the product the other is relatively good at making.

Let's go back once again to the concept of opportunity cost. What is the opportunity cost to the United States of producing one VCR? In other words, to raise VCR output by one unit, what do we give up? We give up two copiers. What is the opportunity cost of producing one VCR in Korea? You guessed it: one-half of one copier.

Now let's consider the opportunity cost of producing copiers. In the United States it's one-half of one VCR; in Korea it's two VCRs. In other words, the opportunity cost of producing VCRs is lower in Korea. But the opportunity cost of producing copiers is lower in the United States.

Now we're finally ready for the *principle of comparative advantage*, which is what this section is all about. Are you ready? Okay, here it comes: The *principle of comparative-advantage* states that *total output is greatest when each product is made by that country that has the lowest opportunity cost*. In our example, copiers should be made in the United States and VCRs in Korea. This is so because the United States has a comparative advantage in copiers, while Korea has one in VCRs. This is true even though Korea can make both copiers and VCRs at a lower cost than the United States can.

15 | CONCLUDING NOTE

In effect, then, we've presented the underlying argument for free trade, which would benefit every nation. In recent years, however, the United States has racked up huge trade deficits, and there are those in and out of Congress who have been calling for legislation to protect us against foreign competition. Although some fairly persuasive arguments have been made in behalf of protection, nearly all economists take a firm stand in support of free trade. The basis for that stand is the existence of comparative and absolute advantage.

Self-Test 5

1. In international trade, what are absolute advantage and comparative advantage?

2. If it costs three times as much to make a car in Nigeria as in Mexico and it costs twice as much to grow wheat in Mexico as in Nigeria, we say that Mexico enjoys an absolute advantage in the production of _____ and Nigeria enjoys an absolute advantage in the production of _____ .

3. If Egypt can produce a ton of cotton at half of what it would cost in the United States and a barrel of oil at one-quarter of what it would cost in the United States:
    A. Which country has a comparative advantage in cotton production and which one has a comparative advantage in oil production?
    B. Therefore, the United States would export _____ and import _____ .
    C. Egypt would export _____ and import _____ .

Answers to Self-Test 5

1. A country has an absolute advantage when it produces a good or service more cheaply than another country; a country enjoys a comparative advantage when the opportunity cost of producing a particular good or service is lower than that of its trading partner.

2. Cars; wheat.

3. A. The United States has a comparative advantage in the production of cotton, and Egypt has one in the production of oil.
    B. Cotton; oil.
    C. Oil; cotton.

CHAPTER 6

Gross National

Product

Gross National Product is a central accounting statistic in economics and the most widely quoted figure. When you have finished this chapter you will know:

- How GNP is defined.
- How GNP is measured.
- The difference between GNP and Real GNP.
- The shortcomings of GNP as a measure of national economic well-being.
- How to calculate per capita GNP.

1 | WHAT IS GROSS NATIONAL PRODUCT?

When Edward Koch was a U.S. Congressman, and later when he was Mayor of New York, he was continually asking people he encountered, "How'm I doin'?" (translation from New Yorkese: "How am I doing?"). If a country asked the same question about itself, it would say, "How big is my GNP?"

What is GNP? It is the nation's *expenditure on all the goods and services produced during the year at market prices.* For example, if we spent $8,000 on each of 7 million American cars, that $56 billion would go into GNP. We'd add in 10 billion Big Macs at $2 each for another $20 billion and 1.6 million new homes at $100,000 each for $160 billion. Then, for good measure we'd add 4 billion visits to doctors' offices at $40 apiece for $160 billion and 18 billion disco admissions at $10 each for $180 billion. Add it all up and we'd get something in the neighborhood of $5 trillion.

We've been throwing around some pretty hefty numbers. If you still don't know your millions from your billions, or your billions from your trillions, reread frames 1–4 of Chapter 2.

2 | HOW IS GNP MEASURED?

There are two basic methods of measuring GNP: the flow-of-income approach and the expenditures approach. Both are illustrated in Figure 6.1.

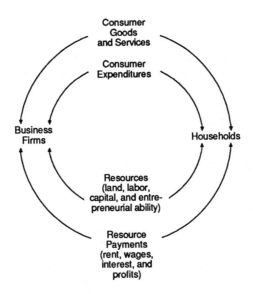

Figure 6.1 Methods of measuring GNP

3 | Flow-of-Income Approach

The flow-of-income approach of determining GNP is shown in the lower half of Figure 6.1. Households provide business firms with resources (land, labor, capital, and entrepreneurial ability). In return for these resources, business firms pay out rent, wages and salaries, interest, and profits to members of those households.

If we were to add up all these resource payments, we'd have National Income. When we include indirect taxes collected by the government (largely sales and property taxes) and depreciation allowances (found on the tax returns of business firms) in this total, we end up with Gross National Product.

The expenditures approach to determining GNP is much more relevant to our purposes and will be useful in the next few chapters. We will not mention the flow-of-income approach again.

4 | Expenditures Approach

When we add up all the money spent by individual consumers, business firms, and the government, we get GNP. This is the expenditures approach. Figure 6.1 assumes that business firms produce all of our goods and services. This is not far from the mark, because in the United States the private sector ultimately does produce over 90 percent of our GNP.

People buy consumer goods from business firms. All of Figure 6.1 illustrates the circular flow of expenditures and income—note that the top and bottom loops are connected. People receive income from business firms in return for their land, labor, capital, and entrepreneurial ability. The money flows right back to the firms in exchange for consumer goods and services. And so the money keeps flowing around and around as more goods are produced and paid for.

If we included business investment expenditures and government expenditures along with consumer expenditures, the total will add up to GNP: *consumer expenditures + investment expenditures + government expenditures = GNP.*

GNP, then, represents spending by three major groups, the largest of which is composed of consumers, who spend about two out of every three dollars of GNP. Consumption spending is designated by the letter C.

Business firms spend hundreds of billions of dollars on plant, equipment, and inventory. We call this sector investment and use the letter I to represent it.

And finally, if we add up all the spending on goods and services by the federal, state, and local governments we have government expenditures, represented by the letter G.

Now we need to add net exports to our GNP equation. We'll designate net exports by X_n:

$$GNP = C + I + G + X_n$$

If we subtract all the money we spend on foreign goods and services from what foreigners spend on our goods and services, we get net exports: *net exports = exports − imports.* This number represents the difference between what we sell to other nations and what they sell to us.

Until very recently, most economists more or less ignored the last item in the GNP equation, net exports. This figure, while positive, was usually less than 1 percent of GNP. More significantly, from the end of World War II to the mid-1970s, net exports was a positive figure virtually every year. But since then, the strong (or overvalued) dollar, weak foreign demand, and a buying binge by American consumers all contributed to our huge balance of trade deficits of the 1980s.

Let's take a look at GNP back in 1986. Using the figures for the fourth quarter, we had a GNP of just over four and a half trillion dollars.

Consumption	$2820.4 (in billions)
Investment	663.2
Government	885.3
Net Exports	−110.2
GNP	4258.7

Self-Test 1

1. What is the definition of GNP?
2. All resources are supplied by _____.
3. Using the expenditure approach, the largest sector of GNP is _____.
4. Suppose that C = 2500 billion, I = 950 billion, G = 800 billion, imports = 350 billion, and exports = 200 billion. How much is GNP?

Answers to Self-Test 1

1. The nation's expenditure on all the goods and services produced during the year at market prices.
2. Households.

3. Consumption.

4. GNP = C + I + G + net exports = (2,500 + 950 + 800 + 200 − 350) = $4,100 (in billions).

5 | GNP VERSUS REAL GNP

Suppose that you have a birthday party every year and invite the same three guests. And every year you send out to the same pizzeria for a large pie with everything. Pretty wild, eh? In 1985, the pie cost $7; in 1986, it cost $7.50; in 1987, it was $8.00; in 1988, it cost $8.75. Since the pie is exactly the same size every year, the only thing that grows bigger is its price. And it's the same way with Real GNP (the pie) and GNP (the price of the pie).

If we wanted to compare our national economic pie, or total production (Real GNP), from one year to the next, we must get rid of the effects of inflation. An example of inflation is the rising price—from $7.00 in 1985 to $8.75 in 1988—of the pizza, which remains the same size.

If our economy produced the same amount of output in 1988 as it did in 1985, then Real GNP did not change. Price went up 25 percent (from $7 to $8.75), but we still produced exactly the same size pie. (We'll be calculating percentage changes in this section. If you need to brush up on this, reread Chapter 2, frames 29–31.)

GNP is the basic measure of how much we produced during a given year. However, comparisons of GNP from one year to the next could be misleading. For example, say the GNP goes from $3 trillion in 1982 to $3.3 trillion in 1983. At first, it appears that we have done extremely well since GNP leaped by 10 percent. But before we get too excited, we should remember that GNP is a measure of all the goods and services produced during a given year *at market prices*. For all we know, perhaps the entire 10 percent increase in GNP was due to inflation. This would obviously be true if prices *did* rise by 10 percent in 1983.

We need to be able to correct GNP for price increases so we can measure the actual rise in production. To do this we use the GNP deflator, which is calculated quarterly by the Department of Commerce. The GNP deflator is really a price index, like the Consumer Price Index. It is used to measure price changes in the items that go into GNP, that is, consumer goods and services, investment goods, and government goods and services.

Let's go back to the problem we posed earlier—GNP rises from $3 trillion in 1982 to $3.3 trillion in 1983. We need to deflate the 1983 GNP to find out how much production rose. In other words, if GNP was $3 trillion in 1982, how much was GNP one year later in *1982 dollars*? To find this out we use the formula:

$$\frac{\text{Real GNP}}{\text{(current year)}} = \frac{\text{GNP}}{\text{(current year)}} \times \frac{\text{GNP deflator (base year)}}{\text{GNP deflator (current year)}}$$

This is a general formula that we'll adapt to specific years. We're comparing 1983 (current year) to 1982 (base year). Therefore, our formula will now read:

$$\text{Real GNP}_{83} = \text{GNP}_{83} \times \frac{\text{GNP deflator}_{82}}{\text{GNP deflator}_{83}}$$

To solve this equation we need to substitute actual numbers for the three variables on the right side of the equation.

We already know that GNP was $3.3 trillion in 1983. By convention, this number is written as 3300. The GNP deflator for 1982, the base year, is 100, again by convention. (The base year of virtually every index is 100.)

We still need to know the GNP deflator for 1983. The Commerce Department publishes this figure, but let's assume for now that it is 110. In other words, prices rose by 10 percent in 1983. Now we'll see if our formula works. We're looking for the Real GNP in 1983, and we see that GNP rose by 10 percent and prices also rose by 10 percent. Real GNP in 1983 should be equal to that of 1982. Substituting into the formula:

$$\text{Real GNP}_{83} = \text{GNP}_{83} \times \frac{\text{GNP deflator}_{82}}{\text{GNP deflator}_{83}}$$
$$= \frac{3300}{1} \times \frac{100}{110}$$
$$= \frac{30}{1} \times \frac{100}{1}$$
$$= 3000$$

Before we move on to a set of problems just like this one, we'll go over a few of the mechanics of our solution. We put the 3300 over 1 because that makes it easier to do cross division and then multiplication. Incidentally, you are allowed to put any number over 1 because that means you are dividing that number by 1. For example, 5 is equal to 5/1, which means that one goes into five, five times.

We also reduced the fractions by division: We divided 3300 by 110, and we got 30. You don't have to reduce fractions, but usually you'll find that smaller numbers are easier to work with.

Here are two more problems:

1. GNP rises from $2.5 trillion in 1980 to $3.0 trillion in 1984. The GNP deflator in 1984 is 125. Find Real GNP in 1984. Find the percentage increase in Real GNP between 1980 and 1984.

2. GNP rises from $3 trillion in 1982 to $5 trillion in 1988. The GNP deflator in 1988 is 150. Find Real GNP in 1988. Find the percentage increase in Real GNP between 1982 and 1988.

Solutions:

1. $$\text{Real GNP}_{84} = \text{GNP}_{84} \times \frac{\text{GNP deflator}_{80}}{\text{GNP deflator}_{84}}$$
$$= \frac{3000}{1} \times \frac{100}{125}$$
$$= \frac{24}{1} \times \frac{100}{1}$$
$$= 2400$$

Percentage change in real GNP from 1980 to 1984:

$$\frac{\text{Change}}{\text{Original number}} = \frac{-100}{2500} = -4\%$$

2. Real $GNP_{88} = GNP_{88} \times \dfrac{\text{GNP deflator}_{82}}{\text{GNP deflator}_{88}}$

$$= \frac{5000}{1} \times \frac{100}{150}$$

$$= \frac{33.33}{1} \times \frac{100}{1}$$

$$= 3333$$

Percentage change in real GNP from 1982 to 1988:

$$\frac{\text{Change}}{\text{Original number}} = \frac{333}{3000} = 11.1\%$$

If we know the Real GNP in the current year, we can compare the economy's output, or production, with that of the base year. In the first problem we found the percentage change in Real GNP between 1980 and 1984 to be −4 percent. Output in 1984 was 4 percent lower than in 1980. In the second problem, output was 11.1 percent higher in 1988 than in 1982.

Self-Test 2

1. GNP rises from $4 trillion in 1986 to $6 trillion in 1992. The GNP deflator in 1992 is 140. Find the percentage increase in real GNP between 1986 and 1992.

2. GNP rises from $4.2 trillion in 1987 to $5.8 trillion in 1995. The GNP deflator in 1995 is 160. Find the percentage increase in real GNP between 1987 and 1995.

Answers to Self-Test 2

1. Real $GNP_{92} = GNP_{92} \times \dfrac{\text{GNP deflator}_{86}}{\text{GNP deflator}_{92}}$

$$= \frac{6000}{1} \times \frac{100}{140}$$

$$= \frac{42.856}{1} \times \frac{100}{1} = 4286$$

Percentage change in real GNP from 1986 to 1992:

$$\frac{\text{Change}}{\text{Original number}} = \frac{285.6}{4000} = 7.1\%$$

2. Real $GNP_{95} = GNP_{95} \times \dfrac{\text{GNP deflator}_{87}}{\text{GNP deflator}_{95}}$

$$= \frac{5800}{1} \times \frac{100}{160}$$

$$= \frac{36.25}{1} \times \frac{100}{1}$$

$$= 3625$$

Percentage change in real GNP from 1987 to 1995:

$$\frac{\text{Change}}{\text{Original number}} = \frac{-575}{4200} = -13.7\%$$

6 | SHORTCOMINGS OF GNP AS A MEASURE OF NATIONAL ECONOMIC WELL-BEING

Any single numerical measure of national economic well-being will exclude things that should be included and include other things that might best be left out. In the next four frames we'll consider four basic shortcomings of GNP.

7 | Production that Is Excluded

Household Production

Household production consists mainly of the work done by homemakers— care of children, cleaning, shopping, and cooking. If a housekeeper is hired to do this work, his or her production would be included in GNP. If two homemakers chose to work for each other as housekeepers (why, I don't know), their work would be counted in GNP. So why not count homemakers' work in their own homes? Because no money changes hands. No payments are recorded.

GNP does not include food grown in backyard gardens, home repairs made by a family member, clothes made at home, and do-it-yourself goods and services that people produce or perform for themselves, their families, and their friends. When a person buys goods or services from other people, however, they are counted, assuming that the sellers report the resultant income.

Illegal Production

Illegal goods and services are not counted in GNP. The big three—dope, prostitution, and gambling—are ignored even though people spend hundreds of billions on these goods and services. If you place a legal bet at a race track or an off-track betting parlor, it counts in GNP, but a bet placed with a bookie is illegal. If you play the state lottery, your bet is counted toward GNP, but not if you play the "numbers" game run on city streets.

Prostitution was legal in France before World War II. Although the same services continued to be provided after the war on an illegal basis, anyone scanning France's GNP figures right after the war might have thought that country had been hit by a depression.

California is our leading agricultural state. Do you know its number one crop? Lettuce? Grapes? Citrus fruit? Sorry, it's none of the above. California's number one crop is grass—as in marijuana.

The Underground Economy

In every large city, on country roads, in flea markets, and even in suburban malls, people are selling everything from watches to watermelons, from corn to collectibles. And the chances are they do not report the proceeds of these sales to the government. They do not pay taxes on this income, and the sales are not reflected in GNP.

Some of the items sold were stolen, but most are goods produced without the government's knowledge. Together with illegal goods and services, these markets form a vast underground economy. How vast? Maybe 10 or 15 percent of GNP.

Who knows? How much of *your* income do you spend in the underground economy? Or, perhaps I should be asking, how much of *your* income *comes* from the underground economy?

Street peddlers, cab drivers, and low-life entrepreneurs aren't the only ones who underreport their incomes. The underground economy also includes a very nice class of people. Doctors, dentists, lawyers, and even, heaven forbid, accountants. In fact, there is a whole branch of accounting dedicated to the underground economy. It's called "creative accounting." This involves keeping three separate sets of books: one for their creditors, showing an inflated profit; one for the government showing very little profit; and one for themselves, so they know how they're actually doing. The next time you're having your teeth realigned, just ask your dentist, "Would you prefer a check or cash?" Then, to make absolutely certain, ask if there's a discount for paying cash.

Let's just step back for a minute and look once again at our definition of GNP: *the nation's expenditure on all the goods and services produced during the year at market prices.*

What exactly is production? For once, economists are in agreement. *Production is any good or service that people are willing to pay for.* And that means *anything*!

You go to a concert and fall asleep. How much did you pay for your ticket? $10? That was $10 worth of production.

You attend a brilliant lecture on the future of the universe. It's free. The speaker doesn't get paid. No production.

You grow tomatoes in your backyard for your own family's consumption. No production.

You take a course in philosophy. The professor walks into the room and lies down on the floor in the front of the class. This happens all term. How much tuition did you pay to take this course? That's how much production took place.

The problem we have, then, is an inconsistency between the definition of GNP and the way the GNP figure is compiled by the U.S. Department of Commerce. There's a lot of production going on out there that the government misses. Why? Is the department understaffed (one of the all-time favorite words of bureaucrats)? Maybe. But the main reason for the discrepancy is that the government refuses to count the underground economy and will not even acknowledge its existence. As a result, underground production does not go into GNP, even as an estimate, so we are grossly (no pun intended) undercounting GNP.

8 | Treatment of Leisure Time

GNP does not take into account leisure time. We have no way of telling, from the GNP, if the people of a country enjoy a thirty-hour week or have to work sixty hours a week. Many immigrant groups—the Vietnamese and Koreans in the 1970s and 1980s, the Cubans in the 1960s, the eastern and southern Europeans from the 1880s to the 1920s, and the Irish in the 1840s—put in longer work hours than native-born Americans. For these immigrants who worked at low wages, long hours were necessary for survival. Workers in other nations also labor for longer hours. The rice farmer in Egypt, the factory worker in Hong Kong, and the manual laborer in India do not enjoy seven-hour work days, paid sick leave, long vacations, paid holidays, and days off for Christmas shopping.

The average work week in the United States and in the rest of the industrial world, however, has gradually declined. Until after World War II, most workers still put in five and a half or six days a week. In 1900 the ten-hour day was common, and when you wanted to take a vacation, if your boss liked you, he reached into his pocket and gave you $5 spending money.

We have made marvelous gains in leisure time, but these gains are not reflected in GNP, nor are the differences in the work weeks of various countries whose GNPs might be compared with ours. For example, the Japanese have nearly caught up with us in per capita real GNP (see frame 11), but they work longer hours.

9 Human Costs and Benefits

Another problem with comparing our GNP with that of other countries, or with our own GNP in previous years, is that GNP does not include the physical, mental, and psychological costs of production and the human benefits associated with it.

First, the costs. These include the strain of commuting long distances along congested routes, the tedium, the dangers, the low status, and the other unpleasantness associated with certain jobs. Other jobs cause anxiety; advertising account executives, air traffic controllers, and bomb squad members are under extreme stress during most working hours. The psychological strain associated with work is called *psychic cost*. These psychic costs detract from one's enjoyment of a job. On the other hand, *psychic income* adds to that enjoyment.

There are also physical strains and benefits associated with work. As I've already noted, the average work week is much shorter than it was eighty years ago, but the amount of physical labor performed on the average job has declined as well. Not only have we shifted nearly completely from human power to mechanical power, but the nature of work has also changed from farming and manufacturing to service jobs, most of which require no physical labor.

There are still a good many jobs that require physical labor or that must be performed under unpleasant circumstances. Just ask the people who work in asbestos, textile, or automobile factories, or talk to a few coal miners, migrant farm workers, and foot patrolmen.

Some people, on the other hand, really enjoy their jobs. Take actors. They are willing to hold all kinds of stopgap jobs while they wait for that big chance. For most, of course, it never comes. In New York, where no more than a thousand people earn their entire livelihood from acting, there are tens of thousands of aspiring actors. Why are they willing to buck such outrageous odds? Because they really love the work. The *psychic income* from working in the theater—the roar of the greasepaint, the smell of the crowd, the adulation, the applause—is the compensation they really seek.

Finally, there are physical benefits from certain kinds of work. For example, my friend Marty, a gym teacher, is always in great shape. And I'll never forget Mr. Spalter, a little bald man who taught gym (How can you *teach* gym?) at

James Madison High School in Brooklyn in the 1950s. The guy must have been close to eighty, but he could climb up a thirty-foot rope in less than fifteen seconds, and do it in perfect form, with his legs exactly perpendicular to his body. The physical benefits of being a gym teacher then—or a farmer or a health club employee—are obvious.

Today's GNP is produced by an entirely different type of labor force doing very different work from that of fifty or one hundred years ago. And our labor force works very differently from that of developing countries. This makes long-term and international GNP comparisons less valid.

10 | What Goes into GNP?

Other problems with GNP as a measure of national economic well-being have to do with the "unproductive production" that goes into GNP. A large part of our production, for example, goes toward national defense, police protection, pollution control devices, cleanups of oil spills, repair and replacement of poorly made cars and appliance; thus, a large GNP is not a very good indicator of how we're doing. Also, a large part of our labor force staffs the myriad bureaucracies of the federal, state, and local governments, as well as those of the corporate world, so we're not all that well off. GNP supposedly tells us how much we produce. We need to ask, How much of what?

In general the problem with using GNP as a measure of national economic well-being is that GNP is just a single number, and no one number can possibly provide us with all the information we need. Try these examples on for size.

My neighbor is doing very well on her diet. She's down to 120 pounds. Of course, she's only 3'6".

How's the weather? It's great. The temperature is 50. Oh, yes, we're having a hurricane.

My friend got straight A's in his college course this semester. Unfortunately, he's taking them in jail where he is serving ten consecutive life sentences for mass murder. Oh, well, nobody's perfect.

Self-Test 3

1. Which of the following are counted in GNP:
    A. Household pi oduction?
    B. Illegal goods and services?
    C. Leisure time?
2. Why *should* illegal production be counted in GNP?
3. What physical benefits are associated with our GNP today compared to those of eighty years ago?

Answers to Self-Test 3

1. None
2. Production is any good or service that people are willing to pay for. Illegal goods and services meet that criterion. GNP should include *all* goods and services produced during the year.

3. Today's labor force does much less physical labor and works under much more pleasant conditions.

11 | PER CAPITA REAL GNP

GNP may be used to compare living standards between various countries or between time periods within one country. We usually make such comparisons on a per capita basis using this formula:

$$\text{Per capita GNP} = \frac{\text{GNP}}{\text{Population}}$$

Using U.S. data for the fourth quarter of 1986, we can plug right into the formula:

$$\text{Per capita GNP} = \frac{\$4,258,700,000,000}{242,000,000} = \$17,600$$

To compare 1986 per capita GNP with that of other years we have to correct for inflation, revising our formula as follows:

$$\text{Per capita Real GNP} = \frac{\text{Real GNP}}{\text{Population}}$$

How does our current per capita Real GNP compare with that of earlier years? As you can see from Table 6.1, it has more than tripled since 1929. Over this same period, incidentally, Real GNP has more than quintupled (from $710 billion to $3677 billion, in 1982 dollars). In recent years, however, especially from the early 1970s to the early 1980s, the gains have been less impressive. In fact, between 1978 and 1982 there was virtually no change.

How valid are per capita Real GNP comparisons over times? Over the short run, say up to ten years, they are quite valid. But comparisons over twenty, thirty, or forty years become more and more like comparing apples and oranges, or like comparing video games and pocket calculators with nine-inch Dumont TVs and big old-fashioned adding machines that were powered by a lever that you pulled every time you entered a number. Over long periods of time, different goods and services go into GNP, and the quality of those goods and services changes.

International comparisons of per capita Real GNP must be made with even more caution. America's per capita real GNP is perhaps one hundred times

Table 6.1. Per Capita Real GNP
for Selected Years, 1929–1986

Year	Per Capita Real GNP
1929	$5800
1949	7400
1969	12000
1986	17600

Sources: 1987 Economic Report of the President; The New York Times, March 19, 1987

larger than India's. Do we produce one hundred times as much per capita? Probably not. The typical Indian, a farmer living in a rural village, is not subject to psychological stresses, commuting problems, pollution, or crime, as is the average American. Furthermore, the average Indian family produces most of its own food, clothing, and shelter—items that are not counted in GNP. Therefore, we are seriously underestimating India's Real GNP.

Perhaps the American Real GNP is not one hundred times greater than India's, but just twenty-five times higher. Per capita Real GNP is not an accurate measure of international differences in production levels, but it does provide a rough measure of these differences. Comparisons of countries at similar stages of economic development are much more accurate, however, than comparisons of countries at different stages.

Self-Test 4

1. Per capita Real GNP is found by dividing _____ by _____ .
2. Our standard of living in 1986 was about _____ times as greater as it was in 1900.
3. If our GNP is $5 trillion and our population is 250 million, what is our per capita GNP?

Answers to Self-Test 4

1. GNP; population.
2. Four.
3. $$\text{Per capita GNP} = \frac{\text{GNP}}{\text{Population}} = \frac{\$5,000,000,000,000}{250,000,000} = \$20,000$$

CHAPTER 7

The Government, Business, and Consumption Sectors

The big three of GNP are consumer spending, investment spending, and government spending. We'll be looking at these expenditures and their economic significance in this chapter. We'll also be talking about taxes, business organization, and saving.

When you have completed this chapter you will:

- Know what the federal, state, and local governments spend their money on and where that money comes from.
- Be familiar with direct, indirect, progressive, and regressive taxes.
- Know how your personal income tax is computed.
- Understand why business firms are organized as proprietorships, partnerships, and corporations.
- Be familiar with the major categories of investment.
- Be able to calculate the average propensity to consume, the average propensity to save, the marginal propensity to consume, and the marginal propensity to save.
- Understand the consumption function.

1 | THE GOVERNMENT SECTOR

The Growth of Government Spending

Big government is a relatively recent phenomenon. Until the 1930s, we had very small government. Local, state, and federal spending totalled just 10 percent of GNP. Today, if we include transfer payments, like Social Security, Medicare, and unemployment insurance benefits, government spending accounts for about one-third of GNP.

Two cataclysmic events brought about this increase in government spending—the Great Depression of the 1930s and World War II. President Franklin Roosevelt was elected in 1932 on a platform pledging to get the country out of the Depression. He set up permanent government institutions that would ultimately spend hundreds of billions of dollars a year on social programs. The Japanese attacked Pearl Harbor, and we entered World War II and embarked on a long-term increase in government spending for defense.

How much money does the government actually spend? In fiscal year 1988, which began on October 1, 1987, the federal budget called for over $1 trillion in spending, while state and local government were spending another $600 billion.

Let's see where this money has gone. The big three of federal government spending are Social Security, defense, and interest on the federal debt. This last item needs some explanation. The national debt stood at a few billion dollars at the onset of the Depression. By 1981 it had risen to $1 trillion; it reached $2 trillion in 1986, and it's fast approaching the $3 trillion mark. As the debt increases, so does the interest. Let's suppose that the interest rate on the debt is 7 percent. How much interest would we owe in one year? Figure it out in the space below using $2.5 trillion at 7 percent interest.

2 | The interest comes to $175 billion. That's a pretty big chunk out of the federal budget. Add to that the other social programs—Medicaid, food stamps, public assistance. Throw in government spending for highway construction, mass transit aid, crime prevention, environmental protection, and the hundreds of other federal programs. You'll come up with a figure well over $1 trillion.

State and local spending have also been on the rise since World War II, but not quite as sharply as federal spending. Well over half of the state and local money goes to education, health, and welfare.

Let's take a look at educational spending. Nearly twenty million Americans are currently attending high school or college. Fifty or sixty years ago most people began working at age fourteen. Now all those teenagers are still in school. And supporting public education has traditionally been the role of the state and local governments, although in recent years Washington has provided supplementary funds.

Another expenditure that has gone up enormously is police protection. Although this is another traditional function of local government, rising crime and the deterioration of neighborhoods have made it necessary to hire many more police.

It is important to distinguish between government spending and transfer payments. Only spending—government spending, business spending, or consumer spending—goes into GNP. Remember, GNP is total spending on goods and services. Transfer payments cannot be counted because they don't represent that kind of spending. However, once people (or government units) spend that transferred money—whether public assistance checks, Social Security checks, or highway funds—it goes into GNP.

In general, then, Americans today look toward the government to provide more and more services. Where does the money come from?

3 | ## Taxation

The Tax Burden

Where does the government get all this spending money? State and local governments raise most of their funds from taxes, and the rest are supplied by the federal government. For example, when an interstate highway is built, improved, or maintained, the federal government will foot 90 percent of the bill. Federal aid to mass transit, education, health, and welfare are also very important sources of funding for state and local programs. Unlike the debt-ridden federal government, state and local governments have been running substantial surpluses since the early 1980s.

The federal government has not had a budget surplus since 1969. In fiscal years 1985 and 1986 our deficits were over $200 billion. The federal government raises 80 to 90 percent of the money it needs from taxes and borrows the rest.

Contrary to popular opinion, Americans are not very heavily taxed in comparison with the citizens of other industrial countries. Taxes in the United States total about one-third of GNP, a figure somewhat higher than Japan's and somewhat lower than West Germany's. But try some of these figures on for size: Sweden, 50.5 percent; the Netherlands, 47.3 percent; Belgium, 45.4 percent; Denmark, 46.2 percent; Italy, 40.6 percent; and France, 44.6 percent. (See *Statistical Abstract of the United States*, 1986, p. 846.)

4   ## Types of Taxes

There are two basic types of taxes: (1) direct and indirect taxes and (2) progressive and regressive taxes.

5   *Direct taxes*   A direct tax is a tax with your name written on it. The personal income tax and the Social Security tax are examples. They are taxes on individuals. If you earn a certain amount of money, you must pay these taxes.

The corporate income tax is also a direct tax, since a corporation is considered a legal person. For example, in court, you would sue a corporation rather than its owners or officers. And so, if a corporation makes a profit, it must pay a corporate income tax, and that is a direct tax.

6   *Indirect taxes*   Indirect taxes are on things rather than on people. Taxes on things include sales and excise taxes. A state sales tax on retail purchases and the excise taxes on tires, gasoline, movie tickets, cigarettes, and liquor are examples of indirect taxes.

7   *Progressive taxes*   A progressive tax places a greater burden on those best able to pay and a lesser burden or no burden at all on the poor. The best example is, of course, the federal personal income tax. The head of a family of four, for example (and the sole support of the family), with an income of less than $12,200 in 1988 ($12,400 in 1989) would pay no personal income tax whatsoever. But as we so well know, the more we make, the more we must shell out to Uncle Sam.

8   *Regressive taxes*   When the burden of a tax falls more heavily on the poor than on the rich, the tax is said to be regressive.

We'll use the excise tax on cigarettes as an example. Suppose that a rich person and a poor person smoke the same number of packs per day; each would pay exactly the same tax, say, $200 a year. Now what's $200 to a person who earns $100,000 a year? It's only 0.2 percent of the individual's income. But

Table 7.1. Social Security Tax Paid at Various Income Levels in 1988*

Level of Earned Income	Taxes Paid	Taxes as a Percentage of Earned Income
$10,000	$751	7.51%
50,100	3582.15	7.51
100,000	3582.15	3.58
1,000,000	3582.15	0.36

In 1989 the maximum taxable wage base rises to $53,400 and the tax rate stays at 7.51 percent. In 1990 the maximum taxable wage base rises to $57,000 and the tax rate rises to 7.65 percent.

a person who earns only $10,000 a year would have to pay 2 percent of his or her income in cigarette excise tax. Obviously, then, the cigarette excise tax is regressive, because it places a greater burden on poor people.

Let's take a close look at sales tax and the Social Security tax to see if these taxes are progressive or regressive. The general sales tax might take, say, 4 percent of everyone's income. Ask yourself which would hurt more: $400 from an annual income of $10,000, or $4,000 from an annual income of $100,00? Although economists are rather reluctant to make interpersonal comparisons of pain, most people would agree that a sales tax hurts the poor much more than the rich and is therefore a regressive tax.

The Social Security tax may at first appear *not* to be regressive, since everyone is taxed at the same rate! 7.51 percent of all wages and salaries in 1988. However, this tax is limited to the first $50,100 of earnings (with increases in the tax base scheduled for 1989 and 1990 shown in Table 7.1).

What this means is that people earning up to $50,100 pay 7.51 percent of their earnings in Social Security tax. Anything beyond that is tax-free, as is such "unearned income" as interest, dividends, rent, and profit. People who earn more than $50,100 pay less than 7.51 percent of their income in Social Security taxes. In other words, the more you earn, the smaller the percentage of your income that you pay. Now, that makes for a pretty regressive tax!

Where does all of this leave us? It leaves us to conclude that the Social Security tax, the general sales tax (which varies from state-to-state), and most excise taxes are regressive.

Self-Test 1

1. Government spending went from about _____ percent of GNP in 1933 to _____ percent at present time.
2. What two cataclysmic events brought about this increase?
3. The federal government spends over $ _____ a year.
4. The national debt is fast approaching the $ _____ mark.

5. Most state and local government spending is directed toward
    (1) _____ , (2) _____ , and (3) _____ .

6. Which statement is true? Since the early 1980s
    A. State and local governments, like the federal government have been running budget surpluses.
    B. State, local, and federal governments have been running budget surpluses.
    C. State and local governments have been running budget surpluses, but the federal government has been running deficits.
    D. State and local governments have been running deficits, while the federal government has been running budget surpluses.

7. The federal government raises about _____ percent of its revenue from taxes.

8. Of these six nations — the United States, Sweden, Japan, France, Italy, and Denmark — which has the lowest tax burden?

9. Is the corporate income tax a direct or indirect tax?

10. Is the sales tax a direct or indirect tax?

11. Which one of the following taxes is progressive?
    A. Sales.
    B. Excise.
    C. Social Security.
    D. Federal Personal income.

Answers to Self-Test 1

1. 10 percent; 33 percent.

2. The Great Depression and World War II.

3. $1 trillion.

4. $3 trillion.

5. Health, education, and welfare.

6. C.

7. 80 to 90 percent.

8. Japan.

9. Direct.

10. Indirect.

11. D.

9 | Sources of Federal Revenue

Personal Income Tax

As we can see from Figure 7.1, the federal government has three main sources of revenue, the largest of which is the personal income tax. This tax was only a minor source of federal revenue until World War II, but it now accounts for nearly one of every two tax dollars collected.

There's a good deal of discussion these days about whether the personal income tax is progressive. Such a question never came up until the Tax Reform Act of of 1986 was passed. Before the "reform" there were fourteen income tax

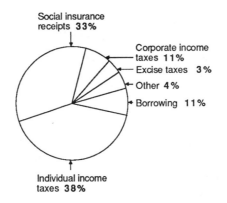

Figure 7.1 Sources of Federal Revenue: Fiscal Year 1988

Source: *The New York Times*, January 6, 1987

brackets ranging from 11 percent to 50 percent. Now there are nominally just two rates: 15 percent for working-class and lower-middle-class taxpayers and 28 percent for those in the loftier income groups. But before you digest that information, we need to make some modifications.

First, there are really four different tax rates: zero for those who are earning relatively low incomes, 15 percent, 28 percent, and then 33 percent for those with extremely high incomes. We'll come back to those rates in a minute.

Second, we are talking about marginal tax rates, not average tax rates. What's the difference?

$$\text{Average tax rate} = \frac{\text{Taxes paid}}{\text{Taxable income}}$$

$$\text{Marginal tax rate} = \frac{\text{Change in taxes paid}}{\text{Change in taxable income}}$$

Let's work out some problems. Suppose you are making $30,000 a year and paying $3000 in taxes. You can compute your average tax rate by plugging these numbers into the formula for the average tax rate. Do it right here:

10   What did you get? Was it 10 percent ($3000/$30,000 = 1/10 = 10 percent)? If so, you calculated correctly. If you are at all uncertain about how to calculate percentages, review Chapter 2, frames 17–28.

Next we'll do the marginal tax rate. Let's say that you got a $10,000 raise to $40,000. Your taxes went from $3000 to $5000 because of this raise. How much is your marginal tax rate? Using the formula for the marginal tax rate, substitute numbers into the formula and solve it.

11   Your marginal tax rate is 20 percent. Let's go over that problem. Your change in taxes paid was $2000. Your change in taxable income was $10,000, since you went from $30,000 to $40,000.

Plug these numbers into the formula:

$$\text{Marginal tax rate} = \frac{\text{Change in taxes paid}}{\text{Change in taxable income}} = \frac{\$2000}{\$10,000} = \frac{2}{10} = 20\%$$

Try this one on for size: Your taxable income goes from $40,000 to $45,000, and your taxes go up by $1500. Figure out the marginal tax rate.

12

$$\text{Marginal tax rate} = \frac{\text{Change in taxes paid}}{\text{Change in taxable income}} = \frac{\$1500}{\$5000} = 30\%$$

Let's deal with the concept of taxable income. We'll use, as our example, a married couple, with no children, filing a joint return for 1980. According to the law, this couple must pay 15 percent on all income below $29,750 and 28 percent on all income between $29,750 and $71,900. On income above $71,900 they would be paying at a marginal rate of up to 33 percent.

Do you follow so far? If so, we need to ask one key question: How much of this income is taxable? Suppose this couple has an income of $50,000. In 1988 they're entitled to two personal exemptions of $1950 each. (In 1989 a personal exemption will be $2000).

But the chances are they could do better. As any accountant will tell you, the name of the income tax game is to get your taxable income as low as possible.

At this point they will have to make a choice: Should they itemize or should they take the standard deduction? The standard deduction would reduce the couple's taxable income by $5000, but I'd be willing to bet they can take off much more by itemizing.

There are five major deductions: (1) mortgage interest, (2) medical expenses, (3) charitable contributions, (4) state and local taxes, and (5) miscellaneous deductions such as home office and employee business expenses. Personal interest—including the interest on credit card, installment, and car loans—will be fully phased out by 1991, but mortgage interest will continue to be fully deductible.

If this couple owns their own home, the chances are they are entitled to a deduction of several thousand dollars for mortgage interest and local property taxes. These two alone may well top $5000.

Most people can't take the medical deduction because these expenses must be over 7.5 percent of their income. But charitable contributions are fully deductible for those who itemize.

Now another biggie—state and local income taxes. If the couple happens to work in a high-tax state like New York, California, or Illinois, this deduction will amount to several thousand dollars.

The miscellaneous deduction is very helpful to people who work at home and are not fully reimbursed by their employers.

In short, if you're making $50,000, and especially if you own your own home and have a fairly high mortgage, you'll be far better off if you itemize your deductions. Unless, of course, you really want to give your money to your favorite charity—the Internal Revenue Service.

Are you ready for another problem? This one will be a little easier. How much tax will a single man earning $10,000 have to pay? We'll assume this man takes the standard deduction. To figure out his taxable income, all we have to do is subtract one exemption ($1950) and the standard deduction for a single taxpayer ($3000) from his income ($10,000): $10,000 minus $4950 equals $5050. What's his tax rate? 15 percent. Figure out what this man must pay?

Table 7.2. Deductions and Exemptions from the
Federal Personal Income Tax*

Exemptions
Self, spouse, dependents 1988: $1950
1989 and after: $2000

Deductions
Single $3000
Joint return   5000
Head of household   4400

* Cost-of-living adjustments will raise these exemptions
and deductions after 1989.

Table 7.3. Federal Personal Income Tax Rates

	Income	
Married couple		
filing jointly	0–$29,750*	15%
	$29,750– 71,900	28%
	over 71,900	up to 33%
Single person	0–$17,850	15%
	$17,850– 43,150	28%
	over 43,150	up to 33%

* Cost-of-living adjustments will widen (or raise) these
brackets after 1989.

13

It comes out to $757.50 ($5050 × .15).

When you prepare your personal income tax return, you have one big decision to make: whether to take the standard deduction or itemize. Once you've made that decision, you have only a few mechanical operations to carry out. I've prepared a couple of tables to summarize the exemptions and deductions you're entitled to and the rates you're subject to. Table 7.2 shows exemptions and deductions; Table 7.3 shows the tax rates. These tables will help you do some of the problems in Self-Test 2.

Self-Test 2

1. A. In effect, how many federal personal income tax rates are there?
   B. List them: _____.

2. A. If you earn $20,000 and are entitled to exemptions and deductions totaling $10,000, your average tax rate (ATR) (on your taxable income) will be _____ percent if you paid $1500 in taxes.
   B. If your taxable income rises from $50,000 to $60,000 and you have to pay $2800 in additional taxes, your marginal tax rate (MTR) will be _____ percent.

3. What is the taxable income of a single person who, in 1989, earns $25,000 and takes the standard deduction?

4. In 1989 a married couple with one child earns a joint income of $40,000. They must now decide whether to take the standard deduction or to itemize.

They should definitely itemize if their deductions come to more than $ _____ .

5. How much income tax will you have to pay in 1989 if you are single, take the standard deduction, and earn $22,000?

6. How much income tax will a married couple have to pay in 1989 if they have two children, earn a joint income of $60,000, and are entitled to a total of $15,000 in deductions (if they itemize)?

7. A family of six (with only one wage earner) would pay no personal federal income tax in 1989 on any income below $ _____ .

Answers to Self-Test 2

1. A. Four.
   B. Zero, 15 percent, 28 percent, up to 33 percent.
2. A. ATR = taxes paid/taxable income = 1500/10,000 = 15 percent.
   B. MTR = change in taxes paid/change in taxable income = 2800/10,000 = 28 percent.
3. $25,000 − $5,000 ($3000 standard deduction plus personal exemption of $2000) = $15,000. $15,000 × .15 = $2250.
4. Standard deduction of $5,000.
5. $22,000 − 5000 = $17,000. $17,000 × .15 − $2,550
6. $60,000 − 23,000 ($15,000 plus four exemptions @$2000) = $37,000 taxable income. The first 29,750 is taxable at 15 percent, and the rest, $7250, is taxable at 28 percent. They would pay a total of $6492.50 ($4462.50 + $2030.00).
7. $4400 + $12,000 (6 exemptions at $2000 each) = $16,400.

14 | Social Security Tax

Up to now we've been talking about the Social Security tax, but technically it is the payroll tax. We make this distinction for two reasons. First, this tax covers not just Social Security but also Medicare. Second, and more important, when a worker pays 7.51 percent of his or her salary, that worker's employer matches this payment. For example, a woman earning $20,000 would pay $1502 in taxes ($20,000 × 7.51 percent), and her employer wold also pay $1502. In effect, then, there is really a 15.02 percent tax on payrolls.

The payroll tax is the federal government's fastest growing source of revenue and now stands second in importance (See Figure 7.1). We have seen that this is an extremely regressive tax, but this regressiveness has been lessened somewhat in recent years as the earning ceiling has been raised. Each time the ceiling is raised, people in higher income brackets pay a higher percentage of their earnings.

15 | The Corporate Income Tax

Until the late 1970s, the corporate income tax was the second largest source of federal revenue. It is now a distant third. The Tax Reform Act of 1986 lowered the tax rate that larger corporations pay from 46 percent to 34 percent, but it also lowered several deductions, so that, in effect, nearly all large corporations are now paying higher taxes.

16 | Excise Taxes

An excise tax is a sales tax that is aimed at specific goods and services. The federal government, for example, taxes tires, cigarettes, liquor, gasoline, and phone calls. Although most excise taxes are levied by the federal government, state and local governments often tax the same items. In many states cigarettes and gasoline are subject to both federal and state excise taxes. In fact, the differential in state excise taxes encourages many people to "smuggle" cigarettes from one state to another.

Excise taxes serve as a source of government revenue, but they also serve another purpose: They tend to reduce consumption of certain products that the federal government looks upon with a jaundiced eye. Not only does the Surgeon General warn us that "Smoking Causes Lung Cancer, Heart Disease, Emphysema, And May Complicate Pregnancy," but he undoubtedly smiles approvingly as the government taxes each pack of cigarettes we buy.

Self-Test 3

1. List the four main federal taxes in order of revenue collected.
2. In 1989 the total payroll tax rate was _____ percent.
3. The top tax rate on corporate income is now _____ percent.
4. List three items that are subject to federal excise taxes.
5. Besides raising revenue, federal excise taxes serve a second purpose. What is that?

Answers to Self-Test 3

1. Personal income, payroll, corporate income, and excise taxes.
2. 15.02 percent.
3. 34 percent.
4. Tires, cigarettes, gasoline, liquor, and phone calls.
5. To discourage the consumption of certain goods.

17 | **THE BUSINESS SECTOR**

Investment, which is carried out primarily by business firms in the United States, consists of the production of new plant and equipment, additions to inventory, and new residential housing. Let's see how businesses are organized. Then we'll examine how they produce investment goods.

18 | **Three Types of Business Firms**

There are three basic types of business enterprise: the proprietorship, the partnership, and the corporation. There are nearly twenty million business firms in the United States. About seven out of ten are proprietorships, one out of ten is a partnership, and two out of ten are corporations. We'll examine each of these three types of enterprise.

19   The Proprietorship

Proprietorships are owned by a single person, and they are almost always small business: groceries, barber shops, dry-cleaning stores, restaurants, candy stores, family farms, and gas stations.

20   The Partnership

A partnership is a business enterprise that is owned by two or more people. Although the typical partnership has two partners, some law firms and accounting firms have hundreds of partners. There are two key advantages to the partnership: (1) two owners can raise more capital than one and (2) the partners can share the work and responsibility of running the business. A typical division of labor between partners would be production and sales, or, in the parlance of business, inside and outside.

These advantages must be weighed against two basic disadvantages: (1) the partnership must be dissolved when one partner dies or decides to leave the business and (2) both partners are liable for all debts run up by their business. For example, if the firm is sued for negligence, both partners are personally liable if the firm is unable to pay the full amount awarded. If one partner absconds with funds, the other partners may lose their homes and cars even though they were innocent victims. The way out of this dilemma is to incorporate.

21   The Corporation

The key advantage of the corporation is limited liability—that is, each owner's liability is limited to the amount of money he or she has invested in the business.

A corporation is a legal person. As such, it can sue and be sued. This attribute is significant because it means that the people who own the corporation—the stockholders—cannot be sued no matter how grievous the transgressions of the corporation.

A second advantage of a corporation is its perpetual life. While a partnership must be dissolved when one of the partners leaves the business, a corporation can continue indefinitely. The stock owned by the principal who wants to pull out is purchased by someone else. In the case of very large, publicly held corporations, such transactions take place routinely at the major stock exchanges.

Still another advantage of incorporating is that the company can sell stock to the public to raise more money. Because the owners have limited liability and the firm itself has perpetual life, the corporation is in a better position than the proprietorship or partnership to go to the public to raise funds, though only a few of them choose to do so.

Most of the nation's three million corporations are small businesses owned by a few individuals. Only about two thousand of U.S. corporations are large companies. These two thousand large corporations, however, include nearly all the nation's largest companies, and it is these giants that go public and that do most of the nation's business. Although corporations account for just under 20 percent of the nation's business firms, they collect over 90 percent of all business receipts.

There are two disadvantages to incorporating: (1) the owners must have papers drawn up and pay a fee for a charter, and (2) the corporation must pay income tax. Although the rates are very low for small corporations, those with large profits must hand over thirty-four cents out of every dollar of profit to the Internal Revenue Service.

Self-Test 4

1. About _____ percent of all American business firms are proprietorships, _____ percent are partnerships, and _____ percent are corporations.
2. What are the two main disadvantages to the partnership form of business?
3. What is the key advantage of incorporating?
4. Which statement is false?
   A. Nearly all corporations are small companies.
   B. Nearly all large companies are corporations.
   C. Most corporations are very large companies.
5. Which statement is false?
   A. A corporation must sell stock to the public.
   B. A corporation must have a charter.
   C. A corporation has to pay income tax.

Answers to Self-Test 4

1. 70 percent; 10 percent; 20 percent.
2. Does not have perpetual life; unlimited liability.
3. Limited liability.
4. C.
5. A.

22 | Investment

Investment makes our economy go. During periods of prosperity, investment is high and rising. During recessions, it is low and falling. Let's define investment and then see how it varies.

Investment, for our purposes, is any new plant, equipment, inventory, or residential housing.

Plant and Equipment Investment

Factories, office buildings, stores, and shipping malls are regarded as plants. Equipment includes assembly lines, machine tools, display cases, cash registers, computer systems, typewriters, and office furniture *purchased by businesses*. In other words, if you buy a car for your personal use, it's not an investment; it is a consumption expenditure. But if Shell Oil buys a car for its executives to drive on company business, it's an investment. If you are adding to your company's plant, equipment, or inventory, then the item you purchase is an investment.

Inventory Investment

Inventory investment is a little tricky. For tax purposes, we include only the net change from January 1 to December 31 of a given year. Take a look at the data in Table 7.4 and figure out how much inventory investment was for General Motors in 1983.

How much was GM's inventory investment in 1983? $25 million? Nope. $395 million? Nope. The answer is $10 million. All you have to do is look at the level of inventory on January 1 and on December 31 and calculate the difference.

Let's try another one. Using Table 7.5's data, calculate the inventory investment in 1984 for Shell Oil.

23

Your answer should be −$10 million. Between the first of the year and the last day of the year, the level of Shell's inventory went down by $10 million. In other words, inventory investment was negative.

That we can have negative inventory investment is very significant. Since investment is one sector of GNP, if inventories decline, this will be a drag on GNP. And that's what happens during recessions.

Most of us are painfully familiar with the distinction between gross income (what your boss tells you you are earning) and net income (what you actually take home after taxes and other deductions). Gross and net investment are parallel concepts. In fact, gross investment − depreciation = net investment.

Gross investment is the nation's entire expenditure on plant, equipment, and inventory. Inventory investment is already a net figure, so we need to take a closer look at depreciation in plant and equipment.

Let's say you started the year with ten machines and bought another six during the year. Your gross investment would be six. Of your original ten machines, if four wore out or became obsolete during the year, your depreciation would be four. Therefore, your gross investment (6) minus your depreciation (4) equals your net investment (2). In other words, you added two machines during the year, raising your total from ten to twelve.

We're almost ready to calculate the nation's gross investment and net investment. Gross investment = expenditures on new plant and equipment + inventory investment. For example, if expenditure on new plant and equipment is $200 billion and inventory investment is $30 billion, then gross investment is $230 billion.

Table 7.4. Hypothetical Inventory Levels of General Motors

Date	Level of Inventory
January 1, 1983	$120 million
July 1, 1983	145 million
December 31, 1983	130 million

Table 7.5. Hypothetical Inventory Levels of
Shell Oil

Date	Level of Inventory
January 1, 1984	$230 million
May 15, 1984	215 million
September 1, 1984	240 million
December 31, 1984	220 million

Now for net investment. Gross investment − depreciation = net investment. If depreciation is $40 billion, then how much is net investment.

What is your answer?

Gross Investment ($230 billion) − Depreciation ($40 billion) = Net investment ($190 billion).

Now we're ready to work out a hypothetical problem. Given all the information in Table 7.6, calculate the nation's gross investment and net investment.

24   Now check your work against these figures: Gross investment = expenditures on new plant and equipment ($120 billion) + inventory change ($10 billion) = $130 billion. Gross investment ($130 billion) − depreciation ($30 billion) = net investment ($100 billion).

Gross investment is designated by the letter I. GNP = C + I + G + X_n (consumption, investment, government expenditures, and net exports). Economists make an important distinction between Gross National Product and Net National Product. The investment component of Gross National Product is gross investment and the investment component of Net National Product is net investment. In short, Gross National Production − depreciation = Net National Product.

Residential Housing Investment

Economists are not in complete agreement about whether new residential housing is a category of investment or consumption. Since the quasi-official position of the profession is that it belongs in the investment category, we'll go along with that position and classify residential housing as investment.

During the twenty-five years following World War II we had a tremendous spurt in residential building, as Americans moved to the suburbs. Today there is continued building, particularly in outlying suburbs, but the postwar housing boom has been over for about two decades.

Table 7.6. Hypothetical Inventory Levels and
Investment and Depreciation Schedules of the
Nation

Date	Level of Inventory
January 1, 1984	$60 billion
July 1, 1984	55 billion
December 31, 1984	70 billion

Expenditures on new plant and equipment:
    $120 billion

Depreciation on plant and equipment:
    $30 billion

Residential building fluctuates considerably from year to year. Mortgage interest rates play a dominant role. For example, from 1979 to 1982, when mortgage rates reached 15 and 16 percent in most parts of the country, new housing starts plunged by nearly 40 percent. Another factor that causes steep declines in home construction is periodic overbuilding. Once the surplus of new homes on the market is worked off, residential construction will go into another boom period.

What this all comes down to is that investment is the most volatile sector in our economy. Fluctuations in GNP are largely fluctuations in investment. More often than not our recessions are touched off by declines in investment and our recoveries are brought about by rising investment.

One more problem and we'll have finished with the business sector. If inventory investment is $30 billion, investment in new plant and equipment is $200 billion, new residential construction is $350 billion, and depreciation is $100 billion, find gross investment and net investment.

Gross investment = investment in new plant and equipment ($200 billion) + inventory investment ($30 billion) + new residential construction ($350 billion) = $680 billion.

Gross investment ($680 billion) − depreciation ($100 billion) = net investment ($580 billion).

Although you have been provided with a cogent explanation of exactly what constitutes investment (the purchase of new plant and equipment, inventory change, and residential construction), some people insist upon confusing other things with investment.

What if you were to purchase 100 shares of New York Telephone? Would that be investment? Does that add (directly) to New York Telephone's plant, equipment, or inventory? It doesn't? Then it is not investment. It's just a financial transaction. When New York Telephone uses those funds to buy plant, equipment, or inventory—*then* it's an investment.

Now that we've looked at two of the big three components of GNP, we will discuss the third component, consumption, which is not only the largest, but also the most stable.

Self-Test 5

1. Investment consists of four things. List them:
2. Which one of the following is investment?
   A. The purchase of 100 shares of IBM.
   B. The purchase of a new car for personal use.
   C. The purchase of a new factory by Exxon.
   D. The purchase of three-year old equipment by Armco Steel.
3. The most unstable sector of GNP is:
   A. Consumption.
   B. Investment.
   C. Government spending.
4. Given the information in the following table, how much was inventory investment in 1986?

Date	Level of Inventory
1/1/86	$100 million
7/1/86	110 million
12/31/86	95 million

5. If inventory investment is $20 billion, investment in new plant and equipment is $250 billion, new residential construction is $370 billion, and depreciation is $165 billion, find gross investment and net investment.

Answers to Self-Test 5

1. New plant, new equipment, additional inventory, and new residential housing.
2. C.
3. B.
4. −$5 million.
5. Gross investment = inentory investment + investment in new plant and equipment + new residential housing: $20 billion + $250 billion + $370 billion = $640 billion. Net investment = gross investment − depreciation: $640 billion − $165 billion = $475 billion.

25 | THE CONSUMPTION SECTOR

Consumption and Saving

Americans usually spend between 90 and 95 percent of their after-tax incomes. In the mid-1980s, however, we went on a spending binge, pushing the savings rate below 5 percent. This was virtually the lowest savings rate among industrial nations and far below the rate of Japan and West Germany, which ran well over 20 percent.

Total spending, or consumption, designated by the letter C, is by far the largest sector of GNP, generally a little less than two-thirds.

Consumers spend about half their money on services such as medical care, eating out, life insurance, interest payments, and legal fees. They spend the other half on durable goods such as television sets and furniture and on nondurable goods such as food and gasoline.

Although consumption is not a steady percentage of disposable income, it is almost always between the 90 and 95 percent mark. John Maynard Keynes noted that consumption is a stable component of income. His theory is called the consumption function, which states that as income rises, consumption rises, but not as quickly. For example, if a country's disposable income rises by $100 billion, its consumption will rise by less than $100 billion. In the United States, when disposable income rises by $100 billion, consumption generally rises by $90 to $95 billion.

26 | The Average Propensity to Consume (APC) and the Average Propensity to Save (APS)

These two measures tell us the percentage of our incomes that we spend and save. They are generally expressed as decimals rather than as percentages. Remember that a decimal may be converted into a percentage by moving the decimal point two places to the right and adding a percentage sign (.80 = 80 percent).

We'll start by finding the average propensity to consume (the part of disposable income that is spent). We'll use the data in Table 7.7.

To find the percentage of disposable income spent, we need to divide consumption by disposable income:

$$APC = \frac{Consumption}{Disposable\ income} = \frac{\$30,000}{40,000} = \frac{3}{4} = .75$$

Let's review how this is done. We use the three-step method of solving this problem. First, write the formula. Then, substitute the numbers into the formula. Finally, solve the formula.

$30,000/40,00 can easily be reduced to 3/4. To change the fraction (3/4) into decimal form, divide 3 by 4. (Remember to always divide the bottom number into the top number.)

$$\frac{.75}{4)3.00}$$

The average propensity to save (APS) is the mirror image of the average propensity to consume (APC). It is the part of disposable income saved. Using the data in Table 7.7, calculate the APS. What's wrong? Oh, is something missing? You don't have the number for savings? But you can figure it out using the numbers you do have. You know the disposable income. You know the consumption. So how much are savings?

Here's the solution: Disposable income ($40,000) − consumption ($30,000) = savings ($10,000). Remember: If you start with a certain disposable income, or take-home pay, you'll spend most of it, and what's left over, you've saved. Now calculate APS.

27 |

$$APS = \frac{saving}{disposable\ income} = \frac{\$10,000}{40,000} = \frac{1}{4} = .25$$

Again, we use the three-step method: write the formula, substitute the numbers in to the formula, and then solve the formula. When you get to 1/4, remember to divide 4 into 1:

$$\frac{.25}{4)1.00}$$

Notice that the APC and the APS add up to one. Now let's work out another one, using the data in Table 7.8.

Table 7.7.

Disposable Income	Consumption
$40,000	$30,000

Table 7.8.

Disposable Income	Saving
$20,000	$1,500

$$\text{APC} = \frac{\text{Consumption}}{\text{Disposable income}} = \frac{\$18,500}{20,000} = \frac{185}{200} = \frac{37}{40}$$

$$\text{APS} = \frac{\text{Saving}}{\text{Disposable income}} = \frac{\$1,500}{20,000} = \frac{15}{200} = \frac{3}{40}$$

```
      .925                .075
40)37.000            40)3.000
  -360xx                280x
      100                200
      -80               -200
      200
     -200
```

Notice that APC and APS add up to 1 again. If they don't, then someone may be trying to tell you something. There are only two things to do with disposable income—spend it or save it. If the percentage spent and the percentage saved don't add up to 100%, then either your arithmetic is faulty or you have a hole in your pocket.

28 The Marginal Propensity to Consume (MPC) and the Marginal Propensity to Save (MPS)

When income changes, so does consumption. When income rises, consumption also rises, but by less than income. That is the consumption function.

The formula for calculation the marginal propensity to consume (MPC) is:

$$\text{MPC} = \frac{\text{Change in consumption}}{\text{Change in income}}$$

Using the data in Table 7.9, calculate the MPC.

29 Solution:

$$\text{MPC} = \frac{\text{Change in C}}{\text{Change in income}} = \frac{\$8,000}{10,000} = \frac{8}{10} = .8$$

When income changes, not only does consumption change, but so does saving. When income rises, both consumption and saving will rise. Similarly, when income falls, both consumption and saving fall.

The formula for calculating the MPS is:

$$\text{MPS} = \frac{\text{Change in saving}}{\text{Change in income}}$$

Using Table 7.9 again, calculate the MPS. (Note: Remember how to find saving when you have disposable income and consumption.)

Table 7.9.

Disposable Income	C
$30,000	$23,000
40,000	31,000

30 | Solution:

Disposable Income	–	Consumption	=	Saving
$30,000	–	$23,000	=	$7,000
40,000	–	31,000	=	9,000

$$\text{MPS} = \frac{\text{Change in saving}}{\text{Change in income}} = \frac{\$2,000}{10,000} = \frac{2}{10} = .2$$

31 | ## The Determinants of Consumption

There are many influences on how much money we spend, but by far the most important is how much money we have. Of couse economists have a name for this: *disposable income*. As the old adage goes, "If yuh ain't got it, yuh can't spend it."

Because the poor have just enough money to get by, they save virtually nothing. Indeed, they often spend more than their incomes. Economists have a word for this too: *dissaving*. Where does this money come from? Most of it is borrowed, and the rest usually comes out of savings.

At the other end of the economic spectrum, we have the rich, who usually manage to save some of their disposable income. Every so often we'll read about a professional athlete or entertainer who has gone bankrupt. But these are the rare exceptions among the rich. The Rockefellers, the DuPonts, the Mellons, and the Fords, for example, spend a lot of money and still manage to save several million dollars a year. Rich people also spend a lot more money than poor people because they *have* more money.

Most Americans are somewhere in the middle. They manage to put away some money in most years, but not very much. During recession years, or when they make major purchases, they dissave. In recent years, the typical middle class American has an APS of about .05.

The most important determinant of consumption, then, is disposable income. Other influences on the level of consumer spending include credit availability, the stock of liquid assets in the hands of consumers, and price expectations. But the level of disposable income will always be the number one influence on the level of consumption.

Self-Test 6

1. The APC in the United States is about _____ .
2. Consumption is generally about _____ of GNP.

3. Americans spend about _____ percent of their disposable income on services.

4. If disposable income is $50,000 and consumption is $42,000, what are the APC and APS?

5. Given the information in the table below, find the MPC and the MPS.

Disposable Income	Saving
$50,000	$42,000
70,000	45,000

Answers to Self-Test 6

1. .90 to .95

2. Two-thirds

3. 50 percent

4. $APC = \dfrac{Consumption}{Disposable\ income} = \dfrac{42,000}{50,000} = .84$

   $APS = \dfrac{Saving}{Disposable\ income} = \dfrac{8,000}{50,000} = .16$

5. $MPC = \dfrac{Change\ in\ Consumption}{Change\ in\ disposable\ income} = \dfrac{17,000}{20,000} = .85$

   $MPS = \dfrac{Change\ in\ saving}{Change\ in\ disposable\ income} = \dfrac{3,000}{20,000} = .15$

32 | Graphing the Consumption Function

The key to reading consumption and other economic variables from a graph is knowing where to look for them. So before we even look at a graph of this sort, let's just talk about them for a while. As you know, on the left side of every graph there is a vertical line or vertical scale. On the bottom of every graph there is a horizontal scale. If you are still unsure about graphs, please go back over Chapter 3.

Every graph in an economics text will have a horizontal and vertical scale. In Figure 7.2 the vertical scale shows expenditures. The numbers 1000, 2000, and 3000 represent expenditures of $1 trillion, $2 trillion, and $3 trillion. By convention, economists write billions of dollars without using dollar signs, for example, $300 billion becomes 300. Notice that the distances between each of these numbers is equal. If you were to take a ruler to measure the distances between 0 and 1000, between 1000 and 2000, and between 2000 and 3000, they would be exactly the same. This is a very important point, because you'll need to estimate distances between these numbers.

The horizontal axis in Figure 7.2 measures disposable income, also in units of 1000, 2000, and 3000. In the graphs you'll encounter in later chapters, the horizontal scale will sometimes be based on units of time or units of output, but here we are measuring disposable income, which is measured in terms of dollars.

Nearly every variable is read from the vertical scale. The only exception we will encounter is disposable income, which is read from the horizontal scale.

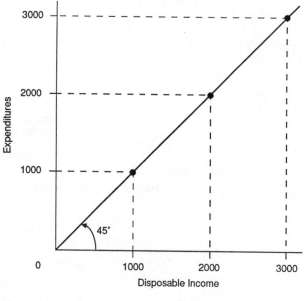

Figure 7.2

The graph in Figure 7.2 shows expenditures along the vertical scale and disposable income along the horizontal scale. Figure 7.2 has only one line on it—a 45 degree line. This line has one purpose: to equate the horizontal scale with the vertical scale, that is, to equate expenditures with disposable income.

Notice the dotted line rising from a disposable income of 1000. It meets the 45 degree line and then moves horizontally to the vertical scale. For a disposable income of 2000, there is another dotted line rising to the 45 degree line and then moving straight across to the vertical scale. The same pattern occurs at a disposable income of 3000.

Now let's take that first point on the 45 degree line, just above 1000 on the disposable income scale and directly across from the expenditures (vertical) scale. That point is exactly 1000 units from both the vertical and horizontal scales. Point 2 is 2000 units from each scale. Thus, we see that points on the vertical scale are equal to their corresponding points on the horizontal scale.

Now we're ready to graph the consumption function. First we'll review our definition of it: *As income rises, consumption rises, but not as quickly.* How should it look on a graph? Suppose that disposable income rises by 1000. By how much should C rise? According to our definition of the consumption function, it should rise by less than 1000.

If the consumption function states that C rises as quickly as income, then can you guess what a graph of the consumption function would look like. That's a hard one. It would look like the 45 degree line. Each point would be the same number of units from the two scales. You didn't get that one? Well, don't worry about it. When Yogi Berra was managing the New York Mets, he was criticized for worrying about what he didn't do back in the fifth inning, rather than planning what he *would* do in the ninth. But he *did* win a pennant in 1973 with the Mets, as well as one with the Yankees in 1964.

Figure 7.3 illustrates that consumption does not rise as quickly as the 45 degree line. Since C does not rise as quickly as disposable income, the points that compose the line are not as high as they were in the 45 degree line in Figure 7.2

Okay, now we're ready to read the graph in Figure 7.3, How much is consumption when disposable income is 1000? How much is it? Don't wait for me to tell you. Find a disposable income of 1000 on the horizontal axis and work your way up to the assumption line (C line). Using a ruler, draw a line straight up to the C line. Now draw a horizontal line across to the vertical axis. Now read the number—1000. Voilà!

There are no guidelines for the next problem. Using the graph in Figure 7.3 once again, find the level of C when disposable income is 2000. Remember: move up from a disposable income of 2000 to the C line and then go straight across. Oops! I'm giving it away. Go ahead; you do it and I'll let you know if you're right or not.

33   What did you get? To me it looks like about 1400. Anything close to 1400 would be fine. Now, how much is the marginal propensity to consume? Figure it out using the three-step method:

$$MPC = \frac{\text{Change in C}}{\text{Change in income}} = \frac{400}{1000} = \frac{4}{10} = .4$$

I hope you're ready for another problem.

How much is C when disposable income is 3000? Do it; don't wait for me to tell you the answer. Did you do it? Then your answer should be around 1800.

Remember that C is measured vertically. Notice that as disposable income (which is measured horizontally) increases, C moves higher and higher. But it doesn't rise as quickly as disposable income.

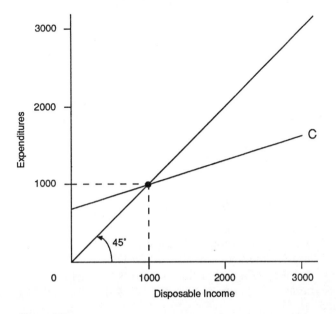

Figure 7.3

At very low levels of disposable income, notice that the C line is higher than the 45 degree line. When that happens, consumption is greater than disposable income. How is that possible? Believe me, it happens, especially during depressions. Hasn't your consumption ever exceeded your income? If your consumption *always* exceeds your income, you won't have any money in the bank, but you should be able to grasp the notion that a nation can spend more than its disposable income.

The way to spend more than disposable income is to borrow or use savings. Although some nations, particularly Mexico, Brazil, Argentina, and now the United States, have gone into debt for tens of billions, we will concentrate on using savings.

34   Graphing the Savings Function

The saving function is virtually the same as the consumption function. *As income rises, savings rises, but not as quickly.*

Now we're ready to find savings on the graph. First, how much is savings when disposable income is 1000? Go ahead and figure it out. Yes,, I know that there's no listing of savings on the graph. But you can still figure out how much savings is from the information you already have, especially the level of C when disposable income is 1000, which you already figured.

Your answer should be zero. If disposable income is 1000 and C is 1000, then savings must be zero. Note that savings is the vertical distance between the C line and the 45 degree line.

Next problem: How much is savings when disposable income is 2000? And after you do that, find savings when disposable income is 3000.

The answers to both questions are worked out in the graph in Figure 7.4. All you need to do is measure the vertical distance between the C line and the 45 degree line.

If you are having trouble measuring these vertical distances, remember that all vertical distances are measured on the vertical axis. Horizontal dotted lines have been drawn in Figure 7.4 to locate points on the vertical axis.

Let's try another graph to make sure we're clear on how to measure consumption and saving at various levels of disposable income. In Figure 7.5, please find the levels of consumption and saving when disposable income is 1500, 3000, and 4500. To check your work, see Figure 7.6.

35   Graphing the C + I Line

Now we're ready to do some more work on the graphs—something I'm sure you've been looking forward to. So far we've had a graph with just one line— the C line, or consumption function. From this one line graph, C and savings could be calculated. To calculate I (actually C + I), a second line is necessary. Figure 7.7 graphs a C + I line, which is parallel to the C line. Actually, this is the same as the graphs in Figures 7.3, 7.4, 7.5, and 7.6, with the C + I line added.

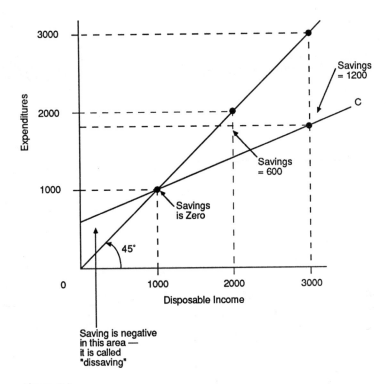

Figure 7.4

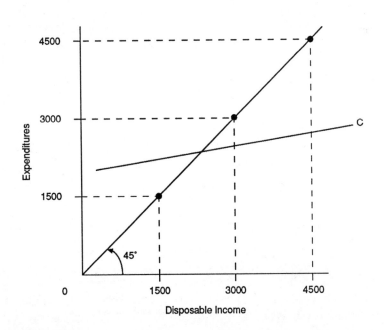

Figure 7.5

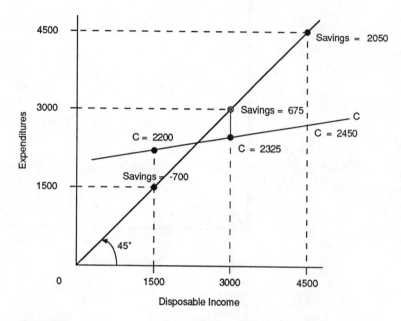

Figure 7.6

Please note: C is the vertical distance between the horizontal axis and the 45 degree line. And C plus savings always equals disposable income. When disposable income is 1500, C is 2200, so savings must be −700. When disposable income is 3000, C is 2325 and savings in 675. When disposable income in 4500, C is 2450 and savings is 2050. These are only approximations. Your answers may vary slightly, as long as your savings and consumption add up to disposable income.

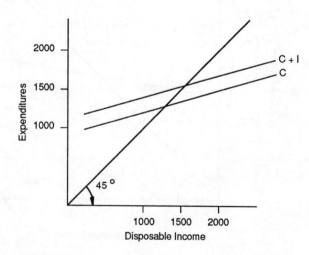

Figure 7.7

Now let's try a three part question: How much is I when disposable income is 1000, 2000, and 3000? Look at the graph and figure out the answers. Keep in mind that the C line and the C + I line are parallel.

36

The answer to all three parts of the question is "around 400" (350, 375, 390, 405, 425, 440, or 450 would be acceptable). More important, since the C line and the C + I line are parallel, the vertical distance between them remains the same. If you estimated I at 375 with a disposable income of 1000, it remains 375 when disposable income is 2000 or 3000.

Self-Test 7

For each of the following three questions, use Figure 7.7

1. When disposable income is 1000, how much are consumption, saving, and investment?

2. When disposable income is 1500, how much are consumption, saving, and investment?

3. When disposable income is 2000, how much are consumption, saving, and investment?

Answers to Self-Test 7

The answers are pictured on Figure 7.8.

1. C = 1200; savings = −200; investment = 200. (Consumption and savings must add up to 1000.)

2. C = 1325; savings = 175; investment = 200. (Consumption and savings must add up to 1500; investment is the same as it was when disposable income was 1000.)

3. C = 1475; saving = 525; investment = 200. (Consumption and savings must add up to 2000; investment remains the same.)

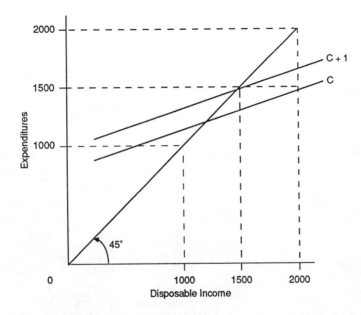

Figure 7.8

37 | The Multiplier

It is obvious that if C goes up, GNP goes up. Or if I goes down, so does GNP. Now we'll add a new wrinkle. When there is any change in spending—that is, in C or I or G—it will have a multiplied effect on GNP.

Money spent by one person becomes someone else's income. And what do we do with most of our income? We spend it. Someone else receives it as income and, in turn, spends most of it. And so, if you spend a dollar, perhaps the person who received that dollar would spend 80 cents, and the next person would spend 64 cents. All spending generated by that one dollar would add up to four or five or six times that dollar. Hence, "the multiplier."

Any change in spending (C, I, or G) will set off a chain reaction, leading to a multiplied change in GNP. How *much* of a multiplied effect? Perhaps a $10 billion increase in G will increase GNP by $50 billion. In that case, the multiplier is 5. If a decline of $5 billion in I causes GNP to fall by $40 billion, then the multiplier would be 8.

First we concentrate on calculating the multiplier, for which we'll use the formula: 1/1-MPC. Then we'll see how it is used to predict changes in GNP.

The formula 1/1-MPC is exactly the same as 1/MPS. Remember, MPC + MPS = 1 (or 1 − MPC = MPS). Since the multiplier (like C) deals with spending, 1 − MPC is a more appropriate formula.

The MPC can be used to find the multiplier, following the three-step procedure used for all our problems: (1) write down the formula, (2) substitute numbers into the formula, and (3) solve the formula.

$$\text{Multiplier} = \frac{1}{1 - \text{MPC}} = \frac{1}{1 - .5} = \frac{1}{.5} = 2$$

Many students get lost at the third step. How do we get .5? How come 1 − .5 = .5? Look at it this way:

$$\begin{array}{r} 1.0 \\ -.5 \\ \hline .5 \end{array}$$

If it's still not clear, think of 1 as a dollar and .5 (or .50) as 50 cents. How much is a dollar minus 50 cents?

Step 4 is just as easy. How many times does 50 cents go into a dollar? Or you can just divide .5 into 1.0. Either way, your answer is 2.

The multiplier is really a shortcut for addition. Look at this example of the derivation of a multiplier illustrated in Table 7.10. Here the consumer spends $1000 of additional money. If the MPC is .5, that means the person who receives this $1000 in additional income will spend $500. This $500 will add to other people's incomes, and—still assuming an MPC of .5—they will spend $250. Ad infinitum. (That's Latin for without limit, forever.)

Are you ready to work out a couple of multiplier problems? First find the multiplier when the MPC is .75. Remember to write the formula, substitute, and solve.

38 | Solution:

$$\text{Multiplier} = \frac{1}{1 - \text{MPC}} = \frac{1}{1 - .75} = \frac{1}{.25} = 4$$

Table 7.10 Derivation of the Multiplier

$1000
500
1500
250
1750
125
1875
62.50
1937.50
31.25
1968.75
15.625
1984.375
7.8125
1992.1875
3.90625
1996.09375
1.953125
1998.046875
.9715625
1999.0184375
.48578125
1999.50421875
.242890625
1999.747109375

After you've substituted into the formula, think of 1 as a dollar and .75 as 75 cents. From there (1/.25) we divide .25 into 1, or a quarter into a dollar.

Here's one more problem: Find the multiplier when the MPC is .8.

Solution:

$$\text{Multiplier} = \frac{1}{1 - \text{MPC}} = \frac{1}{1 - .8} = \frac{1}{.2} = 5$$

Applications of the Multiplier

If we know the multiplier, we can calculate the effect of changes in C, I, and G on the level of GNP. If GNP is 2500, if the multiplier is 3, and if C rises by 10, what is the new level of GNP?

We need a second formula to figure the new level of GNP:

New GNP = Initial GNP + (change in spending × multiplier)

Notice the parentheses. Their purpose is to ensure that we multiply before we add. In arithmetic you must always multiply (or divide) before you add or subtract. Always. The parentheses are there to make sure we do this.

New GNP = Initial GNP + (change in spending × multiplier)

= 2500 + (10 × 3)

= 2500 + (30)

= 2530

To conclude, when consumer spending rises by 10 and the multiplier is 3, GNP will rise by 30. What if G rises by 10? Same thing: GNP would rise by 30. And if I rises by 10? Ditto.

Self-Test 8

1. Find the Multiplier when the MPC is
   A. .4
   B. .6
   C. .9

2. If GNP is 4500, the multiplier is 10, and I falls by 10, what is the new level of GNP?

3. If GNP is 5000, G rises by 20, and the MPC is .5, what is the new level of GNP?

Answers to Self-Test 8

1. Multiplier = 1/1 − MPC
   A. 1/1−.4 = 1/.6 = 1.67
   B. 1/1−.6 = 1/.4 = 2.5
   C. 1/1−.9 = 1/.1 = 10

2. New GNP = Initial GNP + (change in spending × multiplier)

= 4500 + (−10) × 10

= 4500 − 100

= 4400

3. Multiplier = 1/1 − MPC = 1/1 − .5 = 1/.5 = 2
   New GNP = Initial GNP = (change in spending × multiplier)

= 5000 + 20 × 2

= 5000 + 40

= 5040

CHAPTER 8

Inflation

and

Unemployment

The problems of inflation and unemployment have plagued our economy since the days of the founding fathers. During the American Revolution, inflation was so rampant that by the war's end, a dollar (then called a continental) was worth only two cents. "Not worth a continental!" was the lowest appraisal that you could give anything in those times. The Great Depression of the 1930s was preceded by other depressions in the 1870s and 1890s, as well as by several other serious downturns, all of which were accompanied by high unemployment rates.

In the 1970s we managed something completely new: inflationary recessions. About the only economic bright spot of this decade was that economists coined the word *stagflation*—a combination of *stagnation* and *inflation*.

After you've completed this chapter you will:

- Be able to differentiate between demand-pull and cost-push inflations.
- Understand the causes of inflation.
- Understand the psychology of inflation.
- Be able to differentiate between creeping inflation and hyperinflation.
- Be able to compute the unemployment rate.
- Be able to differentiate among frictional, structural, and cyclical unemployment.
- Understand the concept of full employment.
- Know if you are eligible to collect unemployment insurance benefits.

1 | INFLATION AND DEFLATION

Inflation is not necessarily a bad thing. After all, everybody gets to live in a more expensive neighborhood without having to move.

What exactly is inflation? It is a general rise in prices that is usually sustained over several years. In our own lifetimes we have known little but inflation.

Our inflation has been persistent since World War II, particularly in the 1970s when, for much of the decade, it reached double-digit proportions. And yet, when compared to an inflation rate in excess of 100 percent in certain

South American countries, ours is relatively mild. In fact, *relative* is the key word. Given our experience since 1945, most of us would surely settle for a "creeping" inflation of 2 or 3 percent.

If you ask the person on the street about inflation, you'll hear that it means that everything costs more. The Department of Commerce records the prices of all items that consumers buy—cars, appliances, haircuts, TVs, VCRs, steaks, medical services, Big Macs, and so forth—and figures out how much it costs the average family to live. Let's say that in January 1986 it cost the Joneses $20,000 to maintain their standard of living. If it cost them $22,000 to maintain the same standard in January 1989, we would say that the cost of living went up 10 percent.

No one would complain if the cost of living rose 2 or 3 percent a year, but during the ten-year period from 1972 to 1982 the Consumer Price Index rose from 125.3 to 289.1. By what percentage did the cost of living rise? Figure it out right here:

It went up by 130.7 percent! In other words, it cost the typical American family more than twice as much to live in 1982 as it did ten years earlier. If you had trouble with that problem, review frames 29, 30, 31, and 35 of Chapter 2.

*De*flation is a decline in the price level, not for just a month or two but for a period of years. During our last deflation, from 1929 to 1933, prices fell by 50 percent. Significantly, that deflation was accompanied by the Great Depression.

A mild deflation might be good from some consumers, but it would be disastrous for the national economy. Business profits would become losses, and people would be thrown out of work. If a retailer contracted to buy inventory at $100 a unit and hoped to sell it at $120, he or she might end up letting it go for only $110. After paying out all expenses—including rent, salaries, telephone, electric, advertising—the retailer might end up with a loss of $2 or $3 per unit.

Until the inflationary recessions of the 1970s, business downturns were called deflations, since they were invariably accompanied by price declines. As much as businesspeople dislike inflation, particularly that of double-digit proportions, they hate deflation even more.

After an inflation, it is not necessary to bring down prices to their original level, but it is important to bring inflation under control and stabilize prices. To opt for a deflation is to court economic disaster.

2 | A SHORT HISTORY OF LONG INFLATION

During every war in our history, prices have risen sharply. Each war has been accompanied by a combination of money supply increases and large budget deficits.

In 1945, as World War II ended, a tremendous pent-up demand for consumer goods was unleashed. Consumer prices rose sharply. Too many dollars were chasing too few goods. Just as that inflation was being brought under control, the Korean War broke out. This brought on another wave of consumer spending and price increases.

President Eisenhower took office in 1953, pledging to end the war in Korea and the inflation at home. It took him only a month to end the war, but it wasn't until 1960, three recessions later, that inflation was controlled.

Until 1965, consumer prices rose at an annual rate of only 1 percent (see Figure 8.1.) The Vietnamese War, accompanied by huge federal budget deficits, rekindled the inflationary fire.

By this time most Americans had become conditioned to rising prices. They seemed inevitable. When prices have been rising for some time, it is reasonable to assume that they will *keep* rising. So what did we do? We ran out to buy still more goods and services before prices rose still further. And when businesses saw that demand for their products was high, they were encouraged to raise *their* prices.

The result was a self-fulfilling prophecy. So long as people *believe* that inflation is inevitable, it is indeed inevitable.

President Nixon recognized this self-fulfilling prophecy early in his first term. He reasoned that if he could convince people that prices would not rise in the near future, they wouldn't stock up on goods, and prices wouldn't rise. Nixon's reasoning was sound, but no one believed him when he said that prices would level off. The result: continuing inflation.

Since then a lot has happened to affect the rate of inflation. Nixon's wage and price freeze didn't really take, perhaps because it was tried only halfheartedly. When OPEC quadrupled oil prices in the fall of 1973, inflation accelerated (see Figure 8.1.). The deep recession that followed did dampen down the inflation, but in the late 1970s, it returned with renewed vigor. It was not until the back-to-back recessions of 1980 and 1981-1982 that the rate of inflation was finally brought down to acceptable levels.

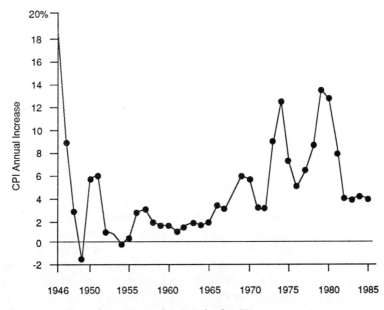

Figure 8.1 Annual percentage increase in the CPI

3 | ANTICIPATED AND UNANTICIPATED INFLATION

Traditionally, inflation has hurt creditors and helped debtors. Throughout our history, farmers have been debtors. As a result, during times of deflation or stable prices, the farmers' cries of anguish are heard loud and clear all the way to Washington. But during times of inflation, they may prosper.

It is easy to see why. Suppose that a farmer borrows $100, which he agrees to repay in one year along with 4 percent interest ($4). In one year he pays back $104. But what if, during that year, prices doubled? The money paid back would be worth much less than the money borrowed.

Let's say that when the farmer borrowed the money, wheat was selling at $2 a bushel. He would have been able to buy 50 bushels of wheat ($100/$2). But farmers don't buy wheat—they sell it. So one year later, this farmer harvests his wheat and pays back the loan. If the price level doubles, we can assume that the price of wheat also doubles. How much wheat would the farmer need to sell at $4 a bushel to pay off his loan? He would need to sell only 26 bushels ($104/$4).

Obviously this farmer, who is a debtor, benefits from unanticipated inflation because he borrowed money worth some 50 bushels of wheat and he later pays back his loan, with interest, in money worth only 26 bushels of wheat. Debtors in general gain from unanticipated inflation because they repay their loans with inflated dollars.

Just as obviously, those hurt by unanticipated inflation are the people who lend the money—the creditors. We generally think of creditors as banks, but banks are really financial middlemen. The ultimate creditors, or lenders, are the people who put their money in banks, life insurance, or any other financial instrument paying a fixed rate of interest. And the biggest debtor and gainer from unanticipated inflation has been the U.S. government. The national debt, which is now approaching $3 trillion, would be a lot easier to pay off if there were a sharp and lengthy inflation.

Unanticipated inflation also benefits businesses. Just as businesses suffer losses on their inventory during deflations, they obtain inventory price windfalls during inflations. Between the time inventory is ordered and the time it is actually sold, prices will have creeped upward, swelling profits.

Who is hurt by unanticipated inflation? People who live on fixed incomes, particularly retired people who depend on pensions other than Social Security. Those who hold long-term corporate or U.S. government bonds are also hurt. And finally, unanticipated inflation hurts workers whose wages are fixed under long-term contracts and landlords who have granted long-term leases at fixed rent.

In other words, under unanticipated inflation, some people gain and others lose. In fact, these gains and losses are exactly equal.

When inflation is fully anticipated, there are no winners or losers. The interest rate takes into account the expected rate of inflation. Normally, without anticipated inflation, the interest rate would be around 5 percent. In 1980 and again in 1981, when the rate of inflation ran at close to 15 percent, the prime rate of interest paid by top credit-rated corporations soared over 20 percent.

In order for inflation to be fully anticipated and built into interest rates, however, people need to live with it for several years. Although we have had relatively high inflation for most of the last dozen years, it was only in 1979 that the prime rate finally broke the 12 percent barrier. Today, though, unanticipated inflation is a thing of the past. Creditors have learned to charge enough interest to take into account, or to anticipate, the rate of inflation over the course of the loan. This would be tacked on to the regular interest rate that the lender would have charged had there been no inflation expected.

Let's work out a few problems. If the real rate of interest—the rate that would be charged without inflation—is 5 percent, and if there is an expected rate of inflation of 3 percent, then obviously the creditors will charge 8 percent.

If the real rate of interest is 4 percent and the expected inflation rate is 6 percent, what will be the nominal rate (the rate actually charged)? Good—I know you said 10 percent. The real rate of interest plus the expected rate of inflation equals the nominal rate of interest.

If the nominal interest rate accurately reflects the inflation rate, then the inflation has been fully anticipated and no one wins or loses. This is a good thing for our economy because it means that no one is hurt and no one is forced out of business because of inflation.

But if the rate of inflation keeps growing—even if it is correctly anticipated—our economy will be in big trouble. In a hyperinflation there are ultimately only losers.

Many wage earners are now protected against inflation by cost-of-living adjustment clauses (COLA agreements) in their contracts. Some retired workers are also protected, since Social Security benefits are now indexed for inflation—that is, they go up by the same percentage as the Consumer Price Index. And so, one way or another, most sectors of our society have learned to protect themselves from at least the short-term ravages of inflation.

Self-Test 1

1. In what decade did inflationary recessions first occur?
2. What is inflation?
3. If the Consumer Price Index rises from 150 to 180, the cost of living rises by _____ percent.
4. What is deflation?
5. Who would be most seriously hurt by deflation?
6. In the 1940s, 1950s, and 1960s, the inflations were generally associated with _____ .
7. What occurred during President Eisenhower's two terms in office that brought inflation under control?
8. If consumers expect inflation, what do they do?
9. During two recent periods, we suffered from double-digit inflation. When were they?
10. Traditionally those hurt by inflation have been
    A. Creditors and people on fixed incomes.
    B. Debtors and people on fixed incomes.
    C. Debtors and creditors.

11. Farmers have generally been _____ by inflation.
    A. Hurt.
    B. Helped.
    C. Neither helped nor hurt.

12. Creditors generally do better when inflation is
    A. Anticipated.
    B. Unanticipated.
    C. Neither.

13. Businesses generally like a little _____ but dislike a little _____ .
    A. Inflation, deflation.
    B. Deflation, inflation.

14. How much will the nominal interest rate be if the real rate of interest is 6 percent and the expected rate of inflation is 5 percent?

15. How are people receiving Social Security retirement benefits protected from inflation?

Answers to Self-Test 1

1. The 1970s.

2. A general rise in price levels.

3. 20 percent.

4. A general decline in price levels.

5. Business people.

6. Wars.

7. Three recessions.

8. They buy a lot of goods and services.

9. The mid-1970s and the late-1970s to early 1980s.

10. A.

11. B.

12. A.

13. A.

14. 11 percent.

15. They are protected from cost-of-living increases because their benefits rise by the same percentage as the Consumer Price Index.

4 | THEORIES OF THE CAUSES OF INFLATION

Demand-Pull Inflation

When there is excessive demand for goods and services, we have demand-pull inflation. Demand is said to be excessive when people are willing and able to buy more output than our economy can produce. In that situation something's gotta give. And that something is always prices.

Demand-pull inflation is often summed up as "too many dollars chasing too few goods." The problem arises when we can't produce any more goods because our economy is already operating at full capacity.

To help explain what happens when there's excess demand, we'll select another term from the economist's glossary: the *aggregate supply curve*. In Figure 8.2 we have a horizontal curve that begins to slope upward to the right and eventually becomes a vertical line. Notice that this happens at full employment.

At very low levels of output—depression levels—it would be easy to increase output without raising prices. After all, with high unemployment and idle plants and equipment, it would be easy to put those resources back to work without raising costs very much. For example, a person who has been out of work for several months will jump at the chance to go back to work at the going wage rate.

As output expands, most of the idle resources will be put back into production. Firms that need more plant and equipment will have to buy them. Employers will have to raise wages to induce new employees to work for them. In effect, then, businesses will have to bid for resources, and, in doing so, they will bid up the prices of land, labor, and capital.

As their costs go up, business firms will be forced to raise their prices. We are now in range 2 of the aggregate supply curve. We're moving closer and closer to full employment. It becomes increasingly difficult to get good help. Companies have to lure workers away from other employers. There's only one way to do this: Pay them more.

These salary increases push costs up still further, until finally we reach the full employment level. Now any further spending on goods and services will simply bid up prices without any corresponding increase in output. Welcome to range 3.

The U.S. economy rarely operates in either range 1 or range 3. Both depressions and runaway inflations are relatively rare occurrences, but they *do* happen.

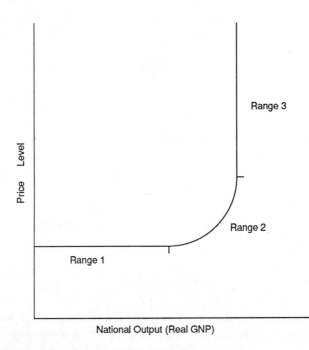

Figure 8.2 Aggregate Supply Curve

Macroeconomic policy has two goals: (1) to avoid depressions and (2) to avoid runaway inflations. But runaway inflations are unavoidable when macroeconomic policy must subordinate itself to military necessity. During World War II, for example, the federal government bought up half our output for military use. That created a problem: Private citizens had plenty of money to spend but not enough output to spent it on. The result was a bidding war between civilians and the government for our limited resources—a classic case of too much money chasing too few goods.

5   Cost-Push Inflation

There are three variants of cost-push inflation: (1) the wage-price spiral, (2) profit-push inflation, and (3) supply-side cost shocks.

The most important variant of cost-push inflation is the wage-price spiral. Because wages constitute nearly two-thirds of the cost of doing business, every significant wage increase is passed along to consumers in the form of higher prices. Higher prices raise everyone's cost of living, creating a demand for further wage increases.

To see how the wage-price spiral operates, let's imagine a 3 percent rise in the cost of living. Labor unions will negotiate for a 3 percent catch-up increase and a 3 percent increase on top of that for an anticipated cost-of-living increase *next* year. That's 6 percent. Now if every labor union gets a 6 percent increase, prices will undoubtedly rise not 3 percent but—you guessed it—6 percent! In the next round of labor negotiations, the unions might demand not just a 6 percent catch-up increase, but a 12 percent rise to take care of the coming year as well. And round and round the wage-price spiral goes; where it stops, nobody knows.

The second variant of cost-push inflation is profit-push inflation. Many industries—including the cigarette, detergent, breakfast cereal, car, and oil industries—are dominated by a handful of giant companies. These firms are so powerful that they can ignore the dictates of supply and demand and can establish prices within the industry. To the degree that they are able to protect their profit margins by raising prices, these firms will respond to any rise in costs by passing those costs on to their customers.

The third type of cost-push inflation is caused by supply-side cost shocks. The oil price shocks of 1973-1974 and 1979 are the clearest example of this variant. The OPEC nations quadrupled the price of oil in the fall of 1973, and that price shock touched off a major recession and a severe inflation. When the price of oil rises, the costs of other products and services rise as well. Those items include electricity, fertilizers, gasoline, heating oil, and long-distance freight transport. And as we've seen again and again, cost increases are quickly translated into price increases.

6   INFLATION AS A SELF-PERPETUATING PROCESS

Have you noticed that once inflation gets under way, it takes on a life of its own? We have already seen what happens when people believe that prices will rise: They act in a way that keep them rising. If we want to curb inflation, then, we have to reverse this inflationary behavior.

Various things can set off an inflationary spiral—wars, huge federal deficits, large increases in the money supply, sudden increases in the price of oil—but once that spiral begins, inflationary behavior takes over. Labor unions seek catch-up wage increases. Businesses raise prices to keep up with those wage increases. Consumers buy more goods and services before prices rise further.

To stop inflation, then, we need to convince workers, business people, and consumers, that prices will stop rising. If we can do that, prices *will* stop rising.

Once we stabilize prices, the inflationary behavior will stop. We will enjoy stability so long as we can avoid triggering another round of inflation. However, this has happened in the recent past only when inflation has been succeeded by recession.

Obviously, then, this "cure" has some unpleasant side effects, particularly for those who lose their jobs during these recessions. After we examine creeping inflation and hyperinflation, we'll turn to the problem of unemployment.

7 | CREEPING INFLATION AND HYPERINFLATION

Because *inflation* is a relative term, one country's creeping inflation would be another country's hyperinflation, and what might have been called creeping inflation ten years ago might now be considered hyperinflation. For example, the United States suffered from double-digit inflation in the mid-1970s and again in the late 1970s and early 1980s. In those days we would have welcomed a rate of 6 or 7 percent as creeping inflation. By the mid-1980s, however, some of us regarded anything above 4 percent as hyperinflation.

Virtually everyone would agree that a 1 or 2 percent annual increase in the Consumer Price Index constitutes creeping inflation. Very few people would be alarmed by this price increase. Most business people would like it because it would swell their profits. And, as we have seen, many wage earners and all Social Security recipients are protected from this kind of inflation.

But once we cross the constantly shifting line between creeping inflation and hyperinflation, we run into trouble. It becomes increasingly difficult to conduct normal economic affairs. Prices rise constantly. It becomes impossible to enter into long-term contracts. No one is sure what the government might do.

Prices serve as a signal to business firms. If prices are rising, business firms will produce more goods and services. But what if costs are rising faster than prices?

Suppose Bethlehem Steel agrees to supply General Motors with 50,000 tons of steel at $30 a ton. But then Bethlehem's costs rise by 50 percent. Will GM be willing to accept a price increase to $45 a ton if it signed a contract at $30 a ton?

Meanwhile, the government may decide to act precipitously. On August 15, 1971, for example, President Nixon suddenly announced the imposition of wage and price controls. In October 1979, to cite another example, the Federal Reserve Board suddenly stopped monetary growth, sending interest rates through the roof and touching off a sharp recession.

The classic hyperinflation took place after World War I in Germany, where price rose 10 percent *an hour*. The German government printed currency in larger and larger denominations—hundred mark notes, thousand mark notes, and eventually million mark notes. The smaller notes became worthless; children used them as play money. This hyperinflation eventually led to a complete economic breakdown, helped touch off a worldwide depression, and paved the way for Hitler's rise to power.

Another classic example of hyperinflation occurred in Hungary during and after World War II. Before the war, if you went into a store with a pengo, you had some money in your pocket. In those days a pengo was a pengo. But by August 1946, a Hungarian consumer needed 828 octillion pengos—that 828 is followed by *27 zeroes*—to buy what one pengo had bought before the war.

When inflation really gets out of hand, people will refuse to accept money as payment and will, instead, barter. This makes it extremely difficult for an economy to function. After all, if you don't have what I want or if I don't have what you want, you and I can't do business.

Does a creeping inflation of 1 or 2 percent a year always spiral into hyperinflation? Definitely not. But there's always the chance that things may get out of control. Inflation is like a fire: If it does get out of control, everybody's in big trouble.

Self-Test 2

1. What is demand-pull inflation?
2. When there are too many dollars chasing too few goods, something has to give. That something is _____ .
3. During several recessions, if demand rises, aggregate supply will rise in the form of higher _____ .
4. If demand rises when we are not at full employment, aggregate supply will rise in the form of higher _____ .
5. What happens when we move through range 2 of the aggregate supply curve toward range 3?
6. In what range of the aggregate supply curve does our economy usually operate?
7. Oil price shocks are a cause of _____ inflation.
   A. Demand-pull.
   B. Cost-push.
8. List the three variants of cost-push inflation.
9. Explain how the wage-price spiral works.
10. How could we put an end to inflationary behavior?
11. Since the Korean War we have had two periods of relative price stability: _____ and _____ . We also had two periods of double-digit inflation: _____ and _____ .
12. Why is there no clear dividing line between creeping inflation and hyperinflation?
13. What two countries experienced classic hyperinflation?
14. Why does hyperinflation lead to economic breakdown?

Answers to Self-Test 2

1. Excessive demand for goods and services (too much money chasing too few goods).

2. Prices.

3. Output.

4. Prices.

5. Both output and prices rise.

6. Range 2.

7. B.

8. Wage-price spiral, profit-push inflation, and supply-side cost shocks.

9. A wage increase, possibly engendered by a rise in the cost of living, is passed on to consumers in the form of higher prices, causing a demand for still further wage increases and price increases.

10. By convincing people that prices will not increase, possibly by attaining a period of price stability.

11. The late 1950s to the mid-1960s and the mid-1980s; the mid-1970s and the late-1970s to early 1980s.

12. Inflation is a relative term: A 6 percent rate might be considered hyperinflation in one country and creeping inflation in another.

13. Germany (during the early 1920s) and Hungary (during and after World War II).

14. It becomes extremely hard to conduct business because it is very hard to adhere to contracts. Eventually, people refuse to accept money as payment for goods and services and the economy must resort to barter.

8 | HOW TO COMPUTE THE UNEMPLOYMENT RATE

The Bureau of Labor Statistics (BLS) compiles statistics on the number of Americans who are employed and unemployed. Where does the bureau get its data? From unemployment insurance offices? No. Only about half of all unemployed Americans collect unemployment insurance. The BLS gets its unemployment statistics from a random survey of 60,000 households.

The Bureau asks a series of questions:

1. Are you working?

2. Did you work at all this month—even one day?

3. Did you look for work during the month?

Those who answer yes to question 1 or 2 are counted as employed. People who say yes to number 3 are counted as unemployed. Those who want to work but have given up looking for a job are classified as "discouraged workers." They are not in the labor force, and they are not considered "unemployed."

The labor force consists of the employed and the unemployed. In March 1987, for example, 113,104,000 Americans were employed and 7,854,000 were unemployed. We can compute the unemployment rate by using this formula:

$$\text{Unemployment rate} = \frac{\text{Number of unemployed}}{\text{Labor force}}$$

What was the unemployment rate in March 1987? Work it out right here:

9

Your first step should have been to figure out how many people are in the labor force. Add up the number of employed people and the number of unemployed; you should get 120,958,000. Then divide 120,958,000 into 7,854,000. If you divided correctly, you found that the official unemployment rate in March 1987 was 6.5 percent. Liberal economists would say that the true rate of unemployment is somewhat higher, perhaps 8 or 9 percent, if we count all the people who are ready, willing, and able to work, but whom the BLS regards as "not in the labor force" or as "discouraged workers."

In *Butch Cassidy and the Sundance Kid*, Paul Newman kept asking Robert Redford about the posse that was pursuing them: "Who *are* those guys?" Let's ask that same question about all the two or three million people who are not working, but are not officially unemployed. If we asked the BLS, "Who *are* these guys?" the bureau would say they're "discouraged workers" who have given up looking for work. Therefore, they don't meet the BLS criteria for being officially unemployed. If a person has not actively looked for a job—sent out a résumé, gone on a job interview, or visited an employment agency—during the last month, then that person is not counted as unemployed. He or she is not in the labor force and, as far as unemployment rate statistics go, is not there at all.

The liberals have a couple of additional criticisms of the BLS definition. A person who worked one day in the last month is counted as employed. Also, someone who works part time but wants to work full time is counted as employed. Doesn't this sort of measurement overstate the number of employed? liberals ask. They maintain that the BLS is overstating employment and understating unemployment, giving us an unemployment rate that is maybe a couple of points too low.

That's the liberal view. As you would expect, the conservatives say that the official unemployment rate *over*estimates the rate of unemployment. Using the BLS definition of an employed person—someone who has not worked this month and who has actively sought work—the conservative focuses on those who are required to report to a government employment office in order to remain eligible for unemployment insurance, welfare, or food stamps. Is this really an effort to find work, asks the conservative, or are these people just going through the motions?

Figure 8.3 is a record of the official unemployment rate from 1948 through 1986. You'll notice a marked upward trend since the late 1960s. The conservatives say that this trend has a lot to do with the rising number of people who are collecting benefits from government programs and who are required to report to government employment offices to get those benefits. They also point to two other important factors: the rising percentage of (1) women and (2) teenagers and young adults in the labor force. The young adults are baby boomers born between 1946 and 1964, who, like all young people, tend to have a relatively high unemployment rate. Many of the women are housewives who are hoping to return to the labor force.

According to the conservatives, a couple of million of the officially unemployed are not really looking for work at all. And according to the liberals, a couple of million people want to work but aren't being counted. Who is right? We'll leave that up to you.

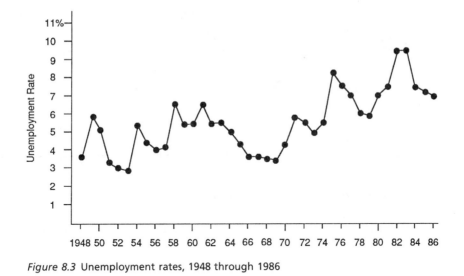

Figure 8.3 Unemployment rates, 1948 through 1986

10 | UNEQUAL BURDENS OF UNEMPLOYMENT

The unemployment rate has varied greatly from group to group in our labor force. Blacks, teenagers, occasionally blue-collar workers, and, in particular, black teenagers have much higher than average unemployment rates.

As you know, the one certain cure for inflation is recession. But the burden borne by the groups who lose their jobs when recessions occur—the same groups just cited—is much greater than that borne by the rest of the labor force.

During the 1981-1982 recession, for example, unemployment in the towns and cities that run across the industrial heartland of western New York and Pennsylvania, Ohio, Indiana, Illinois, and Michigan reached 15 and 20 percent, and the nation's overall unemployment rate hit 10.8 percent, but the black teenage unemployment rate topped 50 percent!

The overall unemployment rate for blacks has been more than double that of whites every year since 1977. In 1983, when the rest of the country was recovering from the recession, the black unemployment rate continued to rise, from 18.9 to 19.5 percent, while the white rate fell from 8.6 to 8.4 percent. No wonder many blacks say that when it's a recession for whites, it's a depression for blacks. Even during 1986, when the white unemployment rate sank to 6.0 percent, the depression continued for blacks, whose unemployment rate was 14.5 percent.

Self-Test 3

1. How does the Bureau of Labor Statistics gather the data it uses to compute the unemployment rate?
2. Which one of the following persons would be considered as unemployed?
   A. Someone who worked three days in the past month and then got laid off.
   B. A person who was ready, willing, and able to work but who gave up looking for a job three months ago.

C. An individual who reported to the state employment office last week but who is not very enthusiastic about finding a job.

3. A person who has not worked in six months and has given up looking for work is officially classified as
    A. Employed.
    B. Unemployed.
    C. Discouraged.

4. Given the following information, compute the unemployment rate: 8 million unemployed, 117 million employed.

5. Why do liberal economists say the official BLS unemployment rate is too *low*?

6. Why do conservative economists say the official unemployment rate is too *high*?

7. Since the mid-1970s, our unemployment rate has almost never dipped below _____ percent.

8. Which groups in our labor force have experience higher than average unemployment rates?

9. Since 1977 how has the unemployment rate for blacks compared with the unemployment rate for whites?

Answers to Self-Test 3

1. The BLS surveys 60,000 households.

2. C.

3. C.

4. Unemployment rate $= \dfrac{\text{Number of unemployed}}{\text{Labor force}} = \dfrac{8}{125} = 6.4\%$

5. Liberals point out that the BLS counts as "employed" two groups of people who are actually unemployed or underemployed: (1) people who worked one day in the last month and (2) people who worked part time but who wanted to work full time. The liberals also point out that the unemployment figures do not include those who would like to work but have given up looking for a job.

6. Conservatives argue that people collecting welfare, food stamps, and other government benefits, and who might not want to work, are required to report to government employment offices and are counted as unemployed.

7. 6 percent.

8. Blacks, teenagers, blue-collar workers, and, especially, black teenagers.

9. The rate for blacks is slightly more than twice the white unemployment rate.

11 | TYPES OF UNEMPLOYMENT

Frictional Unemployment

Frictionally unemployed people are between jobs or just entering or reentering the labor market. At any given time 2 or 3 percent of the labor force is frictionally unemployed. These people include students who are looking for their first full-time jobs, women who are reentering the labor market, and recently discharged members of the armed services. Those who get fired or leave their jobs voluntarily and are searching for better jobs are also classified as frictionally unemployed. Add to these the people who get fired, quit, or are just plumb unhappy, and decide to make a fresh start somewhere else. These people, too, are between jobs, or frictionally unemployed.

12 | Structural Unemployment

A person who is out of work for a relatively long period of time—say, a couple of years—and who cannot find another job is structurally unemployed. The steelworker in Youngstown, Ohio and the coal miner in Kentucky are no longer needed because of the closing of a steel mill and a coal mine. Clerical workers, typists, and inventory control clerks may have been replaced by a computer system. Add to these the people whose companies have gone out of business or whose jobs have been exported to low-wage countries, and you've got another 2 or 3 percent of the labor force structurally unemployed.

Ours is a dynamic economy and opportunities *do* exist for retraining and subsequent employment. But the job prospects for a middle-aged worker who must embark on a second career are not auspicious.

Where do we draw the line between frictional and structural unemployment? The answer is that we don't. There *is* no clear-cut dividing line.

13 | Cyclical Unemployment

Our economy fluctuates constantly, and so does our unemployment rate. During a recession, for example, the unemployment rate may rise to 8 or 9 or even 10 percent. During the Great Depression, the unemployment rate hit 25 percent, and even that alarming figure understated the bleakness of the unemployment picture. Conversely, the unemployment rate may be very low during an economic boom. These changes are known as *cyclical unemployment*.

Some liberal economists insist that we could get the unemployment rate down to 4 percent, but many conservative economists believe that 6 percent is the lowest attainable rate. We'll spit the different and call 5 percent full employment.

If we say that a 5 percent unemployment rate constitutes full employment, then anything above 5 percent would be cyclical unemployment. You may wonder whether 5 percent is a reasonable level of full employment. Surely, we can never expect our unemployment rate to reach zero, since we'll always have some frictionally and structurally unemployed people. Our unemployment rate actually did get down to 1.2 percent in 1944, but only because we were at war. There were 12 million men in the armed forces, and the economy was going at full steam ahead. Employers were desperate for help from anyone who could walk and spell their name.

To determine the cyclical unemployment rate, we add the frictional and structural unemployment rates and subtract the sum of these two rates from the current rate of unemployment. If, for example, the sum of frictional and structural unemployment is 5 percent, and the current rate of unemployment is 7.2 percent, then the cyclical unemployment rate is 2.2 percent (7.2 percent − 5 percent = 2.2 percent).

14 | WHO IS ELIGIBLE TO COLLECT UNEMPLOYMENT BENEFITS?

A lot of people are eligible to collect unemployment benefits, but many of them don't *know* they're eligible. To be eligible, a person must be able to answer yes to these three questions:

1. Did you work for at least part of each of 20 of the last 52 weeks (or 15 of the last 52 weeks and 40 of the last 104)?
2. Did you lose your last job through no fault of your own?
3. Are you ready, willing, and able to work?

The second question is open to argument. Let's say you were fired from your last job. If you provoked your own dismissal—by constant tardiness, say, or by falling asleep on duty—then you can't collect. If you were fired because you and your boss had an argument, however, you may be eligible. Also, if you got fired because your boss just didn't like you, because you couldn't get the hang of the job, or because there was no work for you to do, you could collect. But if you got fired because you were often absent or because you refused to work, you are not eligible for unemployment benefits.

The answer to the second question is not always a clear-cut yes or no, however. As a one-time employee of the New York State Employment Service, I am offering you this advice: If you lose your job and think you *may* be eligible, you should go to your state unemployment insurance office and apply for unemployment benefits. You may win a tax-free, $200 a week, twenty-six week, paid vacation.

15 | CONCLUSION

We have rarely been able to attain a low unemployment rate and stable prices at the same time. A.W. Phillips, a British economist, devised a curve to illustrate that there is a trade-off between price stability and low unemployment. He demonstrated that in the 1950s we attained price stability at the cost of higher unemployment. In the 1960s, according to Phillips, we did the exact opposite: We attained lower unemployment at the cost of price stability.

But in the 1970s, the trade-off that Phillips had observed in earlier years vanished completely. We suffered from both high unemployment *and* rapidly rising prices. In fact, during the presidential campaign of 1976, Jimmy Carter spoke of President Gerald Ford's "misery index," which was the inflation rate and the unemployment rate combined. Anything over 10 was unacceptable, according to Carter. In 1980 Ronald Reagan resurrected the misery index, reminding the voters that it had gone from 10, when President Carter took office, all the way to 20.

I'm not going to burden you further with the misery index, but you're welcome to construct your own by adding the data from Figures 8.1 and 8.3. You'll find that since 1970, the misery index dipped below 10 only once—in 1986. Be that as it may, it is the job of macroeconomic policy to keep that index as low as possible. We'll be examining macroeconomic policy over the next three chapters to learn how things are supposed to work and why they sometimes don't.

Self-Test 4

For questions 1–6 use these choices:

    A. Frictional unemployment.
    B. Structural unemployment.
    C. Cyclical unemployment.

1. An auto worker who is still out of work two years after his plant closed is an example of _____ .

2. A housewife returning to the labor market after an absence of ten years who is looking for work is an example of _____ .

3. A blue-collar worker who is laid off until business picks up again is an example of _____ .

4. People who are between jobs are example of _____ .

5. A person whose skills have become obsolete and is in her mid-fifties would be an example of _____ .

6. When the unemployment rate goes above 5 percent, anything above that 5 percent level is _____ .

7. If the unemployment rate is 9 percent, what is the cyclical unemployment rate?

8. To be eligible for unemployment insurance benefits, you must be able to answer yes to what three questions?

9. According to A. W. Phillips, there is a trade-off between _____ and _____ .

10. The misery index is the sum of the _____ and the _____ .

11. How did the 1970s differ from the 1950s and the 1960s with respect to A. W. Phillips' trade-off?

Answers to Self-Test 4

1. B.

2. A.

3. C.

4. A.

5. B.

6. C.

7. 4 percent.

8. (1) Did you work for at least part of twenty of the last fifty-two weeks? (2) Did you lose your job through no fault of your own? (3) Are you ready, willing, and able to work?

9. Price stability; low unemployment.

10. Unemployment rate; inflation rate.

11. In the 1950s and the 1960s there was a trade-off: As the unemployment rate rose, the inflation rate declined, or vice versa. In the 1970s, we had the worst of both worlds—a high unemployment rate and a high inflation rate.

PART 3

MACROECONOMICS:

THE

SOLUTIONS

CHAPTER 9

Fiscal

Policy

Fiscal policy is the manipulation of the federal budget to attain price stability, relatively full employment, and a satisfactory rate of economic growth. To attain these goals, the government must manipulate its spending level and taxes.

You don't need to be a great economist to see that we haven't been too successful, particularly over the last two decades. As we saw in Chapter 8, from the early 1970s to the early 1980s we were plagued by the twin problems of high unemployment and severe inflation. Our rate of economic growth—about 2.5 percent from 1970 to 1986—was nothing to write home about either.

After reading this chapter you will:

- Be able to recognize inflationary and deflationary gaps and know how to eliminate them.
- Understand when budget surpluses and deficits are appropriate.
- Know how automatic stabilizers and discretionary fiscal policy are used.
- Be able to solve basic fiscal policy problems.
- Understand the magnitude of the national debt and the degree to which is it will be a burden on future generations.

1 | FISCAL POLICY AND EQUILIBRIUM GNP

Fiscal policy was invented by—who else?—John Maynard Keynes. During the 1930s, when Keynes was writing his *General Theory*, people all over the world were demanding that their governments do something to end the depression. The only question was "what?" Until that time, the economic wisdom was to balance the budget and let private enterprise do the rest. But the policy of *laissez-faire* did not seem to be working. The depression kept getting worse and worse.

Keynes suggested that the government follow his two-word policy prescription: *Spend money*. Since the massive government spending during World War II brought us out of the depression, we have continued following the Keynesian dictum—perhaps blindly. The Great Depression ended some fifty years ago, but our government still hasn't gotten the news.

Many people attribute the recent inflation to high level of federal spending and the attendant megadeficits. Others blame the rapid growth of our money supply. Fiscal policy and monetary policy have the same goals: high employment and stable prices. However, people often get the two policies mixed up. Although both fiscal policy and monetary policy have the same ends, their means are very different.

Monetary policy is aimed at regulating the rate of growth of our money supply, while fiscal policy is aimed at manipulating the federal budget. We'll examine fiscal policy in this chapter; we'll discuss monetary policy in Chapter 10.

Before we can delve into fiscal policy, we need to understand the concept of Equilibrium GNP. The equilibrium level of GNP is determined by the forces of aggregate demand (the subject of Chapter 6) and aggregate supply (see frame 4 of Chapter 8). Exactly *how* these forces determine Equilibrium GNP requires a rather complex theoretical exposition that is best left to more advanced texts.

At any given time, a certain amount of money is being spent on consumption, investment, government purchases of goods and services, and net exports. In other words, a certain amount of output is being purchased. This is the equilibrium level of GNP.

In terms of Equilibrium GNP, sometimes we are spending too much, and other times we're spending too little. When Equilibrium GNP is too high, we have an inflationary gap; when it's too low, we have a deflationary gap. Our policy objective is to find a level of GNP that is just right. In this section we will deal with inflationary gaps, and deflationary gaps, and GNPs that are just right.

When Equilibrium GNP is just right, it is buying up exactly the output that would be produced by our labor force if it were fully employed. Using the figure we agreed on at the end of Chapter 8, that would mean an unemployment rate of 5 percent. So we shall call that level of spending *Full Employment GNP*.

2   THE DEFLATIONARY GAP

The deflationary gap—sometimes called the recessionary gap—occurs when Equilibrium GNP is less than Full Employment GNP. In other words, when too little money is being spent to provide enough jobs for everyone, we have a deflationary gap (see Figure 9.1). Another way of expressing this state of economic affairs is to say that we are inside our production possibilities curve. (If you need to review this curve, reread the end of Chapter 4.)

How do we close this gap? By increasing the amount of spending—in other words, by increasing consumption (C), investment (I), government expenditures (G), or some combination thereof. Keynes recommended raising G. We may decide, instead, to lower taxes. Lowering business taxes might encourage more investment, while a cut in personal income taxes would stimulate consumption.

By how much would we have to raise spending to eliminate a deflationary gap? In Figure 9.1 the gap is $50 billion. Anything less than $50 billion would reduce the gap but would not eliminate it.

Notice that Equilibrium GNP is $200 billion less than Full Employment GNP. How much must the multiplier be? If we raise G by $50 billion and thus raise Equilibrium GNP by $200 billion, then the multiplier must be 4.

Notice how the points in Figure 9.1 line up. Equilibrium GNP is to the left of Full Employment GNP. The deflationary gap is directly above Full Employment

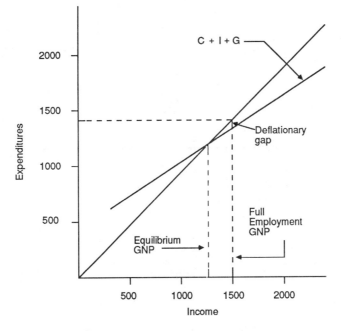

Figure 9.1 Deflationary gap

GNP. It is the vertical distance between the 45 degree line and the C + I + G line.

Notice also that Equilibrium GNP is too low. How much too low? It is $200 billion too low. What can we do, then, to increase it by $200 billion?

We can raise C or I or G or some combination thereof. Suppose we raise C + I + G by a total of $50 billion. This increased spending will give rise to additional spending. How much additional spending? By the time the entire process is over, it will have increased spending by a total of $200 billion (or four times the original increase of $50 billion). So, we can say that an initial increase in spending of $50 billion will ultimately raise Equilibrium GNP by $200 billion. That implies a multiplier of 4. (If the workings of the multiplier still mystify you, please reread frames 37–40 of Chapter 7.)

Let's summarize what we've discussed so far. The Equilibrium GNP, which occurs where the C + I + G line crosses the 45 degree line is where our economy is currently operating. If it is operating below the full employment level, there is a deflationary gap. By pushing Equilibrium GNP up to the level of Full Employment GNP, we will eliminate the deflationary gap.

3   THE INFLATIONARY GAP

The inflationary gap is shown in Figure 9.2. The key difference between this graph and the one in Figure 9.1, showing the deflationary gap, is the position of Equilibrium GNP. When there is an inflationary gap, Equilibrium GNP is to the right of Full Employment GNP. When there's a deflationary gap, Equilibrium

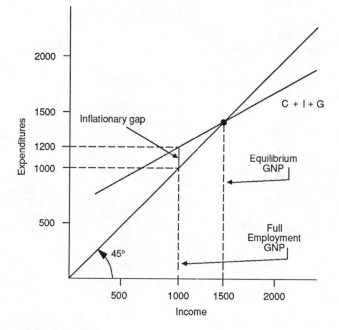

Figure 9.2 Inflationary gap

GNP is to the left. In other words, Equilibrium GNP is greater than Full Employment GNP when there's an inflationary gap and Full Employment GNP is greater than Equilibrium GNP when there's a deflationary gap.

In both graphs the gap is the vertical distance between the C + I + G line and the aggregate supply line (or 45 degree line). And in both graphs the gap is directly above Full Employment GNP.

In a word, when there's a deflationary gap, Equilibrium GNP is too small, and when there's an inflationary gap, it's too big. Keynes would suggest that we cut G and raise taxes to eliminate an inflationary gap. Both actions are aimed at reducing spending and thereby also reducing Equilibrium GNP.

In Figure 9.2 the inflationary gap is $200 billion. Cutting spending by $200 billion would have a multiplied effect on GNP. Equilibrium GNP would decline by $500 billion to the Full Employment level. How much is the multiplier? If Equilibrium GNP falls by $500 billion in response to a spending cut of $200 billion, the multiplier is 2.5.

To summarize, if spending is too high, then equilibrium GNP is above the full employment level. To eliminate the inflationary gap, we cut G and/or raise taxes. If Equilibrium GNP is less than Full Employment GNP, we eliminate the deflationary gap by raising G and/or cutting taxes.

Self-Test 1

1. What is fiscal policy?
2. When was it invented and by whom?

3. What was Keynes' two-word policy prescription for ending the Great Depression?

4. How do fiscal policy and monetary policy differ?

5. What is Equilibrium GNP?

6. When is Equilibrium GNP at just the right level?

7. When Full Employment GNP is greater than Equilibrium GNP, we have a(n) _____ gap; when Equilibrium GNP is greater than Full Employment GNP, we have a(n) _____ gap.

8. If Equilibrium GNP is $100 billion less than Full Employment GNP and there is a deflationary gap of $20 billion, how much is the multiplier?

9. If Full Employment GNP is $400 billion greater than Equilibrium GNP and there is a deflationary gap of $100 billion, how much is the multiplier?

10. If there is an inflationary gap of $200 billion and the multiplier is 2, what should the government do with respect to G?

11. Full Employment GNP implies an unemployment rate of _____ percent.

12. If the mutliplier is 8 and Equilibrium GNP is $200 billion greater than Full Employment GNP, there is a _____ gap of $ _____ .

13. If the multiplier is 10 and Full Employment GNP is $300 billion greater than Equilibrium GNP, there is a _____ gap of $ _____ billion.

Answers to Self-Test 1

1. Fiscal policy is the manipulation of federal government spending and taxation to attain price stability and high employment.

2. It was invented by John Maynard Keynes during the Great Depression of the 1930s.

3. Spend money.

4. Fiscal policy is aimed at manipulating the federal budget; monetary policy is aimed at regulating the rate of growth of the money supply.

5. Equilibrium GNP is the amount of output that is being purchased at any point in time.

6. When there is no inflationary or deflationary gap.

7. Deflationary; inflationary.

8. 5.

9. 5.

10. G should be lowered by $100 billion.

11. 5 percent.

12. Inflationary; $25 billion.

13. Deflationary; $30 billion.

4 | THE NUTS AND BOLTS OF FISCAL POLICY

When we stop to think about the federal government's budget, it is not unreasonable to ask if there really *is* such a thing as fiscal policy, or, indeed, if anyone is even in charge. However desirable the goals of fiscal policy, any reasonable observer might question whether there is any intelligent life form that has some connection with the federal budget.

The main problem faced by fiscal policymakers is that over two-thirds of federal spending simply cannot be cut, either for legal reasons or for political reasons. Add to that the reluctance of most politicians to raise taxes and you've got a surefire prescription for massive budget deficits. Perhaps President Reagan best exemplified this political stance by repeatedly stating that there would be a tax increase only "over my dead body."

So in a very basic way, there *is* no fiscal policy—or regardless of our state of fiscal policy, our de facto policy is to run huge deficits and to create a continuous stream of inflationary gaps.

As we consider the actual workings of fiscal policy, we'll be talking mainly about fiscal policy aimed at fighting recessions. First we'll consider three possible results of any given fiscal policy: budget deficits, budget surpluses, and balanced budgets. Then we'll see how automatic stabilizers and discretionary fiscal policy produce these results.

5 | DEFICITS, SURPLUSES, AND BALANCED BUDGETS

To understand how fiscal policy works, we need to understand these three basic concepts: deficits, surpluses, and balanced budgets. A *budget deficit* occurs when federal government spending is greater than tax revenue. The government is paying out more than it's taking in. How does it make up the difference? It borrows. The United States enjoyed its last surplus in 1969 and has been running budget deficits every year since then; in the mid-1980s we managed to push these annual deficits over the $200 billion mark.

A *budget surplus* would occur if tax revenue were greater than government spending, since the government would be taking in more than it was spending. When President Carter took office in 1977, he promised us a surplus by 1981. When President Reagan took office in 1981, he promised a surplus by 1984. We're still waiting.

Keynes advised the creation of a budget deficit to fight recession and the use of surpluses to fight inflations.

A *balanced budget* exists when government expenditures are equal to tax revenues. Although we've never had a perfectly balanced budget, we have had relatively small surpluses or deficits. If the deficit or surplus were less than $10 billion (less than 1 percent of federal government spending), we'd probably call that a balanced budget.

Some economists think that the federal government should balance its budget every year unless we are at war or threatened by a bad recession. Why do these economists exclude recession years? Because efforts to balance the budget during a recession could turn the recession into a depression. For example, if we tried to balance the budget by cutting expenditures, exactly what would we cut? Food stamps? Welfare? Unemployment compensation? Defense? Any spending cut whatsoever would hurt individuals and would lower overall spending. Trying to balance the budget by raising taxes during a recession would have the same effect.

Self-Test 2

1. When we have a budget deficit, _____ is greater than _____ ; when we have a budget surplus, _____ is greater than _____ ; a balanced budget means that _____ is equal to

   _____ .

2. When does a budget deficit occur and when should it be used (according to Keynes)?

3. When does a budget surplus occur and when would a surplus be useful?

4. When did we last enjoy a federal budget surplus?

5. In the mid-1980s our federal budget deficits reached
   $ _____ a year.

6. Should we try to balance the budget in recession years? Why or why not?

Answers to Self-Test 2

1. Government spending is greater than tax revenue; tax revenue is greater than government spending; tax revenue is equal to government spending.

2. A budget deficit occurs when government spending exceeds tax revenue; it can be used to fight a recession.

3. A budget surplus occurs when tax revenue exceeds government spending; it is useful in fighting inflation.

4. 1969.

5. $200 billion.

6. We should not try to balance the budget in recession years because by doing so we would make the recession much worse.

6 | THE AUTOMATIC STABILIZERS

Three automatic stabilizers are built into our economy and work automatically: (1) variations in tax receipts, (2) unemployment insurance benefits, and (3) personal savings. Congress does not need to pass any laws to create these mechanisms, and no new bureaucracies have to be created to administer them.

Each of these stabilizers protects the economy from the extremes of the business cycle, in other words, from recession and inflation. The stabilizers, by themselves, are not expected to prevent booms and busts, but only to moderate them. Let's examine these economic stabilizers one at a time.

7 | Variations in Tax Receipts

During times of prosperity, tax receipts automatically rise. Individuals pay more personal income tax and Social Security tax, which is matched by employers. Corporations pay more corporate income tax. This leaves less money available for individuals and businesses to spend, thereby lessening inflationary pressures.

During recessions, as incomes fall, individuals and corporations pay lower taxes. This leaves more money available for consumption and investment, thereby moderating the effects of the recession.

8 | Unemployment Insurance Benefits

During recessions, as unemployment increases, more people will become eligible for unemployment benefits. Tens of billions of dollars of unemployment benefits will be paid out, establishing a floor under purchasing power. Because of the benefits, people who are temporarily out of work will continue to spend money. This will prevent retail sales from falling very much, and so, even without further government help, the economy will have time to work its way out of the recession. As the economy recovers and moves toward prosperity, people will return to work and unemployment benefit claims will drop substantially.

Two other important transfer payments also rise *automatically* during a recession as unemployment increases. They are (1) public assistance, or welfare, and (2) food stamps.

9 | Personal Savings

As the economy moves into a recession, savings decline. Many Americans lose their jobs and others get less overtime. As incomes fall, savings must fall as well. However, consumption will rise as a percentage of income.

Take, for example, a family that earns $20,000 a year and saves $2,000 annually. Suddenly, a recession hits, and the family's earnings drop to $12,000. This family will almost certainly stop saving and will reduce spending, say, from $18,000 to $12,000. This means that a decline of $8,000 in income causes the family's consumption to fall by only $6000 (see Table 9.1).

Just as the loss of income is cushioned by a fall-off of saving, the reverse happens when the economy picks up again. When the family's income returns to its prerecession level of $20,000, savings goes up again to $2000. Thus, an $8000 rise in income is accompanied by a consumption increase of only $6000.

10 | Other Transfer Payments

Some people think that when a recession hits, the government automatically raises Social Security benefits. This might make sense, but it doesn't happen.

Table 9.1.

Family Income	Consumption	Savings
$20,000	$18,000	$2000
12,000	12,000	0

Special legislation would have to be passed, which would mean that it isn't automatic.

Two important transfer payments—public assistance and food stamps—*do* rise automatically during a recession because of laws on the books. As unemployment increases, more people become eligible for public assistance and food stamps, since eligibility is based solely on income.

These four automatic stabilizers smooth out the business cycle, keeping the economic fluctuations within a moderate range. Since the 1930s, we have not had severe depression or runaway inflation. Remember, however, that the stabilizers, by themselves, cannot altogether eliminate economic fluctuations.

The automatic stabilizers may be called the automatic pilot of our economy, not very well suited for takeoffs and landings, but fine for the smooth part of the flight. But when the going gets rough, the economy must use manual control. Discretionary policy is our manual control.

Self-Test 3

1. What are the three main automatic stabilizers and how do they work?
2. What three types of federal tax receipts decline during a recession?
3. As incomes fall, what happens to the nation's average propensity to save?
4. In addition to unemployment insurance benefits, what other two transfer payments rise automatically during a recession?
5. With respect to fiscal policy, _____ can be likened to automatic pilot, while _____ would be our manual controls.

Answers to Self-Test 3

1. One, variation in tax receipts: Taxes rise during inflations and fall during recessions. Two, unemployment insurance benefits fall with inflation and rise with recessions. Three, personal savings rise with inflation and fall with recession (and consumption moves in the opposite direction).
2. Personal income tax, corporate income tax, and payroll tax receipts.
3. It falls.
4. Welfare and food stamps.
5. Automatic stabilizers; discretionary fiscal policy.

11 | DISCRETIONARY FISCAL POLICY

We've just seen that the automatic stabilizers kick in as soon as a recession or an inflation begins because of laws that are already on the books. Discretionary fiscal policy requires an additional effort by the president and Congress to counter the effects of a recession or an inflation by passing still more legislation. In the next four frames we'll examine the ways that this is done.

12 | Making the Automatic Stabilizers More Effective

The main automatic stabilizer built into our economy to fight recessions is unemployment insurance. But one problem with unemployment benefits is that they run out in six months, while a recession can drag on for over a year. Extending the benefit period for unemployment benefits is an example of discretionary fiscal policy at work. An increase in the benefit ceiling or a widening or eligibility standards would be other ways of making this stabilizer more effective.

Parallel efforts could be made with respect to food stamps, public assistance, Medicaid, and aid to the homeless during recessions. Then, when the economy returns to prosperity, these programs would be cut back.

13 | Public Works

During the Great Depression, the Roosevelt administration set up several, so-called alphabet agencies to provide jobs for the long-term unemployed. Among them the WPA and the CCC put millions of people to work doing everything from raking leaves on government land to constructing government buildings.

These workers spent their salaries, thereby creating a demand for goods and services in the private sector, and that demand created still more jobs. Public works are probably not the answer for brief recessions, however. Only a very long and severe depression would allow such huge projects to be carried out.

14 | Changes in Tax Rates

Tax increases and decreases are another discretionary policy measure. In 1968, for example, Congress fought an inflation by legislating a 10 percent income tax surcharge sought by President Johnson. Conversely, during the recession of 1981–1982, it passed a tax-cutting measure proposed by President Reagan.

Corporate income taxes, too, could be raised during inflations and lowered during recessions. The investment tax credit, first adapted by the Kennedy administration, is another way of using taxes to manipulate spending.

A key advantage of a change in the tax rate is that it provides a quick economic fix. We have to make sure, however, that temporary tax cuts do not become permanent.

Discretionary fiscal policy dictates that we increase government spending to mitigate recessions and lower government spending to damp down inflation. For example, during a recession the government might increase transfer payments (unemployment compensation, welfare payments, Social Security, and veteran's pensions). Like public works, this would channel money into the hands of consumers who, by spending this money, would create jobs in the private sector. Increased transfer payments would have the added advantage of working very quickly. No plans or blueprints are needed. Just program the computer and put the checks in the mail.

During an inflation, of course, the government would have to cut back on spending. Obviously, this side of discretionary fiscal policy is a lot less popular and may well be tantamount to committing political suicide.

Self-Test 4

1. How is discretionary fiscal policy related to the automatic stabilizers?
2. Would public works projects be an appropriate solution for a short recession?
3. What discretionary fiscal policy would quickly get money into the hands of people who would spend it?
4. Would you raise or lower tax rates to end a recession?
5. Would you increase or decrease government spending to end an inflation?

Answers to Self-Test 4

1. It is aimed at making them more effective.
2. No. They take too long.
3. An increase in transfer payments.
4. Lower them.
5. Decrease it.

15 | FISCAL POLICY: SOME PRACTICAL APPLICATIONS

There is a rule of thumb among economists that a 1 percent rise in the unemployment rate will be accompanied by a $27 billion increase in the federal deficit. There is another rule of thumb among economists that a 1 percent rise in the unemployment rate will be accompanied by a $30 billion increase in the federal deficit. Which rule of thumb is right? Obviously, no one can be sure if either is right.

But let's see if $27 billion and $30 billion are at least ball park estimates. What we'll do is divide up the problem into three parts: (1) When the unemployment rate goes up by 1 percent, how many people lose their jobs? (2) How does this increase in unemployment affect government spending? (3) How does this rise in unemployment affect tax revenue?

We'll deal with first things first—the number of people thrown out of work when the unemployment rate rises by 1 percent. How can we figure that one out? If we knew how many people are in the labor force, we'd be able to take 1 percent of that figure. Let's look it up in the business section of the Sunday *New York Times*. On April 12, 1987, the *Times* reported the March 1987 employment and unemployment figures: 113,104,000 people were working, and 7,854,000 were out of work, which added up to a labor force of 120,958,000 people.

Since the labor force grows by about two million a year, you can figure out approximately how many are in the labor force today—or you could look the figure up in the *Times*, *BusinessWeek*, or some other periodical. For now, let's just pick a number. How does 125 million sound to you?

So, if the unemployment rate goes up by 1 percent from 125 million, how many people lose their jobs? 1.25 million (or 1,250,000). Good!

Now we'll deal with the second question: How does this increase in unemployment affect government spending? We'll assume that 1 million of the 1.25 million newly unemployed are able to collect unemployment insurance for a year. (When it runs out after twenty-six weeks we'll assume they find jobs and another million people collect for the next twenty-six weeks.) How much do they collect? On the average, let's say $150 a week. What does that come to in a year? Go ahead and do it, using a fifty-week year.

What we have, then, is 50 × $150 × 1,000,000. That's $7,500 × 1,000,000 (when you multiply a number by a thousand, or ten thousand, or a million, or any other number with a lot of zeros in it, just tack the zeros on to the original number). $7,500 × 1,000,000 = $7,500,000,000. So the government must pay out $7.5 billion in unemployment benefits to these people who have been thrown out of work by the recession.

Next comes welfare. Some of those who have lost their jobs won't be eligible for unemployment compensation and may have to apply for welfare. Others who *do* collect may be eligible for welfare payments to supplement their unemployment benefits.

How much do these people get? That depends on which states they live in, how large their families are, and on how much income they are receiving. Add to this food stamps, Medicaid, and other government aid and we're talking another $6 or $7 billion. So, we can expect a 1 percent rise in the unemployment rate to raise government spending by somewhere around $14 billion.

Now we're ready for question number three: How does a 1 percent rise in unemployment affect tax revenue? It clearly lowers tax revenue. But by how much? If every newly unemployed worker earned, say, $20,000, what would the government lose in personal income taxes, payroll taxes, and corporate income taxes?

The payroll tax is the easiest to figure. We'll use the year 1990. The tax rate for 1990 is 7.65 percent (see the footnote to Table 7.1.) paid by the employee, and that rate is matched by the employer. So, 15.3 percent of $20,000 is lost to the government for each of the 1.25 million people laid off. How much does that come to?

16   What did you get? 15.3 percent of $20,000 = $3060. $3060 × 1.25 million = 3060 × 1,250,000 (or, 3060 × 125 + 4 zeros). *Answer*: $3,825,000,000, or $3.8 billion.

What about personal income taxes? Of the recently laidoff people earning $20,000, some are single, some are married, some have just themselves as dependents, and some have more than one dependent. But all of them have one thing in common: They're all in the 15 percent personal income tax bracket. What differs is how much of their incomes is taxable. Suppose, on the average, one-half is taxable. How much tax would one person pay if he or she were working? How much would 1.25 million people pay?

17   15 percent of $10,000 = $1500. $1500 × 1,250,000 = (1500 × 125 + 4 zeros) = $1,875,000,000, or $1.9 billion.

So far, so good. Unfortunately the corporate income tax loss will be much harder to figure out with precision. I'm going to go way out on a limb and guess that in 1990 corporate income taxes would come to $180 billion, but that a 1 percent rise in the unemployment rate will cause corporate sales, and consequently corporate income and taxes, to fall by 1 percent, or by $1.8 billion. This guess, by the way, would not be off by more than couple of hundred million.

Okay, go ahead and tote up the entire federal government revenue loss due to the 1 percent rise in the unemployment rate. You should have come up with $3.8 billion + $1.9 billion + $1.8 billion = $7.5 billion. If we add some relatively minor tax losses due to reduced tariff collections and excise tax receipts, we could round out the tax revenue loss to $8 billion.

If a 1 percent rise in the unemployment rate leads to $14 billion of added government spending (and I suspect we've left out a few additional items like more administrative costs, more aid to the homeless, and perhaps more job training programs), then we're up to a good $22 billion, and maybe several billion more. It would seem obvious, then, that the original $27 billion and $30 billion estimates were both in the ball park.

Since you've acquired so much wisdom from the problem we've just worked out, you will be able to dispose of the next two problems in a matter of seconds.

Imagine that the president's budget contemplates no new taxes or spending programs for the next fiscal year, but it expects the current fiscal year's $60 billion deficit to shrink away to zero. Exactly what assumption is the president making?

18

Answer: That the unemployment rate will decline by 2 percent.

If the unemployment rate rises by 4 percent, how much will government expenditures rise as a result in one year?

19

Answer: $7500 × 4 million = $30 billion.

Self-Test 5

1. If there are 130 million people in the labor force and the unemployment rate goes down by 2 percent, total unemployment has declined by _____ percent.

2. If the budget deficit declines by $30 billion in one year with no changes from the previous year in budgeted spending and tax rates, what probably happened to the unemployment rate? Answer as precisely as possible.

3. If the unemployment rate rises sharply, what three types of federal tax receipts will decline?

4. In general, why does a decrease in the unemployment rate reduce the federal deficit?

Answers to Self-Test 5

1. 2.6 million people.
2. It went down 1 percent.

3. Personal income, corporate income, and payroll taxes.

4. Government spending (for unemployment compensation, welfare, food stamps, Medicaid, and aid to the homeless) declines; tax receipts rise.

20 | THE NATIONAL DEBT

In October 1981 the national debt went above the trillion dollar mark. This was our accumulated debt since the beginning of the republic. How much money is a trillion dollars? It's a thousand billion. Written out it looks like this: $1,000,000,000,000.

It took us over 200 years to accumulate this debt. It took us just another four and a half years to reach the $2 trillion mark, which we did in April 1986. Although our rate of debt accumulation has slowed somewhat during the last few years, we are fast approaching $3 trillion.

There is some confusion between the national debt and the federal budget deficit. Let's make sure we understand these two terms. The federal budget deficit is the amount by which federal government expenditures exceed tax receipts. It is an annual total, which exceeded $200 billion in the mid-1980s. The national debt is the cumulative total of all federal budget deficits minus any surpluses. Prior to the mid-1970s, most of this debt was run up during recessions and wars. Although we had a couple of recessions in the early 1980s, most of the increase in the debt since 1975 has been accumulated during years of peace and prosperity.

The national debt is owed to the holders of Treasury bills, notes, certificates, and bonds. If you own any of these, you are holding part of the national debt. About half is held by private American citizens. Foreigners hold more than 20 percent, while the rest is held by U.S. government agencies, including the Federal Reserve.

Is the national debt going to be a burden on future generations, or do we owe it to ourselves? The answers are yes and yes. We do owe an increasing proportion of the debt to foreigners—in 1960 foreigners held just 3 percent of the debt. In recent years, especially as our trade deficits mounted in the mid-1980s, foreigners found themselves holding hundreds of billions of dollars. They have been using a lot of these dollars, as much as $100 billion a year, to buy U.S. government securities. Future generations of Americans will be obligated to continue making interest payments to foreigners, even if we never actually pay off what we owe. In other words, if foreigners are content to continue holding Treasury bills, bonds, certificates, and notes, buying new ones when the old ones fall due, and just keep collecting the interest on them, this will place a continuing financial burden on future generations of Americans.

But we owe most of the national debt to ourselves. Surely, this is not very much of a burden on future generations because all we have to do is keep paying interest to the holders of U.S. government securities. Where do we get the money for this? By taxing all Americans, including those who hold most of the national debt. This amounts to taking money out of one pocket and putting it into another.

Aside from the increasing foreign holdings of the national debt, the debt *does* represent a burden on future generations in a somewhat different sense. The debt was accumulated because the government was spending more money than it was taking in. What was this money spent on? Wars, unemployment benefits, welfare payments, interest on the national debt, and various other government goods and services. If, instead, the government had balanced its budget, the funds it borrowed would have been available to the private sector for investment in plant, equipment, and residential housing.

What this all comes down to, then, is that because we ran huge budget deficits, year after year, especially during the 1970s and 1980s, we invested less in capital goods and housing. And so, in the 1990s and beyond, the generations that come of age will be inheriting less of these assets than they otherwise would have.

Let's fix the blame. Did the national debt cause them to inherit less? Or was it because, year after year, the federal government would not, or could not, live within its means? Any burden on future generations was not caused *by* the national debt itself, but rather by the unending string of deficits the federal government has been running since 1970. The national debt is a symptom, not a cause.

When do we have to pay off the debt? We don't. All we have to do is roll it over, or refinance it, as it falls due. Each year several hundred billion dollars worth of federal securities fall due. By selling new ones, the Treasury keeps us going. But there is no reason why it ever has to be paid off.

A real problem would arise, however, if investors thought the government might go bankrupt. That's what happened to the New York City government in 1975. Suddenly the city was unable to sell its securities, which it needed to do to roll over its debt. Had the pension plans of municipal labor unions and the federal government not helped out, the city would indeed have gone bankrupt. However, the financial position of the governments of New York and the United States are hardly comparable. The federal government has first claim on our tax dollar, which makes its securities the safest possible investment.

Self-Test 6

1. How much is the national debt right now?
2. When did the national debt reach $1 trillion; $2 trillion?
3. What is the national debt?
4. About what percentage of the national debt is held by foreigners?
5. What does the national debt consist of?
6. About half of the national debt is held by _____ .
7. In what two ways is the national debt a burden on future generations?
8. The blame for the national debt should be fixed on _____ .
9. Do we have to pay off the national debt? If not, what do we have to do?

Answers to Self-Test 6

1. Your answer to this question depends on the year in which you are answering. If it is before 1992, your answer should be a little less than $3 trillion. Perhaps sometimes in 1992 or 1993 we'll go over the $3 trillion mark.

2. October 1981; April 1986.

3. It is the sum of all our federal deficits minus the surpluses.

4. A little over 20 percent.

5. Treasury bills, notes, certificates, and bonds.

6. U.S. citizens.

7. To the degree that we owe it to foreigners, future generations will have to pay interest to foreigners and may have to pay off part of the debt (or principal) as well. The debt also represents, but does not cause, a burden because it diverts funds away from investment in capital goods and residential housing, which future generations might have inherited.

8. The federal government for running deficits, especially since 1970.

9. No; just roll it over.

CHAPTER 10

Money, Banking,

and

Monetary Policy

S ince monetary policy has to do with the rate of growth of the money supply, we need to look now at our money supply. After we see how banks create money, we'll see how the Federal Reserve Board conducts monetary policy.

When you finish this chapter you will:

- Understand the three basic functions of money.
- Know what serves as money in the United States.
- Be familiar with the equation of exchange and the quantity theory of money.
- Have learned the origins of banking.
- Know how the FDIC protects bank deposits.
- Know how the Federal Reserve is organized.
- Be able to calculate interest rates.
- Have learned the basic tools of monetary policy and how the Federal Reserve uses them.
- Understand why monetary policy is more effective at fighting inflation than recessions.
- Be familiar with the Depository Institutions Deregulation and Monetary Control Act of 1980.

1 | MONEY

The Three Jobs of Money

Money has three jobs. It serves as (1) a *medium of exchange*, (2) a *standard of value* (sometimes called a unit of account), and (3) a *store of value*, or of wealth.

Without money, we would have to do business by bartering: "How many quarter sections of beef do you want for that car?" or "Will you accept four pounds of sugar for that 18 ounce steak?" In order for barter to work, we need a double coincidence of wants. I must want what you have, and you must want what I have. This makes it pretty hard to do business. Money makes it much easier to buy and to sell, because it is universally acceptable. If I have enough money, I can go out and buy whatever I want. Similarly, a seller will sell to anyone who offers enough money. Money, then, provides us with a shortcut in doing business. By acting as a medium of exchange, money performs its most important function.

Money performs well, too, as a standard of value. If I told you I got a gallon of gasoline for 60 cents, you'd immediately ask of the location of that gas station. Or if I said I bought a cheeseburger at a fast food place for $8, you'd just shake your head at my stupidity. A job that pays $2 an hour would be nearly impossible to fill, while one paying $50 an hour would be swamped with applicants.

Money performs poorly as a store of value, however. This is so because of inflation, since money loses value as prices rise. However, over relatively short periods of time—say, a few weeks—money does not lose very much of its value. More significantly, during periods of price stability, money is an excellent store of value. Of course, the best time to hold money is during deflation, because the longer you hold it, the more it's worth. For example, if you had kept money hidden in your mattress from late 1929 to early 1933, it would have doubled in value during those years.

2 | OUR MONEY SUPPLY

What does our money supply consist of? Gold? No. U.S. government bonds? No. Diamonds? No. Money consists of just a few things: currency (coins and paper money), demand (or checking) deposits, and checklike deposits (commonly called NOW—or Negotiable Order of Withdrawal–accounts). Coins (pennies, nickels, dimes, quarter, half-dollars, and silver dollars) and paper money (dollar bills, fives, tens, twenties, fifties, hundreds, and five-hundred dollar bills) together are considered currency.

Demand deposits are payable on demand. When you write a check, your bank must honor it, provided, of course, that you have enough money in your account to cover the check. These deposits constitute close to three quarters of the money supply. We have to be careful, however, to distinguish between checks and demand (or checking) deposits. Jackie Gleason used to tell a story about two guys who got into an argument in a bar about who was cheaper. Suddenly, one of them pulled out a dollar bill and a book of matches, lit the bill, and let it burn to a crisp. Not to be outdone, the other guy pulled out a five, lit it, and watched it burn to a crisp. Then the first guy did the same thing with a ten. The other guy didn't want to look bad, so he reached into his pocket, pulled out his checkbook, wrote a check for $1,000, lit it, and watched it burn to a crisp.

Checks are *not* money. Checking deposits (and NOW deposits) *are*.

3 | THE EQUATION OF EXCHANGE

The equation of exchange and the quantity theory of money are easily confused, perhaps because the equation of exchange is used to explain the quantity theory. I warn my students every term about how easy it is to write down the equation of exchange when asked for the quantity theory, or vice versa. Despite my warnings, however, many of my students remain faithful to the tradition of confusing the two concepts.

Here is the equation of exchange: MV = PQ. (Some economists prefer to use T, total number of transactions, instead of Q.) What do these letters stand for? M is the number of dollars in the nation's money supply—the currency, demand deposits, and check-like deposits. V is the velocity of circulation, or the number of times per year that each dollar in our money supply is spent. M times V, or MV, is our money supply multiplied by the number of times per year each dollar is spent, in other words, total spending. And total spending by a nation during a given year is GNP. Therefore, MV = GNP.

Now look at the other side of the equation. P represents the price level, or the average price of all the goods and services sold during the year. Q stands for the quantity of goods and services sold during the year. By multiplying P times Q, we get the total amount of money received by the sellers of all the goods and services produced by the nation that year. This is also GNP. Since MV equals GNP and PQ also equals GNP, the MV equals PQ.

We'll get a better idea of how this equation works by replacing the letters with numbers. For M we'll use $900 billion, which will probably be approximately the level of our money supply by the time you read this book. According to empirical studies, V is about 9.

$$MV = PQ$$
$$900 \times 9 = PQ$$
$$8100 = PQ$$

This gives us a GNP of 8100, or $8.1 trillion. (As a shorthand, economists will write billions of dollars without the dollar sign. The money supply of $900 billion becomes 900 and the GNP of $8100 billion becomes 8100.)

So far we have MV = 8100, and therefore PQ also = 8100. Now how much are P and Q? We don't know. All we *do* know is that P × Q = 8100.

For now let's say that P is $81. Why $81? Because that figure will be easy to work with. Now if P equals $81 and PQ equals 8100, Q must equal 100 (economists' shorthand for 100 billion). Therefore:

$$MV = PQ$$
$$900 \times 9 = 81 \times 100$$
$$8100 = 8100$$

That's the equation of exchange. It must always balance, as must all equations. If one side goes up by a certain percentage, then the other side must go up by the same percentage. For example, if MV rises to 9000, then PQ will also rise to 9000.

4   THE QUANTITY THEORY OF MONEY

There are two versions of the quantity theory of money—a crude version and a sophisticated version. The crude quantity theory of money says that when the money supply changes by a certain percentage, the price level changes by that same percentage. For example, if the money supply were to rise by 10 percent, then the price level would rise by 10 percent. Similarly, if M were to double, then P would also double. Using the figures we have assigned to the equation of exchange, let's see what happens if M and P double:

$$MV = PQ$$
$$900 \times 9 = 81 \times 100$$
$$1800 \times 9 = 162 \times 100$$
$$16,200 = 16,200$$

If we double M, then MV doubles also. And if we double P, then PQ also doubles. Since both sides of the equation must be equal, it appears that the crude quantity theory of money works out.

There are only two problems here. We are assuming that V and Q remain constant. Do they? If they do, then the crude quantity theory is correct. But what if they don't? For example, what if M, P, and Q all double. In order for the equation to balance, V would have to go down by 50 percent. Similarly, what if M doubles and V declines by 50 percent? In that case, the rise in P would be cancelled by the decline in V. If M doubles and MV stays the same, could we expect an automatic doubling of P?

Let's take closer look at V and then at Q. Since 1950, V has risen fairly steadily from about 3 to a little more than 9. In other words, individuals and businesses are spending their dollars much more quickly. Alternately, they are making more efficient use of their money balances.

There are several explanations for the rise of V. First, there's inflation. Why hold large money balances when they lose their value over time? Second, why hold idle cash balances when they could be earning interest. Finally, the use of credit cards, especially during the last two decades, has allowed people to carry less cash. As a result, V has more than tripled since the mid-1950s.

Now let's see about Q, the quantity of goods and services produced. During recessions, production—and therefore Q—will fall. For example, during the 1981–1982 recession, Q fell at an annual rate of about 4 percent during the fourth quarter of 1981 and the first quarter of 1982. During recoveries, production picks up, so we go from a declining Q to a rising Q.

Obviously, then, we cannot regard V or Q as constants. Therefore, the crude version of the quantity theory is invalid in this instance.

Today's monetarists, those who believe that changes in M are the key economic variable, have come up with a more sophisticated quantity theory. They assume that any short-term changes in V are either very small or predictable. Q, however, is another story.

Let's say M rises by 10 percent and V stays the same. MV will rise by 10 percent and PQ will rise by 10 percent. So far so good. In fact, so far the crude and sophisticated quantity theories are identical. But what happens next depends entirely on the level of production, Q.

If there's considerable unemployment and we increase M, most, if not all, of this increase will be reflected in an increase in production, Q. Money flowing into the economy will lead to increased spending, output, and employment. Will it lead to higher prices as well? Probably not. Although our recent experience during recessions makes us wary of large surges in the money supply, it is not unreasonable to expect most of the rise in M to be reflected in a rise in Q.

As we approach full employment, however, further increases in M will begin to lead, more and more, to increases in P, the price level (see Figure 10.1).

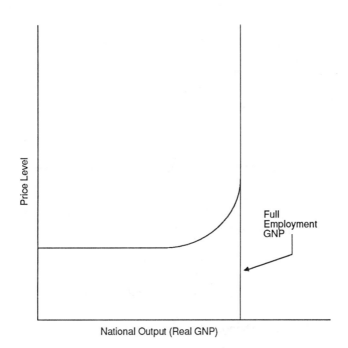

Figure 10.1

And it is there that the sophisticated quantity theory becomes operative. We therefore can summarize the sophisticated quantity theory in two statements:

1. If we are well below full employment, an increase in M will lead mainly to an increase in Q.
2. If we are close to full employment, an increase in M will lead mainly to an increase in P.

That's the sophisticated quantity theory of money. Please don't confuse it with the crude quantity theory of money, and don't confuse either of those theories with the equation of exchange.

Self-Test 1

1. What are the three jobs of money?
2. Which is the most important?
3. The U.S. money supply consists of _____ , _____ and _____ .
4. About three quarters of our money supply consists of _____ .
5. Money performs most poorly as
   A. A medium of exchange.
   B. A standard of value.
   C. A store of value.

6. If M rises and V stays the same
    A. P will definitely rise.
    B. Q will definitely rise.
    C. PQ will definitely rise.
    D. PQ will definitely fall.
7. State the equation of exchange.
8. What is the velocity of circulation?
9. If M is 600 and V is 10, how much is PQ?
10. According the crude quantity theory of money, if M increases by 10 percent, what will happen to V, P, and Q?
11. Over the last thirty-five years or so, what has happened to V?
12. What proof can you offer that Q is not constant over time?
13. Summarize the sophisticated quantity theory in two statements.

Answers to Self-Test 1

1. Medium of exchange, standard of value, store of value.
2. Medium of exchange.
3. Currency, demand deposits, and checklike deposits.
4. Demand deposits.
5. C.
6. C.
7. MV = PQ.
8. The average number of times each dollar in our money supply is spent per year.
9. 6000 ($6 trillion).
10. V and Q will stay the same; P will increase by 10 percent.
11. V has more than tripled.
12. During recessions Q declines; during recoveries and prosperities it rises. Also, over the years, Q rises.
13. (1) If we are well below full employment, an increase in M will lead mainly to an increase in Q. (2) If we are close to full employment, an increase in M will lead mainly to an increase in P.

5 | BANKING

There are some 15,000 commercial banks in the United States. These are defined as banks that hold deposits. Other banks—primarily savings banks—have NOW accounts, which are checklike deposits and which constitute part of our money supply. We can see, then, that the distinction between commercial banks and other savings institutions is becoming somewhat blurred.

The first banks, as we know them, were run by goldsmiths back in the Middle Ages. These fellows invented not only banking but paper money as well.

6 | The Goldsmiths

Back in medieval times many people kept their money in the safes of the goldsmiths, where it would be safe from thieves and fire. When a goldsmith accepted money for safekeeping, he would give the owner a receipt. No one is sure who first used goldsmiths' receipts as paper money, but it might well have happened like this: A knight was having his castle completely redone—new tapestries, new bearskin rugs, new dungeon, new drawbridge, the works! When the job was finally completed, the contractor handed him a bill for 32 gold pieces.

The knight told the contractor, "Wait right here. I'll hitch up the team and take the ox-cart into town, and I'll get 32 gold coins from the goldsmith. I shouldn't be gone more than three days."

"Why bother to go all the way into town for the coins?" asked the contractor. "When you give them to me, I'll have to ride all the way back into town and deposit the coins right back in the goldsmith's safe."

"You mean you're not going to charge me for the job?" The knight, while able to count past ten, came up short in certain areas.

"Of course I want to get paid," replied the contractor, "Just give me your receipt for 32 gold coins."

It took the knight a little while to figure this out, but after the contractor went over it with him another six or eight times, he was finally able to summarize their transaction: "If I give you my receipt, we each save a trip to the goldsmith." And with that, paper money began to circulate.

Now the goldsmiths were not only able to count higher than anyone else in town, but they generally had a little more upstairs as well. And some of them began to figure out that they could really start to mint money, so to speak. First of all, they recognized that when people came in to get back their gold coins, they did not insist on receiving the identical coins they had left. They also noticed that more and more people were paying their debts with receipts. And so, the goldsmiths were struck with this thought: Why not lend out some of these gold coins that are just sitting in our safes?

And at this moment, modern banking was born. As long as the total number of receipts circulating was equal to the number of gold coins in the safe, the banking system did not exist. But when the number of receipts in circulation exceeded the number of coins in the safe, a banking system was created. In other words, as long as a goldsmith had 1000 coins in his safe and receipts for 1000 coins circulating, he wasn't a banker. But what if he decides to lend out 10 of those gold coins? He still has receipts for 1000 coins circulating, but he has only 990 coins in his safe. *Now* he's a banker. The receipts (paper money) issued by the goldsmith are no longer fully backed by gold. But he has nothing to worry about because he knows that all of his depositors will never show up at the same time for their gold. And meanwhile, of course, the goldsmith is collecting interest on the 10 goldpieces he has lent out.

"By why stop there?" asks the goldsmith. "Why not lend out 100 gold coins, or even 500?" And so he does. With 500 coins lent out, he still has 500 in his safe to cover the 1000 receipts in circulation. And what are the chances that half his depositors will suddenly turn up demanding their coins?

Now we have 500 coins backing up 1000 receipts, or a reserve ratio of 50 percent. As long as there are no panics, 50 percent is certainly a very prudent reserve ratio. As their ratio declines (from 100 percent to 50 percent), let's see what happens to the money supply, the gold coins, and the goldsmith's receipts in the hands of the public (see Figure 10.2).

Initially we had 1000 coins in the safe (or bank) and 1000 receipts circulating. The reserve ratio was 100 percent (1000 coins backing 1000 receipts). Now we have 500 coins in the safe and 500 circulating, along with the 1000 receipts in circulation. Our reserve ratio is 50 percent (500 coins backing 1000 receipts). And our money supply? It's grown to 1500—1000 receipts and 500 coins in circulation. Thus, as the reserve ratio declines, the money supply rises.

Let's go a step further and have the goldsmith lend out an additional 250 gold coins. See if you can figure out the reserve ratio and the size of the money supply.

Since there are now 250 coins backing 1000 receipts, the reserve ratio is 25 percent. Meanwhile, the money supply has grown from 1500 to 1750, because in addition to the 1000 receipts, we have 750 coins in the hands of the public.

If the goldsmith continues to lend out gold coins, he will end up with none in his safe. His reserve ratio will sink to zero, and the money supply will be 2000 (1000 receipts and 1000 coins).

The goldsmith, however, has noticed that his receipts circulate as easily as gold coins. And so, he doesn't lend out all his coins, which he really needs as reserves, or backing for his receipts. Instead, he begins to lend money in the form of receipts. For example, suppose you need to borrow 10 gold coins. The goldsmith merely writes up a receipt for 10 gold coins, hands it to you, and you spend it, since it's paper money.

If the goldsmith writes up a receipt for everyone who wants to borrow, he is now *printing money*. For example, with his original 1000 gold coins tucked away in his safe, the goldsmith prints up 2000 receipts. How much would the reserve ratio be and what would be the size of the money supply?

Since there would be 1000 coins backing up 2000 receipts, the reserve ratio is 50 percent. The money supply consists of the 2000 receipts in the hands of the public. Now suppose the goldsmith lends out another 2000 money units in the form of receipts. The reserve ratio would be 25 percent (1000 coins backing 4000 receipts), and the money supply would be the 4000 receipts.

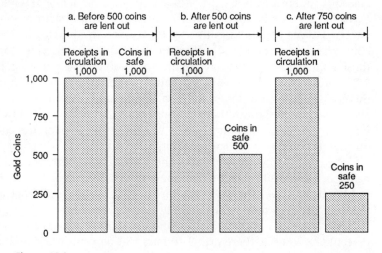

Figure 10.2

The goldsmith could even print up 10,000 receipts, which would bring about a reserve ratio of 10 percent (1000 coins backing 10,000 receipts) and a money supply of 10,000 receipts. Or he could lend out 100,000, bringing the reserve ratio down to 1 percent (1000 coins backing up 100,000 receipts) and a money supply of 100,000 receipts.

The system works only as long as the goldsmiths do not get too greedy and as long as the depositors maintain their confidence in the goldsmith's ability to redeem his receipts in gold coins. When a goldsmith goes too far in lending out money, whether in the form of gold coins or receipts, his depositors begin to notice so many receipts in circulation. They ask themselves if the goldsmith has enough coins in his safe to redeem all those receipts. And when they realize he might not have enough coins, they rush into town to withdraw their gold before it's too late. If too many people do this, a panic will ensue and the goldsmith won't be able to meet the demands of his depositors. In effect, then, he will go bankrupt, and those left holding his receipts will find them worthless. Of course, that was all before the days of the Federal Deposit Insurance Corporation (which we'll get to in frame 8), so there was no one to turn to.

7 | MODERN BANKING

Today's bankers, like the early goldsmiths, don't keep 100 percent reserve backing for their deposits. First of all, if a bank kept all of its deposits in its vault, it would lose money from the day it opened. The whole idea of banking is to borrow cheap and lend dear. The more you lend, the more profits you make.

Banks like to keep about 2 percent of their deposits in the form of vault cash. As long as their depositors maintain confidence in the banks—or at least in the FDIC—there is really no need to keep more than 2 percent on reserve.

Unhappily for the banks, however, they are generally required to keep a lot more than 2 percent of their deposits on reserve. All of the nation's 15,000 commercial banks, as well as the 18,000 credit unions, 3000 savings and loan associations, and 400 savings banks now have to keep up to 12 percent of their checking deposits and up to 3 percent of their savings deposits on reserve (see Table 10.1).

Table 10.1. Legal Reserve Requirements, May 1987*

Checking Accounts:	
$0 to $36.7 million	3%
Over $36.7 million	12%
Time Deposits	
(By original maturity):	
Less than 18 months	3%
18 months or more	0%

*Effective December 29, 1983 this amount was raised from $26.3 million to $28.9 million; on January 1, 1985, to $29.8 million; effective December 31, 1985, to $31.7 million; and effective December 30, 1986, the amount was increased to $36.7 million.

Source: *Federal Reserve Bulletin*, March, 1987, page A7.

Banking today is not all that different from the banking conducted by the goldsmiths back in the Middle Ages. Of course, today's bankers all have the Federal Reserve looking over their shoulders, not to mention the state banking authorities, and the FDIC. Why all this regulation? Basically because people want to know that their money is safe.

8   THE FEDERAL DEPOSIT INSURANCE CORPORATION (FDIC)

After the massive banking failures of the 1930s, Congress set up the FDIC— a classic case of closing the barn door after the horse had made its departure. The FDIC taxes its members 1/12 of 1 percent of its deposits in exchange for insuring all member bank deposits of up to $100,000. (The amount insured has progressively been raised, the last time in 1980, when the ceiling was raised from $40,000.)

The purpose of the FDIC is to avert bank panics by assuring depositors that the federal government stands behind their bank, ready to pay off if the bank should fail. The very fact that the government is ready to do this has apparently provided enough confidence in the banking system to avoid any situation that could lead to widespread panic.

Over 99 percent of all banks are members of the FDIC. If you want to make sure that yours is, see if there's a sign in the window attesting to this fact. If there isn't, ask one of the bank officers. If the answer is no, walk calmly up to a teller and withdraw all your money.

Less familiar than the FDIC is the Federal Savings and Loan Insurance Corporation, which, as its name indicates, insures the shares, or deposits, or savings and loan associations. Nearly all credit union deposits, as well, are insured.

All of this means that your money is safe and that we will probably never have a repetition of the runs on the banks that occurred back in the 1930s.

Self-Test 2

1.   Who were the first bankers?
2.   At what moment was modern banking born?
3.   If a goldsmith kept 100 gold coins in his safe and had receipts for 200 in circulation, what was his reserve ratio and how much was the money supply?
4.   If a goldsmith kept 1000 gold coins in his safe and had receipts for 4000 in circulation, what was his reserve ratio and how much was the money supply?
5.   If the goldsmith had 250 gold coins in his safe, lent out 250 coins, and had 500 receipts in circulation, what was his reserve ratio and how much was the money supply?
6.   About what percent of their deposits do bankers keep as vault cash?
7.   What percentage of their checking deposits must all banks, savings and loan associations, and credit unions keep on reserve?
8.   The FDIC insures bank deposits of up to $ _____ .
9.   The main purpose of the FDIC is to avoid _____ .

Answers to Self-Test 2

1. The goldsmiths.
2. When goldsmiths issued paper receipts for more gold coins than were stored in their safes.
3. 50 percent; 200 coins.
4. 25 percent; 4000 coins.
5. 33 1/3 percent; 750.
6. 2 percent.
7. 12 percent.
8. $100,000
9. Runs on banks, or bank panics.

9 | THE FEDERAL RESERVE SYSTEM

The Organization of the Federal Reserve System

The Federal Reserve District Banks

The nation is divided into twelve Federal Reserve Districts, each with its own bank. Each bank prints currency to meet the business needs of its district. All the currency issued by the Boston Federal Reserve District Bank, in the First District, has an "A" on the face side of the bill about an inch and a half from the left side. Currency issued by the Second Federal District Bank in New York has a "B." That issued by the Philadelphia Bank, in the Third District, has a "C," and so forth.

Each Federal Reserve District Bank is owned by the several hundred member banks in that district. A commercial bank becomes a member by buying stock in the Federal Reserve District Bank. However, effective control is really exercised by the Federal Reserve Board of Governors in Washington.

10 | The Board of Governors

The seven members of the Federal Reserve Board of Governors are nominated by the President of the United States, subject to confirmation by the Senate. Each board member is appointed for one fourteen-year term and is ineligible to serve a second term. Their terms are staggered so that vacancies occur every two years. That way, in every four-year term in office, a president will get to appoint two members to the Board of Governors.

The Chairman of the Board, who generally exercises considerable influence over the board, serves a four-year term. This is part of his fourteen-year term as a member of the board. He is also appointed by the president and may serve more than one four-year term as chairman.

The Fed has come in for its share of criticism and praise over the years. Some of its critics feel that an unelected group of seven should not have sole authority over how fast our money supply grows. Those who support the Federal Reserve Board, however, feel that hard, unpopular monetary policy decisions must be made by people who are insulated from the wrath of the voters. Tight money, for example, is an unpopular policy. The Federal Reserve Board may decide to follow this policy because they think it will help control inflation. Their supporters believe they should be able to make such a decision without fear of angering voters.

Of course, the members of the Board of Governors are not immune to the reactions of the public, but their independence does permit them to follow unpopular policies they feel to be in the best economic interest of the nation. Although attempts have been made to make the Federal Reserve Board more responsive to the wishes of Congress, none has been successful to date.

11 | Legal Reserve Requirements

The Federal Reserve has various jobs, the most important of which is to control our money supply. When the Reserve was set up, in 1913, the framers of the Federal Reserve Act envisaged the Fed as a "lender of last resort." The record of widespread bank failures in the early 1930s is a sad commentary on how well the Fed was able to do that job.

Before we consider how the Fed works today, we will look at the focal point of the Federal Reserve's control of our money supply: legal reserve requirements. The member banks are legally required to hold a certain percentage of their deposits on reserve, either in the form of deposits at the Federal Reserve District Bank or in their own vaults. Federal Reserve deposits and vault cash do not pay interest, and many of the member banks were unhappy about the Fed's relatively high reserve requirements compared to those of the state banking authorities. In fact, many member banks left the Federal Reserve System between 1950 and 1980 because of these high requirements.

The passage of the Monetary Control Act of 1980 (which will be discussed in detail toward the end of this chapter) called for uniform reserve requirements for all financial institutions: commercial banks, savings banks, savings and loan associations, and credit unions. Table 10.1 lists the Fed's legal reserve ratios as of May 1987: Notice that the reserve requirements for time deposits are lower than those for demand deposits. Why? Because time deposits tend to be left in the banks for relatively longer periods of time. Demand (or checking deposits) are payable on demand and must be available for day-to-day transactions of individuals and business firms.

Banks *must* keep the required percentage of their deposits on reserve. There are no ifs, ands, or buts about this. I said earlier that bankers, for the sake of prudence, would want to hold about 2 percent of their deposits on reserve. But the Fed currently requires them to hold 12 percent of their demand deposits on reserve. It stands to reason that bankers are unhappy about being required to hold so much in reserve. Let's see why this requirement displeases them.

The banker, like everyone else, is in business to make a profit. How big a profit? As big as possible. How does the banker do this? By borrowing money from depositors at relatively low interest rates and lending it out to businesses and individuals at relatively high interest rates.

What does all of this have to do with reserves? Just one thing: The more the banker has to hold in reserve, the less she or he has available to lend out. Keep in mind that reserves held in the form of vault cash pay no interest. Similarly, if the reserves are held at the Federal Reserve District Bank, they don't draw any interest.

It would be fair to assume, then, that bankers strive to keep excess reserves as low as possible, so their actual reserves invariably equal the required reserves. If actual reserves minus required reserves equals excess reserves, then excess reserves will be pretty close to zero. And ideally, these excess reserves *will* be zero.

Suppose the Fed required that banks hold 10 percent of their checking deposits on reserve. Now suppose that Bank of America has $70 billion in checking deposits. How much reserves would Bank of America actually hold?

12   It would hold $7 billion in reserve. Remember that it would hold only what it *had* to.

Now we'll try another bank. Assuming a 10 percent reserve requirement, how much would Chase Manhattan hold if it had deposits of $55 billion. And how much would its excess reserves be?

13   It would hold $5.5 billion in reserve, and its excess reserves would be zero. In other words, it would hold exactly what it was legally required to hold.

14   ## MONETARY POLICY

The Goals of Monetary Policy

Monetary policy—-and, for that matter, fiscal policy as well—has two basic goals: (1) to avoid inflation and (2) to avoid high unemployment. Stated positively, monetary policy seeks to attain (1) price stability and (2) high employment. In pursuit of these two goals, the Fed regulates the rate of growth of the nation's money supply. Much of its effort centers on the reserves held by banks. The most important tool used by the Fed to control bank reserves—and, indirectly, the money supply—is open market operations.

15   ### Open Market Operations

Open market operations are the buying and selling of U.S. government securities in the open market. What are U.S. government securities? They are Treasury bills, notes, certificates and bonds. The Fed does not market new securities. That's the Treasury's job. Rather, the Fed buys and sells securities that have already been marketed by the Treasury, some of which might be several years old. The Fed is legally limited to buying no more than $5 billion in newly issued government securities a year, which is less than 1 percent of what the Treasury issues.

Open market operations, then, consists of the buying and selling of chunks of the national debt. The Fed does this by dealing with government bond houses, which are private bond dealers. If the Fed wants to buy, say, $100 million worth of Treasury notes that will mature within the next three months, it places an order with a few of these bond houses. The bond houses then buy up the securities for the Fed. When the Fed wants to sell securities, it asks the government bond houses to do the actual selling.

When the Fed wants to increase the money supply, it buys U.S. government securities on the open market. You might ask, "What if people don't want to sell?" Remember the line from *The Godfather*: "Make him an offer he cannot refuse"? Well, that's exactly what the Fed does. It tells the government bond houses, "Buy us thirty thousand Treasury bills, no matter what the price."

If the Fed goes on a buying spree in the open market, it will quickly drive up the prices of U.S. government securities. All this buying will also push down interest rates. Let's see why.

Suppose a bond was issued by the Treasury with a face value of $1000 and an interest rate of 8 percent. That means the bond costs the initial buyer $1000 and pays $80 a year interest. The price of the bond will fluctuate considerably over its life, but when it matures, the Treasury will have to pay the owner $1000, its face value, and during every year of the bond's life, the Treasury must pay the owner $80 interest.

Using the formula:

$$\text{Interest rate} = \frac{\text{Interest paid}}{\text{Price of bond}}$$

we can observe that a $1000 bond paying $80 interest pays an interest rate of 8 percent:

$$\frac{\$80}{\$1000} = 8\%$$

Suppose the Fed bought enough government securities in the open market to bid up their price to $1200. Remember that these securities still pay $80 a year interest. Let's calculate their new interest rate:

$$\text{Interest rate} = \frac{\text{Interest paid}}{\text{Price of bond}} = \frac{\$80}{\$1200} = 6\frac{2}{3}\%$$

As we had predicted, when the Fed goes into the open market to buy securities, it bids up the price of securities and lowers their interest rates. This process, as we shall soon see, also expands the money supply.

When the Fed wants to contract the money supply, or at least slow down its rate of expansion, it *sells* securities in the open market. In this process, it lowers bond prices and raises interest rates.

When selling securities, the Fed again utilizes the "Godfather principle": It makes an offer that can't be refused. In this case, it offers to sell securities at prices low enough to ensure the sale of a certain amount.

If the Fed bids bond prices down to $800, we use the same formula to find that the interest rate has risen to 10 percent:

$$\text{Interest rate} = \frac{\text{Interest paid}}{\text{Price of bond}} = \frac{\$80}{\$800} = \frac{1}{10} = 10\%$$

When the Fed sell securities on the open market to reduce the money supply, bond prices fall and interest rates rise. Falling bond prices and rising interest rates generally accompany a tightening of the money supply.

We should add that although the Fed deals only with U.S. government securities, interest rates and bond prices are broadly affected in the same way as are the government securities. Therefore, when the Fed depresses the price of U.S. government securities, all government and corporate bond prices tend to fall. And when the Fed pushes up the interest on U.S. government securities, all interest rates tend to rise.

Remember that we are talking about just those U.S. government securities that have already been issued and are circulating. The Fed occasionally does buy some securities directly from the Treasury to help the government with its cash flow just before tax payments are due, but it is legally barred from holding more than $5 billion in securities purchased directly from the Treasury (which amounts to a mere drop in the bucket).

Are you ready for a couple of interest rate problems? What would be the interest rate on a bond that pays $100 a year in interest and is currently selling for $800?

16

$$\text{Interest rate} = \frac{\text{Interest paid}}{\text{Price of bond}} = \frac{\$100}{\$800} = 12.5\%$$

What would be the interest rate on a bond that pays $120 in interest and is currently selling for $1440?

17

$$\text{Interest rate} = \frac{\text{Interest paid}}{\text{Price of bond}} = \frac{\$120}{\$1440} = 8.3\%$$

If you've gotten the hang of it, go on to frame 20; otherwise, go to frame 18.

18   What will be the interest rate on a bond that pays $90 in interest and is currently selling for $1200?

19

$$\text{Interest rate} = \frac{\text{Interest paid}}{\text{Price of bond}} = \frac{\$90}{\$1200} = 7.5\%$$

20   Open market operations are conducted by the Federal Open Market Committee (FOMC), which consists of twelve people. Eight are permanent members: the seven members of the Board of Governors and the President of the New York Federal Reserve District Bank, who is a permanent member because nearly all open market purchases are made in the New York Federal securities market. The other four members of the FOMC are the presidents of some of the other eleven Federal Reserve District Banks, who serve on a rotating basis.

The FOMC meets about once every three weeks to decide what policy to follow. This is not to say that every three weeks the committee changes directions from buy to sell to buy again.

Assume the FOMC decides to ease credit a bit, perhaps because of the threat of a recession. The committee might decide to buy $100 million of securities in the open market. The New York bank, as the agent of the Federal Reserve, places orders with several government bond houses. These bond houses buy the securities and then resell them to the New York Federal Reserve Bank.

The end result of this operation is an increase in the money supply. The New York Fed buys $100 million in U.S. government securities and pays the government bond houses with checks totaling $100 million. The bond houses deposit these checks in the commercial banks at which they have deposits. What do the commercial banks do with these checks? They send them to the New York Federal Reserve District Bank. And the New York Fed credits the reserves of these commercial banks for a total of $100 million.

Let's go over this transaction. The Fed buys $100 million of U.S. government securities. They pay for them by check. The checks are deposited in various commercial banks, which send them to the New York Fed. And the bottom line is that the reserves of these commercial banks are increased by $100 million.

Assuming that these banks were not carrying any excess reserves—because banks hate to carry any more reserves than they are legally required to carry—they now have a total of $100 million excess reserves. So what do they do with this money? They lend it out, and by doing so, they increase our money supply.

You see, when money is sitting in a bank, it's not part of our money supply. It's just bank inventory. Remember that our money supply consists basically of currency and checking deposits in the hands of the public. The banks lend out this reserve money either by giving currency to borrowers or by putting money in the borrowers' checking deposits. Generally, of course, borrowers prefer to have the money transferred to their checking deposits, because it would not be wise to walk out of a bank with $10 million in cash. Especially in tens and twenties.

So when the Federal Reserve wants to increase the money supply, it goes into the open market and buys U.S. government securities. Now guess what it does when it wants to decrease the money supply? You got it; it *sells* securities.

Now let's say that the Fed wants to increase the money supply by selling $100 million of securities. By how much will this move increase the money supply? By $100 million? No! By a lot more than that. How much more? Let's find out.

Remember our discussion of the multiplier back in frame 37 of Chapter 7? When someone spends a dollar, it ends up in someone else's pocket. And that person spends part of that dollar. How much the person spends depends on his or her marginal propensity to consume. Now if you're really sharp, you'll even remember the formula for the multiplier: $1/1-MPC$.

This formula also applies to bank lending. Suppose that a bank receives $100 million in excess reserves. How much will that bank lend out? The whole $100 million? No. Keep in mind that banks strive to hold exactly zero in excess reserves, but if a bank lends out $100 million by providing some corporation with a $100 demand deposit, it still has to hold a certain percentage of reserves against that deposit. How much? The legal reserve requirement would be around 12 percent, but let's assume a reserve requirement of just 10 percent, since that's a much easier number to work with.

So suppose the Bank of America receives $100 million excess reserves. It there's a 10 percent reserve requirement, how much will it lend out? I'm sure that you said 90 million, which is correct. Now what do you suppose will happen to that $90 million loan? Obviously, the company that borrowed it will spend it. Suppose it spends the whole $90 million for inventory and writes a check to its supplier for $90 million. The supplier deposits the check in its bank, Mellon National, and that bank's excess reserves go up by $90 million. How much does Mellon National lend out? It will lend out $81 million (90 percent of $90 million)—in other words, it will hold a reserve of 10 percent ($9 million) on a $90 million dollar loan.

If we continue this process, we'll have successive loans of $72,900,000, $65,610,000, $59,049,000, $53,144,100, and so on ad infinitum. If we continue this process for the next few weeks and then add up all these loans, can you guess what their grand total would come to? It would be $1 billion.

Luckily for us, there is a faster and easier way to figure out how much our money supply would be increased if the Federal Reserve decided to buy $100 million of securities. It's called the monetary multiplier. Its formula is 1/required reserve ratio. Using this formula, figure out how much the monetary multiplier is for the problem we've been doing, assuming a reserve ratio of 10 percent.

21

$$\text{Monetary multiplier} = \frac{1}{\text{Reserve ratio}} = \frac{1}{.10} = 10$$

So when the Fed increases excess reserves by buying $100 million on the open market, the money supply could increase by 10 times that amount, or $1 billion.

22   Now suppose that the Fed buys $200 million of securities, assuming that the reserve ratio is 12 percent, by how much could our money supply increase?

23   Excess reserves × monetary multiplier = potential expansion of the money supply. $200 million × 1/.12 = $200 million × 8.3* = $1,660,000,000. *(We rounded after one decimal and got 8.3. If you rounded after four decimals, you would have gotten 8.3333, which would have given you a deposit expansion of $1,666,660,000.)

There is, of course, no guarantee that the banks will lend out all, or even most, of their excess reserves. We will discuss this further in frame 28.

By selling securities on the open market, the Fed could force a contraction of the money supply. Assuming that banks carry virtually no excess reserves, we could ask these same questions in reverse: By how much could the Fed force a contraction of the money supply by selling securities on the open market?

If you need further practice with the monetary multiplier, go to frame 24; otherwise, go to frame 26.

24   By how much could our money supply increase if the Fed buys $150 million of securities and the reserve ratio is 12.5 percent?

25 $150 million × 1/.125 = $150 million × 8 = $1.2 billion.

26   ## DISCOUNT RATE CHANGES

The discount rate is the interest rate paid by member banks when they borrow at the Federal Reserve District Bank (the Fed). Banks borrow primarily because they are having trouble maintaining their required reserves. However, by frequently resorting to borrowing from the Fed, the member banks are calling attention to their difficulties, perhaps inviting closer audits when they are visited by their Federal Reserve inspectors. Also, there is always the chance of being turned down for these loans.

The original intent of the Federal Reserve Act of 1913 was to have the district banks lend money to the member banks to take care of seasonal business needs. In the busy period before Christmas, for example, firms would borrow money from their banks, which would, in turn, borrow from the Federal Reserve District Banks. Borrowing, then, was really *note discounting*. In note discounting, someone might borrow $1000, but the bank would deduct the interest—$80 for a one-year loan at 8 percent—in advance. The borrower, then, would get only $920 but would have to pay $1000. The commercial banks could take these IOUs, or commercial paper, to the Federal Reserve District Bank and borrow money to cover these loans. This was called *rediscounting*.

Banks no longer rediscount their commercial paper. Instead, they borrow directly from the Federal Reserve, and the interest they pay is known as the *discount rate*. Each district bank sets its own discount rate, but they agree on the same rate virtually all of the time, perhaps with an occasional prod from the Board of Governors.

Day-to-day open market operations are the most important policy weapon of the Fed. If the Fed sells securities in the open market and still fails to get the commercial banks to cut back enough on their loans, the Fed can raise the discount rate.

27 | CHANGING RESERVE REQUIREMENTS

The nuclear bomb is the ultimate weapon, but it is almost never used. The Fed also has an ultimate weapon that it seldom uses: *changing reserve requirements*. In 1980 the reserve requirement for checking deposits were set by law for 1987 at 12 percent. The Fed has the power to change this rate, but it does so only as a last resort.

Like the nuclear bomb, this powerful weapon is rarely used because it is *too* powerful. For example, if the Federal Reserve Board were to raise the reserve requirement on demand deposits by just one-half of 1 percent, the nation's bank and thrift institutions would have to come up with over $5 billion in reserves.

Prior to 1980 the Federal Reserve Board changed the reserve requirements, on the average, about once every fifteen months. When they wanted to slow the rate of growth of the money supply, they would raise the requirements, and when they wanted to raise the rate of monetary growth, they would lower the requirements.

But all that is history. Don't look for many future changes in reserve requirements unless there's a major recession (when reserve requirements might be lowered) or a high rate of inflation (when reserve requirements would be raised).

28 | MONETARY POLICY: FIGHTING INFLATIONS AND RECESSIONS

The monetary policy of the Federal Reserve, in a nutshell, is to raise the rate of growth of the money supply when a recession is in the offing and to lower it when the economy is threatened by inflation.

Federal Reserve policy in fighting inflation has been likened to pulling on a string. When the Fed fights inflation, it gets results—provided, of course, it pulls the string hard enough. But fighting a recession would require *pushing* on that string, and of course no matter how hard the Fed pushes, it often gets no results.

First we'll consider fighting inflation. Assume the Fed has used all three basic policy tools: It has sold securities on the open market, it has raised the discount rate, and, as a last resort, it has even raised reserve requirements. The results: Bond prices have plunged, interest rates have soared, and money supply growth has been stopped in its tracks. Banks find it impossible to increase their loan portfolios. There's a credit crunch, and there's credit rationing. Old customers can still borrow, but their credit lines are slashed. My own line of credit, for example, was cut by Citibank during the 1980 crunch from $3500 to $500. New customers are nearly all turned away.

During times like these, the rate of inflation has got to decline. It's hard to raise prices: People aren't buying anything because they don't have any money. Of course, the Fed is reluctant to tighten up very much or very long because such a policy generally brings on recessions.

But the Fed has an even harder time dealing with a recession. Again, assume that the Fed has used the standard tools: It has purchased securities on the open market, it has lowered the discount rate, and it has even lowered the reserve requirements. All of this has created excess reserves for the banks. But now the $64 question: What do the banks *do* with these reserves?

Lend them out? To whom? To a business that needs a loan to keep going? To a firm that can't meet its next payroll without a loan? To individuals who have lost their jobs and can't meet their car payments? Banks simply can't afford to take the risk of lending money to these people. A banker's first question has got to be "Will we get paid back?" Bankers, in other words, have to keep in mind the first law of banking: Never lend out money to anyone who needs it. (If you want a bank loan, you've got to convince the loan officer that you don't really need the money.) Businesses that might be good credit risks during prosperity often become poor risks during recessions. Individuals as well lose credit worthiness during recessions, particularly if they've just been laid off. And so the very segment of the economic community most in need of help during recessions is least likely to be accommodated.

Meanwhile, even many of the top credit-rated corporations are not coming in to borrow very much money. During recessions, those companies to which the banks *would* lend money do not borrow. Why? Because business isn't so great for them either. Would you borrow to buy more equipment—even at low interest rates—if one-third of your equipment was idle? Would you expand your factory if sales were down by 20 percent? Even if the interest rate fell to 4 percent?

At the very time, then, when the Fed is expanding bank reserves, loan demand is falling. And the people who really want to borrow can't get any money. All of this means that the Fed can lead a bank to more reserves, but it can't force the bank to lend those reserves out.

29 THE DEPOSITORY INSTITUTION'S DEREGULATION AND MONETARY CONTROL ACT OF 1980

The 1970s and 1980s were decades of swift and significant change in American banking. During this period the distinction between commercial banks and thrift institutions—savings banks, savings and loan associations, and credit unions— blurred to the point where it became hard to tell which institutions were banks and which were not banks.

Until 1980 the line of demarcation was very clear. Commercial banks could issue checking deposits. Savings banks, savings and loan associations, and credit unions could not. The only problem was that more and more of them were doing just that. The thrift institutions got around the law by calling their checking deposits Negotiable Order of Withdrawal Accounts (NOW accounts). And so, technically, people who had deposits at these thrift institutions were not writing checks; they were writing negotiable orders of withdrawal.

Federal Reserve regulation prohibited commercial banks from paying interest on checking deposits, but the thrift institutions were paying their depositors about 5 percent interest on their NOW accounts. Since these were technically savings accounts rather than checking accounts, and they were able to pay interest on them, which gave them a considerable competitive advantage over commercial banks.

The commercial banks complained to the Fed and to anyone else who would listen, but to little avail. Finally, Congress took matters into its own hands and passed the Depository Institutions Deregulation and Monetary Control Act of 1980. This act had three key provisions:

1. All depository institutions were now subject to the Fed's legal reserve requirements. Thrifts and commercial banks that were not members of the Federal Reserve—about one-third of all commercial banks were members— were also now subject to these requirements. The other commercial banks and thrift institutions were subject to state reserve requirements, which were substantially lower.

2. All depository institutions were now legally authorized to issue checking deposits, and these deposits could be interest bearing. Until then, commercial banks had been forbidden to pay interest on checking accounts, while the thrift institutions claimed to be paying interest on savings accounts.

3. All depository institutions could now enjoy all the advantages that only Federal Reserve member banks formerly enjoyed, including check clearing and discounting, or borrowing from the Fed. (Check clearing is the mysterious process by which all the checks you wrote last month are mailed to you by your bank at the end of the month. The Federal Reserve system processes, or clears, billion of checks a year.)

Self-Test 3

1. How many Federal Reserve District Banks are there, and how many members serve on the Federal Reserve Board of Governors?

2. Monetary policy is made by which group within the Federal Reserve?

3. Currently the legal reserve requirement on checking deposits is _____ percent.

4. The most important job of the Federal Reserve is to _____ .

5. Are reserve requirements higher for time deposits or for demand deposits? Why?

6. What are the two goals of monetary policy?

7. What are open market operations?

8. The interest rate is obtained by dividing the _____ by the

   _____ .

9. What is the interest rate on a bond that pays $120 a year in interest and is currently selling for $960?

10. What committee conducts open market operations and who is on this committee?

11. When the Fed wants to expand money supply what does the Federal Open Market Committee do?

12. When the Fed wants to contract the money supply, what does the Federal Open Market Committee do?

13. The interest rate charged by the Federal Reserve District Banks to banks that borrow funds from them is called the _____ .

14. Which Federal Reserve monetary policy weapon is used least often? Why?

15. Is monetary policy more effective in fighting inflation or recessions? Why?

16. Why was the Depository Institutions Deregulation and Monetary Control Act passed and how did it improve the banking environment?

17. By how much could our money supply increase if the Fed buys $300 million of securities and the reserve ratio is 14 percent?

Answers to Self-Test 3

1. Twelve banks; seven board members.

2. The Board of Governors or, alternatively, the Federal Open Market Committee.

3. 12 percent.

4. Regulate the rate of growth of the money supply.

5. Reserve requirements are higher for demand deposits, because these deposits are more volatile than time deposits—that is, they are more likely to be withdrawn in the short term.

6. High employment and stable prices.

7. The buying and selling of U.S. government securities on the open market.

8. Interest paid by the price of the bond.

9. 12.5 percent.

10. The Federal Open Market Committee, which is comprised of the Federal Board of Governors, the President of the New York Federal Reserve District Bank, and the presidents of four other district banks, who serve on a rotating basis.

11. It buys U.S. government securities on the open market.

12. It sells U.S. government securities on the open market.

13. Discount rate.

14. Changing reserve requirements. This weapon is so powerful that if requirements were raised, banks would have a hard time coming up with necessary funds.

15. It is more effective fighting inflation. An inflation is fueled by monetary growth. If we cut off the increase in the money supply, the inflation can be brought under control. It is hard to increase the money supply during recessions if businesses and individuals don't want to borrow.

16. Nonbanking institutions were issuing checking accounts on which they paid interest. At the same time, these institutions were subject to relatively low reserve requirements. The 1980 law made it legal for the thrift institutions to issue checking accounts but made them subject to the same reserve requirements as the banks that were members of the Federal Reserve.

17. $300 million $\times$ 7.14 = $2,142,000,000.

CHAPTER 11

Twentieth Century

Economic

Theory

Economists are not easy to follow when they talk about familiar, day-to-day events like unemployment rate changes and the Consumer Price Index. But when they talk theory, even their fellow economists have difficulty understanding what they are saying. In fact, there is a theory that if all the economists in the world were laid out end to end, they still would not reach a conclusion.

In this chapter I will outline some of the underlying ideas of each of the five main schools of economics of this century. What conclusion will you reach at the end of this chapter? Some economics students choose to defend one school of economic thought while attacking all the others. But I hope that you will consider each theory carefully, ferreting out what you can't accept and appreciating the cogency of the arguments that have been advanced.

After you've read this chapter you will have a better understanding of the basics of:

- Classical economics.
- Keynesian economics.
- The monetarist school.
- Supply-side economics.
- Rational expectations theory.

1 | CLASSICAL ECONOMICS

The classical school of economics dominated mainstream economics from roughly 1775 to 1930. Adam Smith's *The Wealth of Nations*, which was a plea for laissez-faire (no government interference), was the bible of economics through most of this period. The classical economists believed that our economy was self-regulating: Recessions would cure themselves, and a built-in mechanism would always push the economy toward full employment.

Over the course of American history, we have been plagued by the twin problems of recession and inflation. The classical economists introduced the quantity theory of money, which said that if the money supply grew at a certain rate, the price level would rise at the same rate. In other words, if the money supply grew by 10 percent, prices would rise by 10 percent. If the money supply doubled, prices would double. Despite its apparent simplicity, however, this theory led to great economic debates, which we will discuss in the next two sections.

For now, though, let's examine the belief that our economy could regulate itself without government interference. To back up this belief, classical economists pointed out that very bad recessions, and even depressions, had occurred in the 1830s, 1870s, and 1890s, but we always recovered eventually. If the government *did* try to get us out of a recession, said the classical economists, it would only make things worse.

Their reasoning was based largely on Say's Law. Jean Baptiste Say, a French economist back in the late eighteenth century, had formulated this law, which was simplicity itself: Supply creates its own demand.

Why do people work? asked Say. *To make money.* And what do they do with that money? *They spend it.* Voila! Everything you earn, you spend. Therefore, everything you produce, you sell. In other words, supply creates its own demand.

So far so good. But what if we don't spend our entire income? What if we save some of our earnings? No problem, said the classicals, as long as business firms borrow the money we save and invest it in new plant and equipment.

Suppose, for example, that we produced $5 trillion worth of output. For this we received $5 trillion in income. If we spent $4 trillion, we would have saved $1 trillion. Suppose we put that $1 trillion in the bank, and the bank lent that money to business firms to invest in new plant and equipment. Say's Law would hold up: All of our income would be spent, and all of our production would be purchased.

Still, some critics were not entirely convinced. They asked the classical economists a hard question: Why are you so confident that business firms will invest exactly the same amount that people save? The classicals had an answer ready. They pointed to the old supply-and-demand graph in Figure 11.1. This time, supply is the supply of savings, and demand is the demand for investment funds.

Let's examine these curves. The supply of savings curve goes upward to the right, indicating that at higher interest rates people will put more money in the bank. Is this a reasonable assumption? How much money would you put into the bank each week at 2 percent interest? At 20 percent? At 100 percent?

Now look at the demand curve. As you'll notice, it goes downward to the right. At lower interest rates, business firms borrow more for investment purposes. Why? Because at very high interest rates, very few investment projects are worthwhile. Suppose you were starting a business and your friendly bank loan officer said you would have to pay 80 percent interest. You might do better dealing with a loan shark.

As the interest rate declines, however, more and more investment projects become profitable. If the interest rate fell to 2 or 3 percent, there would be a tremendous demand for funds by business firms.

The rate of interest at any given time is determined by the intersection of the supply and demand curves. In Figure 11.1, the interest rate happens to be 10 percent. Now, if the interest rate were temporarily at 12 percent, there would be a surplus of savings relative to the demand for funds, but the interest rate would automatically fall to 10 percent because some savers (or lenders) would

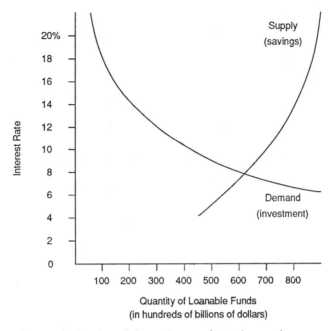

Quantity of Loanable Funds
(in hundreds of billions of dollars)

Figure 11.1 Supply and demand curves for savings and
investment

be willing to accept lower interest and would make deals with some borrowers at 11 percent and eventually 10 percent interest.

What all this means, the classical economists claimed, was that Say's Law held, even if people saved part of their income. Supply would still create its own demand, even though part of that demand would be for new plant and equipment. Everything that was produced would still be sold.

The classicals even had a fallback position—wage and price downward flexibility. Workers who lost their jobs and remained unemployed for a few months would soon be willing to settle for somewhat lower wages. Employers who couldn't afford to pay higher salaries would snap up those workers who were willing to accept lower pay.

Similarly, retail stores, wholesalers, and manufacturers, having gotten stuck with unwanted inventories, would be willing to sell them off at reduced prices. And so, everything that got produced would get sold. Which, of course, once again verifies Say's Law.

Since the classical economists had been able to demonstrate that the economy automatically cured its own recessions and always tended toward full employment, they believed that the government should not interfere with the workings of this magnificent economic machine. They were saying, in short: If it ain't broke, don't fix it.

Self-Test 1

1. State and explain Say's Law.

2. According to the classical economists, what should the government do to end a recession?

3. The classical economists, applying Say's Law, believed that all our income would be _____ , all our production would be _____ , and all our savings would be _____ .

4. According to the classicals, if the amount of money people wanted to save was greater than the amount of money business firms wanted to borrow for investment purposes, what would happen to set them equal to each other?

5. What was the classical fallback position if a change in the interest rate did not bring us out of a recession?

6. If the money supply were to grow by 25 percent, what does the quantity theory of money predict will happen to the price level?

Answers to Self-Test 1

1. Supply creates its own demand. People work only for money, which they will spend, thus buying up everything that they have produced.

2. Nothing.

3. Spent; purchased; invested.

4. The interest rate would fall.

5. Wage and price downward flexibility.

6. It will rise by 25 percent.

2 | KEYNESIAN ECONOMICS

The Great Depression marked the end of the dominance of classical economics. Herbert Hoover—perhaps the last political leader to support the theories of classical economics—kept insisting that recovery was just around the corner. But despite his show of confidence, the unemployment rate continued to rise, production plummeted, and soup kitchens proliferated. More and more Americans began to demand that the federal government do something to end the depression. In 1932 they elected Franklin Roosevelt by a landslide after he promised that the government would do whatever was necessary to bring about recovery.

It was during this period that John Maynard Keynes wrote his landmark work, *The General Theory of Employment, Interest, and Money*. In his book, Keynes provided a blueprint for recovery. The problem, he said, was inadequate aggregate demand. People were just not buying enough goods and services to employ the entire labor force. In fact, aggregate demand was so low that only the government could spend enough money to provide a sufficient boost.

What type of spending was necessary? Any kind, said Keynes. Quantity was much more important than quality. Even if the government paid some people to dig holes and others to fill them up, Keynes said, it would help us spend our way out of the Depression.

But where would the government get the money to hire people? There were two choices: print it or borrow it. If we printed it, wouldn't that cause inflation? Keynes thought this unlikely; in fact, during the Great Depression we had been experiencing *de*flation, or falling prices. Sellers wouldn't raise prices when they had trouble finding customers.

If we borrowed the money, would that cause budget deficits? Nothing improper about deficits during recessions and depressions, said Keynes. We needed to prime the pump by sucking up the idle savings that businesses were not borrowing and using those funds to get the economy moving again.

Once government spending got under way, people would finally have some money in their pockets. And what would they do with that money? You guessed it—they'd spend it. This money would then end up in other people's pockets, and they, in turn, would spend it once again.

That money would continue to be respent again and again, putting more and more people back to work. And as that happened, the deficit would melt away. The government could but back on its spending programs while tax receipts swelled. So we could view the budget deficits as a temporary means to get the economy on the move.

But what about the automatic mechanism that the classical economists had talked about, the mechanism that ensured that the economy would always move toward full employment? In the long run, Keynes conceded, maybe it really *did* work. But in the long run, noted Keynes, "We'll all be dead."

Why didn't the classical mechanism work in the short run? Keynes observed that interest rates fell to about 2 percent during the Depression, but business firms still did not borrow much to build new plant and equipment. They wouldn't invest in new plant and equipment when factories were operating at only 30 or 40 percent of capacity. Besides, said Keynes, at an interest rate of 2 percent, many people would not be willing to lend out their savings. Why tie them up at such a low interest rate? Why not just sit on the money until interest rates rose again? So much for the interest rate mechanism.

Well, then, what about downwardly flexible wages and prices? The problem with those was the existence of institutional barriers: Labor unions opposed lower wage rates, while highly concentrated industries preferred output decreases to price cuts during recessions.

Keynes also raised some objections to the quantity theory of money. Most significantly, he asked what would happen to the money that would be printed or borrowed if the government *did* decide to increase the money supply. The classicals had assumed that the money would be spent, thus pushing up prices. This *could* happen, conceded Keynes. But during a bad recession, maybe people would just hold their money and wait for interest rates to rise before they lent it out.

Poor people would spend, of course, but where would poor people get money in the first place? If the money supply were increased during a bad recession, said Keynes, that extra money would simply be held as idle cash balances by relatively well-to-do people, who would not invest that money until interest rates rose and more investment opportunities became available.

By the mid-1930s, the classical school of economics had lost most of its adherents, but not everyone became a Keynesian. Conservative economists, in particular, could never fully reconcile themselves to the vastly increased economic role that the Keynesians awarded to the federal government. In fact, the monetarists, the supply-siders, and the rational expectationists all railed against the evils of big government.

But big government was here to stay. Although the massive spending programs of Franklin Roosevelt's New Deal did not get us all the way out of the Great Depression, the much bigger defense spending during World War II certainly did. There was no question that Keynes had been right. After the war, however, we were plagued not only by periodic recessions but also by almost unending inflation. There was a growing feeling that perhaps Keynesian economics was just recession and depression economics and could not curb inflation.

Keynesian economics did enjoy a brief renewal of success in 1964, however, when personal income tax rates were cut by about 20 percent. This tax cut, combined with increased military spending during the Vietnam War, brought about a rapid rate of economic growth in the middle to late 1960s. This growth was accompanied by increasing inflation that reached double-digit proportions in the early 1970s. By the time Richard Nixon proclaimed himself a Keynesian, the influence of this school of economics had already begun to decline. By the 1970s, Keynesianism was "out" and monetarism was "in."

Self-Test 2

1. John Maynard Keynes said that during recessions and depressions the main problem was _____ .
2. To solve that problem, Keynes suggested _____ .
3. In what two ways could the government raise money to fight recessions?
4. If we could put money in peoples' pockets during the Depression, reasoned Keynes, what would they do with the money and how would that help end the Depression?
5. Why don't business firms borrow during a depression when the interest rate is low?
6. What were the main institutional barriers to downward wage and price flexibility?
7. When did the classical school of economics lose most of its adherents?
8. To what principle of Keynesian economics did conservative economists object most strongly?
9. What was the main success of Keynesian economics in the 1960s?
10. What objection did Keynes raise to the quantity theory of money?

Answers to Self-Test 2

1. Insufficient aggregate demand.
2. Increased government spending.
3. Print money and borrow money.
4. They would spend it. More goods and services would be purchased, inventories would be depleted, and employers would hire back their workers.
5. There are very few favorable investment opportunities.
6. Labor unions and concentrated industries.
7. During the mid-1930s, or during the Great Depression.
8. The large economic role of the federal government.
9. The tax cut of 1964.
10. People might hold on to additional funds instead of spending them, and therefore the price level might not rise.

3 | THE MONETARIST SCHOOL

The monetarist school of thought begins and ends with one obsession: the rate of growth of the money supply. Monetarists believe that most of our major economic problems—especially inflations and recessions—are due to the Federal Reserve's mismanagement of our rate of monetary growth. When the money supply grows too quickly, we have inflation; when it grows too slowly, we have recessions.

Milton Friedman, who has long been the leading exponent of monetarism, did exhaustive studies of the relationship between the rate of growth of the money supply and the rate of increase in prices. He reached a couple of conclusions that will startle no one: (1) we have never had a serious inflation that was not accompanied by rapid monetary growth and (2) when our money supply has grown slowly, we have had no inflation.

Building on the quantity theory of money, the monetarists agreed with the classicals that if the money supply grows, the price level will rise, albeit not at exactly the same rate. But the monetarists rejected Keynes's argument that if the money supply is increased during a recession, people might hold on to these added funds. Like the classicals, the monetarists assumed that to get it is to spend it, not necessarily on consumer goods, but on stocks, bonds, real estate, and other noncash assets. If people *do* spend this additional money, prices will be bid up. In other words, the monetarists were saying, the quantity theory does basically hold true.

So far so good. Now, how about recessions? What causes them? According to the monetarists, when the Federal Reserve increases the money supply at less than the rate needed by business—say, anything less than 3 percent a year—we're headed for trouble. Sometimes, in fact, the Fed does not let it grow at all and may even cause it to shrink slightly.

By and large, the monetarists' analysis has been borne out by the course of events. Without a steady increase in the money supply of at least 3 percent a year, a recession is highly likely to occur.

According to the monetarists, the Fed is like a student driver approaching a red light. First, he slams on the brakes and comes to a screeching halt 200 yards from the light. Next, he hits the gas. Then he slams on the brakes again. In fits and starts he makes his way to the light. Similarly, the Federal Reserve allows the money supply to grow much too quickly. Then, alarmed by the growing rate of inflation, the Fed slams on the monetary brakes. Soon an economic slowdown commences. So what does the Fed do next? It hits the monetary accelerator, and the economy picks up speed until the Fed must deal with the ensuing inflation.

The monetarists also reject Keynensian fiscal policy. When there's a recession, the Keynesians tell us to run a large budget deficit. Fine, say the monetarists, but where does the government get the money to finance the deficit? Print it? That's inflationary. Borrow it? That takes needed investment funds out of the private sector and crowds private borrowers out of the financial markets. This they called the "crowding out effect." Of course the Keynesians had an answer to this. Which private borrowers would be crowded out of the financial markets during a bad recession? they asked. They pointed out that the main problem during a recession is that business firms do *not* borrow because they're doing very little investing. The government is not crowding them out, said the

Keynesians; it's merely substituting for them in their absence. They called this the "crowding in effect."

This raises the two questions that the monetarists and the Keynesians have been batting around since the early 1960s: (1) during a recession, should the government run budget deficits or not? and (2) which is more effective—fiscal policy or monetary policy? Since these questions have never really been answered, we'll pass on them, at least for now.

So what *do* we do? The monetarists have a policy prescription, called "the monetary rule," that calls for having the Fed increase the money supply by 3 to 4 percent a year. No more, no less.

But what if there's a recession? Should the Fed increase the money supply at, say, 10 percent a year? No, answer the monetarists. This would only cause inflation further down the road. Besides, the Fed does not have the expertise to fine tune the rate of monetary growth, accelerating it during recessions and decelerating it during inflations. If you aren't convinced of this, just look at the record of the Federal Reserve.

Interestingly, the Fed at one point acted on the advice of the monetarists, and this may have led to the decline of the monetarists. In October 1979, Federal Reserve Chairman Paul Volcker announced a major policy shift: No longer would the Fed focus only on keeping interest rates steady; from now on, the Fed would set monetary growth targets and stick to them.

The Fed followed this new policy for most of the next three years. The double-digit inflation of 1979 and 1980 was finally brought under control by late 1982. But at great cost.

First, interest rates went through the ceiling in early 1980, touching off a sharp recession. The prime rate of interest, which large, top credit-rated corporations pay banks, went above 20 percent. After the Fed eased off, the recession ended, but a year later, in mid-1981, we went into another recession when the Fed again decided to adhere to its monetary growth policy. This time the prime broke the 21 percent mark, and the recession went on for sixteen months. Finally, in the summer of 1982, the Board of Governors eased off the monetary brake, and by late fall the recession ended.

Even though the Fed had finally followed the advice of the monetarists— at least to a large degree—and even though the nagging inflation rate of the last thirteen or fourteen years had finally been wrung out of the economy, people began to look elsewhere for an economic guru. And many of them found their guru in the White House, which had become a stronghold of the supply-side school of economics.

Self-Test 3

1. To the monetarists, the most important thing is
   _____ .

2. What do the monetarists think of the Fed's performance in managing our money supply?
3. According to the monetarists, what is the one reason for inflation?
4. What is the monetarist version of the quantity theory of money?

5. According to the monetarists, what would people do with their money during recessions if the Fed increased the money supply?

6. The monetarists say that recessions are caused by

_____ .

7. Explain the monetary rule.

8. Explain the crowding out effect.

9. What happened when the Fed decided to concentrate on monetary growth targets?

Answers to Self-Test 3

1. The rate of growth of the money supply.

2. It is so bad that their power to control the rate of monetary growth should be removed.

3. The Fed has let the money supply grow too quickly.

4. If the money supply grows at a certain rate, the price level will rise, but not necessarily by exactly that rate.

5. They would hold on to most of it.

6. The Fed not allowing the money supply to grow by at least 3 percent a year.

7. The money supply should grow at 3 to 4 percent a year.

8. Private investors are crowded out of the financial markets by the federal government.

9. Interest rates rose very sharply and we had two recessions.

4 | SUPPLY-SIDE ECONOMICS

Supply-side economics came into vogue in the early 1980s when Ronald Reagan assumed the presidency. Supply-siders felt very strongly that the economic role of the federal government had grown much too large and that high tax rates and onerous government rules and regulations were hurting the incentives of individuals and business firms to produce goods and services. President Reagan suggested a simple solution: Get the government off the backs of the American people. How? By cutting taxes and reducing government spending and regulation.

The objective of supply-side economics, then, is to raise aggregate supply — the total amount of goods and services we produce. The problem, said the supply-siders, was that high tax rates were hurting the work incentive. All we had to do was cut taxes and production would go up.

To understand the importance of incentive, let's look at a man who works thirty-five hours a week. This worker adamantly refuses to work overtime, even though he has countless opportunities to earn more money by doing so. He also turns down countless part-time job offers. Why? Is he lazy? No, say the supply-siders. This man won't work harder because he doesn't want to pay higher taxes. The government is robbing him of his incentive to work by forcing him to pay high tax rates.

Let's suppose that you could earn $20 an hour in overtime. If you're in the 50 percent federal income tax bracket, how much of that $20 would you be left with after taxes? $10, right? Not so fast. Uncle Sam isn't quite through with you. You also must pay Social Security tax, which is, say, 7.15 percent. That's another $1.43 out of your paycheck, so now you're down to $8.57. Do you get to keep that? No. Your state and local governments may step in and take some of it for income tax, disability and unemployment insurance deductions, and perhaps a few other minor things. Suppose they limited themselves to 57 cents. That leaves you with exactly $8 out of your hard-earned $20.

Supply-siders reached the conclusion that a lot more people would be willing to put in extra time at $20 an hour than at $8 an hour. If they could cut federal income tax rates substantially, they reasoned, then they could give people a much greater incentive to work additional hours. And the more people work, the more goods and services they produce. Therefore, the ways to increase aggregate supply is to cut federal income tax rates.

But, you may ask, if the tax rates are cut, won't federal tax revenue fall precipitously? Some supply-side economists feel that this would not be an entirely bad development. After all, they point out, the more the federal government takes in, the more it spends. But Arthur Laffer, an orthodox supply-side economics professor, said that a tax rate cut could in fact lead to a rise in tax revenue. In other words, au contraire. (That's French for just the opposite.)

Imagine that we're at point A on the Laffer Curve shown in Figure 11.2. We cut the marginal tax rate from 50 percent to 40 percent, and tax revenue rises from $1200 billion to $1400 billion. Is that sophistry? (That's Greek for pulling a fast one.)

Let's see how this works by looking at the case of a specific individual. Suppose a woman pays $120,000 in taxes on an income of $240,000. If her tax rate is lowered to 40 percent, she will pay only $96,000 in taxes. Right?

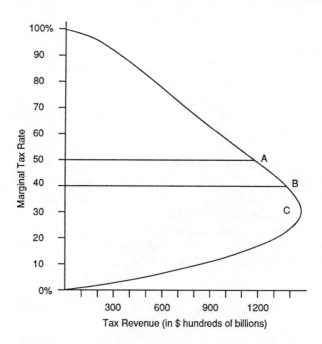

Figure 11.2 The Laffer Curve

Wrong! say the supply-siders. She will now have an incentive to work harder. How much harder? Hard enough, say, to earn a total of $350,000, by working every available hour of overtime or by taking on a second job.

How much is 40 percent of $350,000? Exactly $140,000. The government collected only $120,000 from this woman before the tax cut. By cutting the tax rates, say the supply-side economists, the government will end up collecting an extra $20,000 from her.

Is this true? If we go back to the Laffer Curve, apparently it is. At least at very high tax rates. But when we cut taxes in 1981 and 1982, tax revenue actually declined. Of course there was a recession going on.

Suppose we were at, say, point C on the Laffer Curve and we cut tax rates. What would happen to federal tax revenue? Obviously, it would decline.

The only problem, then, is to figure out where we are on the Laffer Curve, or what the parameters of the curve itself are, before we start cutting taxes. There really *is* a Laffer Curve out there. The trouble is that we don't know exactly where. So trying to use it as a policy tool is kind of like playing an economic version of pin the tail on the donkey. You run the risk of missing the donkey completely. And this game is played for somewhat higher stakes.

During the last two years of the Reagan administration, it became apparent that supply-side economics, like the administration, was an idea whose time had gone. Although inflation had been brought under control and interest rates had declined (largely because of the efforts of the Federal Reserve), the supply-side policies had not led to the rapid rate of economic growth that the public had been led to expect.

But conservative economists, many of whom had never been entirely comfortable with supply-side economics, had still another banner to rally around. This was the flag of rational expectations economic theory.

Self-Test 4

1. Supply-side economists believe they can give people a greater work incentive by _____ .

2. In the early 1980s, supply-side economists felt that the economic role of the federal government was _____ .

3. The main objective of supply-side economics was to

    _____ .

4. If we are at some point on the downward sloping section of the Laffer Curve and we cut tax rates, what will happen to tax revenue?

5. In 1981 and 1982 when federal income tax rates were cut, what happened to tax revenue?

6. Did the supply-side tax cuts of the Reagan administration lead to faster economic growth?

Answers to Self-Test 4

1. Cutting tax rates.

2. Too large.

3. Increase aggregate supply (the output of goods and services).

4. It will increase.

5. It fell.

6. No.

5 | RATIONAL EXPECTATIONS THEORY

Whatever else you have learned about economic policy, you have certainly learned that economists don't all agree on what policies we should follow. Nevertheless, with certain notable expectations, most economists today would more or less agree that we should fight inflation by lowering the rate of growth of the money supply and reducing federal government budget deficits and that we should fight recessions by increasing the rate of growth of the money supply and increasing the size of the deficits. Granted, some economists would admit to only partial agreement with these policies, but we could claim a greater consensus for these policies than for any others.

In the movie *Monty Python and the Holy Grail*, a group of knights distinguished themselves solely by saying "Nuh." If "nuh" meant "no," these knights were the rational expectations theorists, or the new classical economists, of their day.

And like the "old" classical economists, the rational expectationists say no to any form of government economic intervention. They believe that such intervention, no matter how well intended, will do a lot more harm than good. In fact, they maintain that antiinflationary policy and antirecessionary policy, at best, will have no effect whatsoever on the economy. More likely, say the new classical economists, these policies will make things worse in the long run.

Rational expectations theory is based on three assumptions: (1) that individuals and business firms learn, through experience, to instantaneously anticipate the consequences of changes in monetary and fiscal policy; (2) that they act instantaneously to protect their economic interests; and (3) that all resource and product markets are purely competitive.

Now we'll translate. Imagine that the Federal Reserve decided to sharply increase the rate of growth of the money supply in order to stimulate output and raise employment. According to the Fed, this action would produce the following results: (1) the money supply would rise; (2) business firms would be created, and output would rise; (3) wages would not rise right away, but prices would; (4) since prices rise and wages would stay the same, profits would rise; (5) eventually, wages would catch up to prices, profits would go back down, and the expansion would come to an end.

This may have happened in the old days, say the rational expectations theorists, but surely people have learned something from all of this experience. Everybody knows that when the Fed sharply increases the monetary growth rate, inflation will result. Business firms, of course, will raise prices. But what about labor? In anticipation of the expected inflation, wage earners will demand wage increases *now*. No more playing catch-up after the cost of living has already risen.

If wage rates are increased along with prices, do profits increase? No! If profits are not rising, there goes the main reason for increasing output and hiring more people. Which, of course, was why the rate of monetary growth was raised in the first place.

Let's return to the rational expectations theorists' three assumptions. The first one is plausible enough—that through experience, we learn to anticipate the consequences of changes in monetary and fiscal policy. So, if a sharp increase in the rate of growth in the money supply always leads to inflation, eventually we will all learn to recognize this pattern.

It would follow from the next two assumptions that the intended results of macroeconomic policy shifts will be completely frustrated. Why? Well, if you knew the prices would be increasing, would you be willing to sit back and passively accept a decline in your standard of living? Wouldn't you demand higher wages to keep pace with rising prices? The rational expectations theorists say that people can always be expected to promote their personal economic interests and that in a purely competitive market they are free to do so.

In a purely competitive labor market, workers are free to leave one employer for another who offers higher wages. In a purely competitive products market, all firms are subject to the law of supply and demand and will automatically pass along any wage increases in the form of higher prices.

Most macroeconomic policy changes, say the rational expectations theorists, are very predictable. When there's inflation, there are extended debates in Congress and demands for cuts in government spending, tax increases, and a slowdown in the rate of monetary growth. Both Congress and the Federal Reserve generally telegraph policy moves, often months in advance. And when these moves are made, no one is surprised. Because the public anticipates them, the intended effects of these policy changes are cancelled out by the actions taken by individuals and business firms to protect their economic interests. Policies aimed at raising output and employment produce more inflation.

What should the government do? As little as possible, say the rational expectations theorists. Like the classical economists, they believe that the harder the government tries to be an economic stabilizing force, the more destabilizing it will be.

Basically, then, the federal government should figure out the right policies to follow and stick to them. What *are* the right policies? As you might expect, the rational expectationists have taken up the conservative economists' agenda: (1) steady monetary growth of 3 to 4 percent a year—the monetarists' monetary rule—and (2) a balanced budget—favored by the classical economists, among others.

Like every other school of economics, rational expectations theory has come in for its share of criticism. In fact, only a small minority of economists today would consider themselves new classical economists. Most economists feel that the rational expectationists overestimate the rationality of the general population (and of economists as well).

Is it reasonable to expect individuals and business firms to accurately predict the consequences of macroeconomic policy changes when economists themselves come up with widely varying predictions, most of which are wrong? And since economists place so little faith in each other's rationality, would it be rational to expect them to ascribe to the general population a greater prescience than they accord to themselves?

In a world of constant change, is it possible for people to accurately predict the economic consequences of policy changes? Indeed, when a constantly changing cast of policymakers, each with a different economic agenda, seems to be calling for entirely new economic approaches every few years, it's awfully hard to tell the players without a scorecard. And it's even harder to predict the final score.

A second criticism of the rational expectations school is that our economic markets are certainly not purely competitive, and some are not competitive at all. Labor unions are not an economist's idea of purely competitive labor market institutions. Nor are concentrated industries—such as automobiles, petroleum, cigarettes, and breakfast cereals, each of which have just a handful of firms producing most of the output—considered very competitive.

Finally, the critics raise the question of the rigidity of most contracts. A labor union with a two- or three-year contract cannot reopen bargaining with employers when greater inflation is anticipated because of a suddenly expansionary monetary policy. Nor can business firms that have long-term contracts with customers decide to charge them higher prices because they perceive more inflation in the future.

Does all this mean that we should dismiss the rational expectations school out of hand, since it is so vulnerable to criticism? Most economists would probably concede that this school is correct in calling attention to the importance of expectations in affecting the outcome of macroeconomic policy changes. In recent years, then, economists have become more aware that, to the degree that policy changes are predictable, people will certainly act to protect their economic interests. To some degree they will succeed. And in doing so, they will partially counteract the effect of the macroeconomic policy of the government.

In other words, rational expectations theory has a certain validity, as do all of the other theories we discussed. It's up to us to decide how valid each theory is in relation to the others.

Self-Test 5

1. Most economists would agree with at least part of these policies:
   A. To fight inflation the proper fiscal policy would be to
   _____ , and the proper monetary policy would
   be to _____ .
   B. To fight recessions the proper fiscal policy would be to
   _____ , and the proper monetary policy would
   be to _____ .

2. The rational expectations theorists are also known as the
   _____ .

3. On what three assumptions is rational expectations theory based?

4. If the Fed raised the rate of monetary growth, it would expect, as a consequence, that output and employment would grow. But according to the rational expectations theorists, what would happen?

5. What fiscal and monetary policies should the federal government follow, according to the rational expectations theorists?

6. What has been the major contribution of the rational expectations theorists?

Answers to Self-Test 5

1. A. Lower budget deficits; lower rate of monetary growth.
   B. Raise budget deficits; raise rate of monetary growth.

2. New conservative economists.

3. (1) Individuals and business firms learn, through experience, to instantaneously anticipate the consequences of changes in monetary and fiscal policy; (2) they act instantaneously to protect their economic interests; and (3) all resource and product markets are purely competitive.

4. Workers would demand instant wage increases, thus canceling out expected profits. Without profits, business firms would not expand output and employment. Therefore, we would end up with higher prices.

5. Just increase the money supply at 3 to 4 percent a year and balance the federal budget every year.

6. They have called attention to the importance of expectations in affecting the outcome of macroeconomic policy changes.

6 | CONCLUSION

What policies *should* we follow? The classical economists, like Thomas Jefferson, believe that "The government that governs best governs least." Since recessions will cure themselves, say the classicals, the government should adhere to a laissez-faire policy, allowing the private economic system to function without interference.

The Keynesians stress fiscal policy. During recessions, they say, we should run federal budget deficits, and during inflations, we should run surpluses. Monetary policy? The latter-day Keynesians concede that an expansionary monetary policy would be helpful. But Keynesian economics always stresses the primacy of fiscal policy.

The supply-side school, sometimes considered the flip side of the Keynesian school, stresses the importance of tax rate cuts to give people a greater work incentive. Although they basically believe in balanced budgets, temporary deficits are justified as unfortunate by-products of the tax rate cuts.

The monetarists want rules, namely, a 3 to 4 percent rate of monetary growth and balanced budgets. Why? Because we simply do not know enough about the workings of our economy to successfully practice discretionary macroeconomic policy.

Finally, we have the new classical economists, who believe that macroeconomic stabilization policy is self-defeating because everybody anticipates government actions and acts to protect his or her own economic interests, so that the intended effects of the government policy is immediately and fully canceled out.

So where does all of this leave us? Just about where we started at the beginning of this chapter: About the only thing economists can agree on is to disagree. Thus, you are free to draw your own conclusions about macroeconomic theory and policy. Don't dwell on them too long, though, because we're ready to go on to microeconomics.

PART 4

MICROECONOMICS:

DEMAND

AND SUPPLY

CHAPTER 12

Demand

and

Supply

W̱e now return to drawing and interpreting graphs. If you are still not at ease with graphs, reread frames 1 through 6 of Chapter 3, which cover demand and supply, the subjects of this chapter. You may want to buy a package of graph paper at this point, since you will need an extra thirty sheets on which to do the graphs in the text and the Self-Test problems in this chapter, Chapters 13 and 14.

After you read this chapter you will

- Understand the definition of demand and the law of demand.
- Be able to distinguish between individual demand and market demand.
- Understand the definition of supply and the law of supply.
- Be able to distinguish between individual supply and market supply.
- Be able to graph demand and supply curves.
- Be able to find equilibrium price and quantity.
- Understand what brings about changes in demand and supply.
- Recognize the graphs of price floors and price ceilings.

---

1 | DEMAND

What Is Demand?

Demand is the schedule of quantities of a good or service that people are willing and able to buy at different prices.

Table 12.1 provides an illustration of a demand schedule for pizza. Using the data in this table, we can draw the demand curve shown in Figure 12.1. So, both the graph and the table illustrate the demand for pizza.

You'll notice that people buy more and more pizza as the price declines, which is pretty much what you would expect. But we need to understand *why* people buy more at low prices than at high prices.

Why would *you* buy more of something a a lower price? Because you feel you're getting a bargain? Because you can afford to buy more? Let's test these suppositions. We'll take something you really want: ten compact discs of your favorite groups.

Table 12.1. Hypothetical Demand for Dino's Pizza

Price	Quantity Demanded
$2.50	1
2.25	3
2.00	8
1.75	19
1.50	40
1.25	73
1.00	116
.75	178

Let's suppose that if CDs sold for $15 each, you'd buy just one. But if the CDs were on sale at $10 apiece, why not stock up? At an even lower price of, say, $5, you might snap up all ten CDs. Why? Because the price is a real bargain, and because you can afford to buy a lot more CDs at $5 apiece than at $15 apiece. So we know you would buy at least three times as many CDs at $5 as you would at $15.

Now let's take another example. Would you pay someone to chain you to a wall and whip you? Suppose that the service provider usually charges $10 for ten lashes, but when the shop is running a special, you can get twenty lashes for $10. Would you take advantage of that bargain?

Probably not, since most people would not want to be whipped. I would also like to point out to you that since you are not willing to be whipped, you would not take advantage of this "service," even if it were free. The word *willing* is a very important element of the definition of demand.

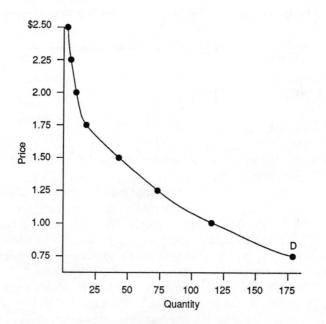

Figure 12.1 Demand curve for pizza

People are hedonists. We like to maximize our pleasure and minimize our pain. So, implicit in our demand for various goods and services is the assumption that we are buying things that give us pleasure. What about the person who pays to get whipped? That person enjoys it, otherwise there would be no demand for that service.

Let's sum up the law of demand: *All other things being equal, price and quantity demanded are inversely related.* In other words, as price falls, people buy larger quantities. Or, alternatively, as price rises, people buy less.

"All other things being equal" means that nothing changes: that is, people's tastes and incomes remain the same as do the prices of substitute products. If tastes and incomes did change, maybe those changes would cause changes in the quantity demanded. We'll consider changes in taste, income, and the price of substitutes in frame 3 of this chapter.

2 | Individual and Market Demand

Individual demand is what we've just discussed. It is the schedule of quantities of a good or service that an individual is willing or able to buy at different prices. Market demand is the sum of all the individual schedules in a market. Let's suppose that Lisa, Diane, Alex, and Jason are also in the market for CDs. When we add up their demand for CDs, together with yours, as we've done in Table 12.2, we end up with the market demand for CDs.

The market demand, then, is the sum of the demand schedules of all the individual buyers in the market. But what *is* the market? That depends on the good or service being purchased.

The market for groceries, for example, is very local. You will shop at a supermarket that's close to your home. Why? Because you don't want your food to spoil on the way home. Have you ever eaten refrozen ice cream? I guarantee that it is a treat you would never try more than once.

How about the market for used cars? How far would *you* be willing to go and buy a used car at a bargain price? Maybe a hundred miles? Or even two hundred miles? So, the market for used cars would be within, say, a couple of hundred miles of where you live. How many used car markets are there in the United States? Probably over a hundred.

Table 12.2. Hypothetical Demand for CDs

Price	Yourself	Lisa	Diane	Alex	Jason	Market Demand
$15	1	0	1	1	0	3
14	1	0	2	1	1	5
13	2	1	2	1	2	8
12	2	1	3	2	3	11
11	2	1	4	2	4	13
10	3	2	5	3	4	17
9	3	3	5	3	5	19
8	3	3	6	4	7	23
7	4	4	7	6	8	29
6	5	4	8	8	9	34
5	6	5	10	11	12	44

What about new car markets? Perhaps a little less than a thousand, because people might be willing to travel somewhat further to get a good deal on a new car than on a used car.

There are national markets and even international markets for certain goods and services. Business firms in New York do business with suppliers in Los Angeles, while firms in Japan sell to buyers in the United States.

3 | Changes in Demand

A change in demand is any departure from the demand schedule. If any change whatsoever occurs in the quantity of a good that is purchased at least one price, a change in demand has taken place. For example, in Table 12.3 we have a change in demand from schedule 1 to schedule 2.

Usually a change in demand will be reflected by an increase in the quantity demanded at all prices, in which case we would say there has been an increase in demand. Alternatively, if quantity demanded at all prices decreases, then there has been a decrease in demand.

This is illustrated in Figure 12.2. If we go from curve D_1 to D_2, there has been an increase in demand. And if we were to go from D_2 to D_1, then demand has decreased.

There are three main causes for increases or decreases in demand. First, if people's incomes increase, their demand for most goods will rise. However, the demand for "inferior goods" will decrease. Inferior goods are those items that people buy only when they are short of money. Thus, as their incomes rise, people buy smaller quantities of these goods, which include rice, spaghetti, potatoes, and Hamburger Helper-type products.

A second possible cause of an increase or decrease in the demand for a particular good or service is a change in taste. In the 1960s a lot of men bought Nehru jackets. But when President Nixon made his historic trip to China in 1973, Nehru jackets were out and Mao jackets were in. Since "cholesterol" became part of our vocabularies in the 1950s, the demand for red meat has declined. This would reflect another change in taste.

The third main cause of an increase or decrease in demand for a good or service is a change in the prices of substitute products. If the price of chicken fell to 25 cents a pound, what do you think would happen to the demand for

Table 12.3. Two Hypothetical Demand Schedules

Price	Quantity Demanded 1	Quantity Demanded 2
$20	1	1
19	2	2
18	4	5
17	8	9
16	14	13
15	23	22

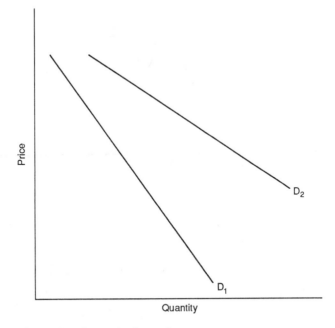

Figure 12.2 Change in demand

steak? Or if the price of steel doubled, what would happen to the demand for aluminum, plastics, and other steel substitutes?

Self-Test 1

1. What is the definition of demand?
2. State the law of demand.
3. What are the two reasons why people buy more of a particular good or service at lower prices than at higher prices?
4. Use these data to draw a demand curve.

Price	Quantity Demanded
$8	2
7	3
6	5
5	9
4	18

5. In the previous problem, you drew a demand curve. Label that curve D_1 and draw a second demand curve, D_2, illustrating an increase in demand.
6. What are the three main reasons for changes in demand?

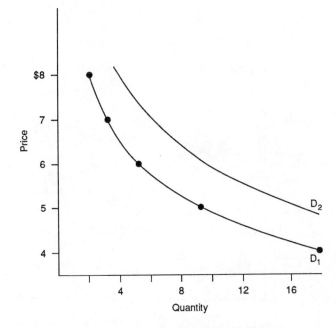

Figure 12.3 Answer to questions 4 and 5 of Self-Test 1

Answers to Self-Test 1

1. Demand is a schedule of quantities of a good or service that people are willing and able to buy at different prices.
2. All other things being equal, price and quantity demanded are inversely related.
3. They can afford more and feel they are getting a bargain.
4. See Figure 12.3.
5. See Figure 12.3.
6. Changes in income, taste, and the prices of substitute products.

4 | SUPPLY

Supply Defined

One of the nice things about microeconomics is its simplicity. For instance, take the definition of supply. Change just two words in the definition of demand (at the beginning of frame 1) and you've got it: *Supply is the schedule of quantities of a good or service that people are willing and able to sell at different prices.*

We can do the same thing with the law of supply. Change just two words in the law of demand and you've got the law of supply (stated near the end of frame 1): *All other things being equal, price and quantity supplied are directly related.* In other words, as price rises, people sell larger quantities. Or, alternatively, as price falls, people sell less.

Table 12.4 illustrates the law of supply with a supply schedule. Draw the supply curve in Figure 12.4, using the data from the table. Then check your work against Figure 12.5.

Table 12.4. Hypothetical Supply Schedule

Price	Quantity Supplied
$12	28
11	25
10	20
9	12
8	3

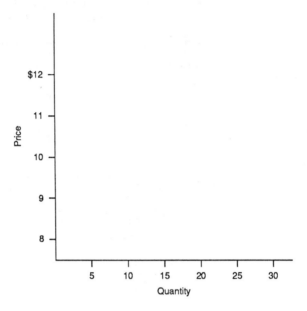

Figure 12.4

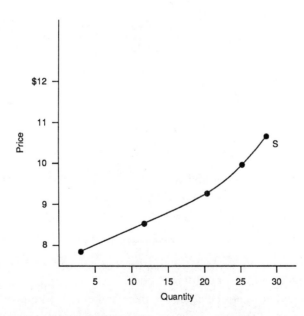

Figure 12.5 Supply curve

195

Why does the supply curve slope upward to the right? Why are greater quantities supplied at higher prices than at lower prices? There are two answers to these questions.

First, at any moment in time there are a fixed number of sellers, or firms, in an industry. Right now there may be nine firms making cars in the United States, and perhaps there are three unisex hair salons in your town.

Let's see what happens when prices go up. The auto makers will increase their output, operating their plants on double or even triple shifts. The unisex hair salons will stay open longer hours and will hire more barbers and beauticians.

But over time, if prices stay high, new firms will be attracted to these industries, increasing output still further. So ultimately, if prices rise and stay high for a fairly long time, the quantity supplied will increase for two reasons: (1) existing firms will produce more and (2) new firms will be attracted to the industry.

If this analysis strikes you as a bit simplistic, it is. We've kind of swept the subtleties of short-run and long-run supply under the rug. But we'll pull the rug out from over them in the next chapter.

Self-Test 2

1. What is the definition of supply?
2. State the law of supply.
3. What are the two reasons why the supply curve slants upward to the right?
4. Use the data in this table to draw a supply curve.

Price	Quantity Supplied
$15	40
14	37
13	31
12	22
11	8
10	2

5. In the previous problem, you drew a supply curve. Label that curve S_1 and draw a second supply curve, S_2, illustrating an increase in supply.

Answers to Self-Test 2

1. Supply is the schedule of quantities of a good or service that people are willing and able to sell at different prices.
2. All other things being equal, price and quantity supplied are directly related.
3. Existing firms produce more and new firms enter the industry.
4. See Figure 12.6.
5. See Figure 12.6.

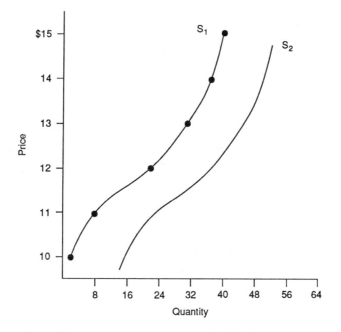

Figure 12.6 Answer to questions 4 and 5 of Self-Test 2

<table>
<tr><td>5</td><td>

THE GRAPHING OF SUPPLY AND DEMAND

Equilibrium

The equilibrium point is where the demand and supply curves cross. At that point quantity demanded equals quantity supplied.
</td></tr>
<tr><td>6</td><td>

You've already graphed the demand and supply curves separately. Are you ready to put them together on the same graph? Use the data from Table 12.5 to fill in Figure 12.7. After you've completed the graph, find the equilibrium price and quantity.
</td></tr>
<tr><td>7</td><td>

Check your work against Figure 12.8. If it came out about the same, go on to frame 10; if it differs markedly, go to frame 8.
</td></tr>
<tr><td>8</td><td>

Using the data in Table 12.6, fill in Figure 12.9. Check your results against Figure 12.10.
</td></tr>
<tr><td>9</td><td>

How did you do *this* time? If you came reasonably close, go directly to frame 10; if not, turn back to frame 6 of Chapter 3 and go over supply and demand once again.
</td></tr>
<tr><td>10</td><td>

Changes in Demand

Now we're ready to see what happens to price and quantity when demand changes. First, let's look at the increase in demand shown in Figure 12.11. How much were the original equilibrium price and quantity (when demand was D_1)? And how much are the new equilibrium price and quantity (when demand is D_2)?
</td></tr>
</table>

Table 12.5. Hypothetical Demand and Supply
Schedules

Price	Quantity Demanded	Quantity Supplied
$20	1	31
19	4	29
18	9	25
17	18	16
16	28	6

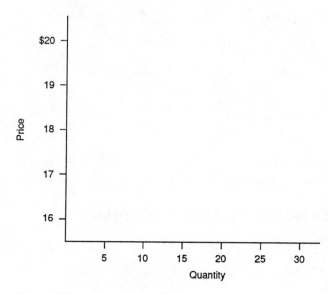

Figure 12.7

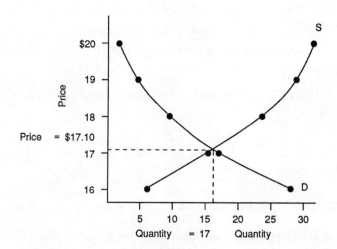

Figure 12.8 Supply and demand curves

Table 12.6. Hypothetical Demand and Supply Schedules

Price	Quantity Demanded	Quantity Supplied
$25	1	30
24	2	28
23	4	24
22	8	17
21	15	9
20	27	2

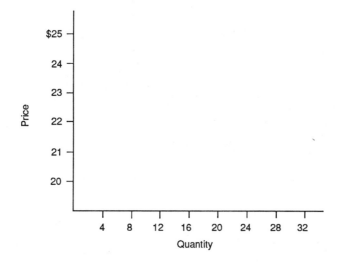

Figure 12.9

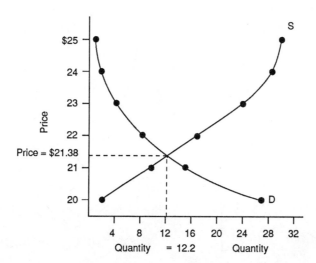

Figure 12.10 Supply and demand curves

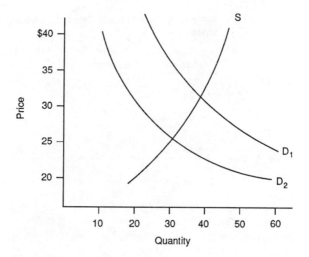

Figure 12.11 Change in demand

11 At the old equilibrium point, price was $25.80 and quantity was 30.2. At the new equilibrium point, price is $31.80 and quantity is 38.5.

If you got this right, go on to frame 13; otherwise, go to 12. Keep in mind that our answers are just visual approximations and cannot be expected to agree to the last decimal.

12 According to the graph in Figure 12.12, how much were the old equilibrium price and quantity when demand was D_1? Find the new equilibrium price and quantity when demand shifts to D_2.

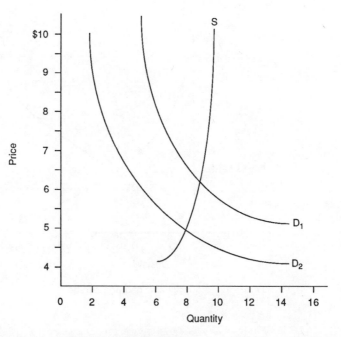

Figure 12.12 Change in demand

13 | At the old equilibrium point, price was $7.73 and quantity was 8.47. The new price is $5.85, and the new quantity is 6.72.

14 | ## Changes in Supply

Changes in supply parallel changes in demand. Using the information in Figure 12.13, state the original equilibrium price and quantity (when supply was S_1). Then state the new equilibrium price and quantity, when supply is S_2.

15 | At the old equilibrium point, price was $17.10 and quantity was 230; at the new equilibrium point, price is $14.52 and quantity is 423.

If your answers were reasonably close to these, go on to frame 18; otherwise go to 16.

16 | Using the information in Figure 12.14, state the original equilibrium price and quantity (when supply was S_1) and the new equilibrium price and quantity (when supply is S_2).

17 | The old equilibrium price was $5.49, and the quantity was 94. The new equilibrium price is $6.79, and the new quantity is 76.

18 | ## Summing Up: The Effects of Changes in Supply and Demand on Price and Quantity

What is the effect of an increase in supply on equilibrium price and quantity?

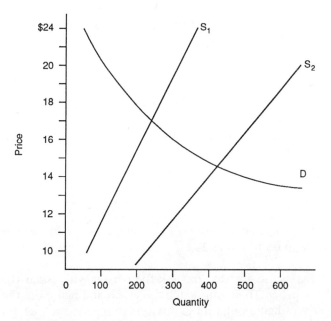

Figure 12.13 Change in supply

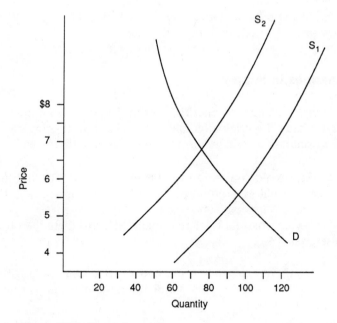

Figure 12.14 Change in supply

19   Price will decline and quantity will rise. Check back to Figure 12.13.
     What is the effect of an increase in demand on equilibrium price and quantity?

20   Price and quantity will increase, as shown in Figure 12.11.
     Next: What is the effect of a decrease in demand on equilibrium price and quantity?

21   The effect will be just the opposite: price and quantity will decrease. This is shown in Figure 12.12.
     One more problem: What is the effect of a decrease in supply on equilibrium price and quantity?

22   Price rises and quantity declines (see Figure 12.14).

23   How can you remember all this stuff? If a stranger were to walk up to you on the street and ask, "What is the effect of a decrease in demand on price and quantity?" would you have a ready answer?
     If you memorized the answers to these four questions, you certainly would be ready. Or if you happened to have Figures 12.11 to 12.14, you could refer to them.
     Isn't there an easier way of coming up with the right answer? Think about it. Then go on to frame 24.

24   Here's the answer. You ask the person who asked you the question for a piece of paper. Then you sketch the graph and figure out the answer. And that's the way to figure out a lot of answers to microeconomic questions.

25 | Price Floors and Ceilings

Price floors and price ceilings will be easy to understand if you start out by wiping from memory your conception of floors and ceilings. Usually, you look up at a ceiling and down at a floor. Am I right? If you're indoors right now, glance up. What do you see? The ceiling! And when you look down, there's the floor.

You can't go any higher than a price ceiling; you can push up against it, but you can't go above it. Similarly, you can't go lower than a price floor; you can stomp on it, but you can't go below it.

But, as you might expect in economics, certain things are upside down. And so, you'll find the price floors near the top of your graphs and the price ceilings near the bottom.

The reason for this is that in economics we have a different kind of gravity. Price always seeks the equilibrium level. When price is above the equilibrium point, it falls. And when it is below that point, it rises.

26 | Case 1: When Market Price Is Above Equilibrium Price

Figure 12.15 shows an equilibrium price of $10. At that price, quantity demanded and quantity supply are equal. Sellers want to sell a quantity of 15 and buyers want to buy a quantity of 15.

At equilibrium price, there are no dissatisfied sellers or buyers. No sellers can say, "Gee, I would have taken a price of $10, but I just couldn't find any buyers." Nor can any buyers complain about not being able to find a seller with a price of $10.

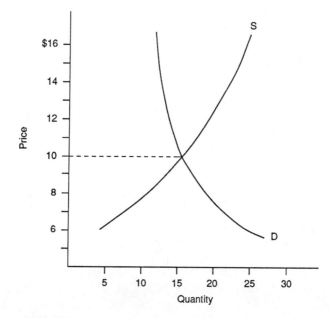

Figure 12.15

At equilibrium, every seller who is willing to sell at $10 can find a buyer, and every buyer willing to pay $10 can find a seller. So at equilibrium, there are no dissatisfied buyers or sellers.

But suppose that the market price—that is, the actual price in that market at that time—happened to be $12. It would *have* to fall to $10. But why?

Many buyers will be unhappy when the price is above $10. They'll be *so* unhappy that they just won't buy. But that's already known from their demand curve. And those buyers aren't really *that* unhappy, because it's not as if they wanted to buy at that price and couldn't find a seller.

But those who will *really* be unhappy when the price is $12 are some of the sellers. Which ones? The ones who were *willing* to sell at $12 but who can't find buyers. How many of them are there? See if you can estimate how many from Figure 12.15.

It looks like about 5. That's how much quantity supplied exceeds quantity demanded.

If you happened to be one of those unhappy sellers who got stuck with these unsold goods, what could you do?

You could lower your price. If you lowered your price to $11, maybe you could sell your goods. Would a price of $11 clear the market?

Evidently not, but it would reduce the market surplus from 5 to about 2 1/2. But there would still be some dissatisfied sellers. So what do you think they would do? That's right, they would lower their price to $10.

There are a couple of other things going on here that you should take note of. When the price was reduced from $12 to $11, the quantity supplied declined from about 18.5 to about 17.5, while the quantity demanded rose from about 12.5 to 13. And when price declined from $11 to $10 the quantity supplied went down and the quantity demanded went up.

We can sum up these findings by saying that if market price is above equilibrium price, the market price will fall to equilibrium price. When that happens, quantity demanded rises, while quantity supplied declines, until the surplus is eliminated.

Here's one last observation: When some sellers lower their price from $12 to $11, other sellers are forced to follow suit. Why? Because why would anyone buy from them when they can buy from the sellers who are charging only $11? And finally, when the price falls to $10, which is the equilibrium price, everyone who wants to buy and sell at that price can do so; thus, there is no tendency for the price to change. In fact, the only thing that can make the price change (short of a shift in the demand or supply schedule) is dissatisfaction on the part of the buyers or sellers.

Case 2: When Market Price Is Below Equilibrium Price

When market price is above equilibrium price, we have a surplus and dissatisfied sellers. Can you guess what we will have when market price is below equilibrium price?

If the market price is $8, there will be an irresistible tendency for the price to rise to $10. Who pushes it up? The dissatisfied buyers. At a price of $8 there's a shortage of about 7.5. When the dissatisfied buyers, some of whom are willing to pay more than $8, bid the market price up to $9, the shortage is reduced to about 3.3. But some buyers are still dissatisfied because they are unable to buy the good; all these buyers bid the price up to $10, where everybody is happy. The shortage is completely eliminated, and the market price will remain at the equilibrium level unless there is a shift in the demand or supply schedule.

All of this has been a prelude to price floors and ceilings. These are artificial mechanisms introduced by the government to maintain prices either above or below the equilibrium level.

28 | Price Floors and Surpluses

Keep in mind that price floors are not found in the lower part of a graph, where you'd expect them to be. You'll find floors near the top of a graph. Over the years, the federal government has established a floor under the price of agricultural products such as wheat and corn. Why? To keep the price of those products higher than they would otherwise have been. Why? So that the farmers would make a better living and not be forced to give up farming.

Figure 12.16 illustrates a price floor. Notice where the floor is located on the graph: $2 above equilibrium price. The floor prevents the price from falling to the equilibrium level of $10.

The government wouldn't help the farmers very much if it merely decreed that the price of wheat and corn should be $12 a bushel. There would still be a surplus of 5 units or, say, 5 million bushels. To maintain the price floor the government buys the surplus.

29 | Price Ceilings and Shortages

Price ceilings are symmetrical to price floors. They are located below the equilibrium price, and they keep the market price from rising to the equilibrium level. A price ceiling is illustrated in Figure 12.17. At that price, $8, there is a shortage of nearly 8 units.

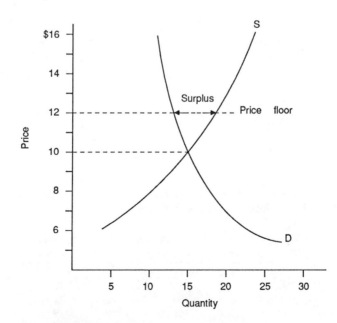

Figure 12.16 Price floor

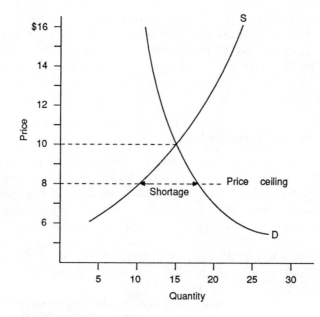

Figure 12.17 Price ceiling

The federal government has imposed price ceilings to keep prices below the equilibrium level. During World War II the government instituted a price freeze. In August 1971 President Nixon imposed a temporary freeze on prices, and during the 1970s there was a ceiling on the price of oil. The government imposed those ceilings in an attempt to fight inflation by legally holding down prices.

Unavoidably under a system of price ceilings there are shortages. During World War II the government issued ration coupons that entitled people to buy limited amounts of various food items, gasoline, and other goods.

Most economists oppose price ceilings because they feel that the ceilings distort the price mechanism. That mechanism automatically eliminates surpluses and shortages. As long as price is free to seek its equilibrium level, quantity supplied and quantity demanded will be equal—or as they say, "You can't repeal the law of supply and demand."

Self-Test 3

1   Using the data in the table, draw a graph of the demand and supply curves. State the equilibrium price and quantity.

Price	Quantity Demanded	Quantity Supplied
$10	1	24
9	2	17
8	4	12
7	7	9
6	12	7
5	21	6

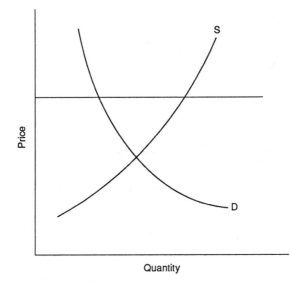

Figure 12.18

2. Draw another supply curve, S_2, illustrating an increase in supply.
3. When demand rises, what happens to equilibrium price and quantity?
4. When supply declines, what happens to equilibrium price and quantity?
5. A. Does the graph in Figure 12.18 show a price ceiling or a price floor?
   B. Is there a shortage or a surplus?

Answers to Self-Test 3

1. See Figure 12.19.

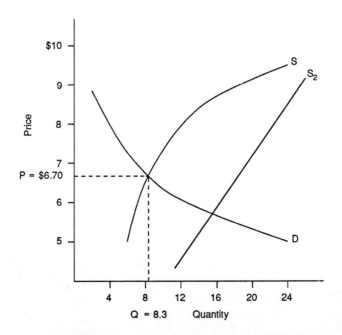

Figure 12.19 Answers to questions 1 and 2 of Self-Test 3

2. See Figure 12.19.
3. They both rise.
4. Equilibrium price rises and quantity declines.
5. A. It shows a price floor.
   B. There is a surplus.

CHAPTER 13

Supply in the

Short Run and

the Long Run

In our discussion of long- and short-run supply, as in much of microeconomics, we will start with some very simple concepts: fixed cost, variable cost, and total cost. We will end up, however, with some pretty complex graphs. You may need to reread parts of Chapter 3 as well as parts of this chapter in order to master certain concepts.

When you have completed this chapter you will:

- Understand the concepts of fixed, variable, and total cost.
- Be able to calculate average fixed cost, average variable cost, average total cost, and marginal cost.
- Be able to differentiate between the short run and the long run.
- Be able to graph a firm's demand, marginal revenue, average variable cost, average total cost, and marginal cost curves.
- Calculate a firm's total profit.
- Be able to find a firm's shutdown and break-even points.
- Identify a firm's short-run and long-run supply curves.

1 | FIXED, VARIABLE, AND TOTAL COST

All of a business firm's costs may be divided into two categories: fixed costs and variable costs. Variable costs vary with output, while fixed costs do not. In other words, as output rises from 1 to 2 to 3 to 4, variable cost also rises. But fixed cost, as its name implies, remains constant.

2 | Fixed Costs

Fixed costs include rent, salaries of contract workers, insurance premiums, depreciation on plant and equipment, and interest payments on a corporation's bonds. Even if output were to fall to zero, the firm would still be legally obligated to meet these costs.

3 | **Variable Costs**

Variable costs include wages of production workers, fuel, electricity, and the cost of materials used for production. These costs would fall to zero if the firm shut down and produced nothing.

4 | **Total Cost**

Total cost is the sum of fixed cost and variable cost at every possible level of output. If fixed cost is constant and variable cost rises with output, what happens to total cost as output rises?

5 | Obviously, it rises. This should become clear when you complete Table 13.1.

6 | The solution for Table 13.1 appears in Table 13.2.

Now we're just about ready to discuss a major axiom in economics—or at least in capitalist economics. We'll approach this axiom by making a statement that shouldn't surprise anyone: All firms are in business to make a profit.

Sure, you can think of exceptions. The occasional saint or altruist may be interested only in performing good works. Others may be like my old friend Jonathan, who for years operated a karate school not for profit, but as a means of meeting women. As far as we're concerned, however, profit is the name of the game.

Are you ready for the important axiom? Here it comes: *Every business firm attempts to maximize its profits.* Never mind the exceptions; just keep in mind the rule. All of the analysis from this moment on right through to the end of the book is predicated on this axiom. If it isn't true, we're in big trouble.

7 | **THE SHORT RUN AND THE LONG RUN**

The dividing line between the short run and the long run is the time it takes a firm to enter or leave the industry. Another way to distinguish between the two is that in the short run there are some fixed costs, but there are no fixed costs in the long run.

Table 13.1.

Output	Fixed Cost	Variable Cost	Total Cost
0	$500	$0	
1	500	200	
2	500	350	
3	500	500	
4	500	700	

Table 13.2.

Output	Fixed Cost	Variable Cost	Total Cost
0	$500	$0	$500
1	500	200	700
2	500	350	850
3	500	500	1000
4	500	700	1200

8   The Short Run

The short run is the length of time it takes all fixed costs to become variable costs. As long as there are any fixed costs, we are in the short run. How long is the short run? The short run may be just a day or two, or it may last for a few years. A street peddler has a very short run. How long would it take him to sell his inventory? That's as long as his short run lasts. (How can a fixed cost become a variable cost? Your rent is a fixed cost as long as you have a lease. Suppose your lease runs out and you reach an agreement with your landlord to rent space on an as-needed basis from month to month. Your rent is now a variable cost.)

On the other end of the scale, we've got steel mills, auto makers, and professional baseball, football, and basketball teams. Professional teams all have players under long-term contracts, some of them for quite a few years. The longest contract on record is the twenty-year agreement between Magic Johnson and the Los Angeles Lakers. He signed for 20 years. Even if the Lakers should decide to never play another game, Magic Johnson will continue to draw his paychecks.

A firm can shut down and cease operations, but it cannot go out of business until it has met all of its contractual obligations. In addition, an operation like a steel mill will need to pay people to close down the furnaces, fill any remaining orders, and bring everything to a halt in an orderly manner.

9   The Long Run

In the long run, the firm has the option of staying in business or going out of business. In the long run, all fixed-cost obligations will have expired and the owners of the firm will be free to decide what to do.

What they do will depend on whether or not the firm is making a profit. If the firm is losing money, it will go out of business in the long run. Let's take a closer look at how the firm's owners decide what to do in the short run and the long run. That decision depends on the firm's profits or losses.

10   THE SHUTDOWN AND GO-OUT-OF-BUSINESS DECISIONS

The Shutdown Decision

A firm has two options in the short run. It can operate or shut down. If it operates, it will produce the output that will yield the highest possible profits, or, if it is losing money, it will operate at the level of output at which losses are minimized.

If the firm shuts down, its output will be zero. Shutting down does not mean zero total costs, however. The firm must still meet its fixed costs. Table 13.2 shows that at an output of zero, fixed costs, and therefore total costs, are $500.

Why can't the firm go out of business in the short run? Because it still has fixed costs. It must discharge these obligations. It must also sell off any plant, equipment, inventory, and raw materials. All of this takes time. How long? Anywhere from a day to a few years.

11   Before we begin to work out shutdown decision problems, let's go over that important axiom: *Every business firm attempts to maximize its profits.* See if you can derive from that axiom the corollary that applies to the firm that is going to lose money. I'll start you off: *Every business firm (that is losing money) attempts to* _____ .

12   The answer is: *minimize its losses.*

'Why is this firm in business in the first place, you may ask, if it is losing money? Of course people don't go into business if they think they will lose money—at least in the long run. But if a firm starts losing money, the owners can't do too much about it in the short run except try to minimize those losses. They don't have the option of going out of business in the short run.

One more thing and we'll be ready to work out shutdown decision problems. When a firm operates, it produces output, which it then sells. Producing this output will cost something, and the firm will take in money from its sales.

What will the firm take in from sales when it shuts down and its output is zero? Sales will be zero. How about costs? Will total cost be zero? Remember what we said back in frame 10. At an output of zero, total cost is equal to fixed cost. This is also shown in Table 13.2.

13   Let's work out some problems involving the shutdown decision. If a firm has fixed costs of $5 million, variable costs of $6 million, and prospective sales of $7 million, what can it do in the short run? It has two choices: (1) to continue to operate or (2) to shut down.

If you owned this firm, what would you do? Keep in mind that no matter what you do, you'll lose money.

14   First, you should ask yourself two questions: (1) How much will I lose if I continue to operate? (2) How much will I lose if I shut down?

15   If I continue to operate, I'll take in $7 million from my sales and I'll pay out $11 million in total cost (fixed cost of $5 million plus variable cost of $6 million). So if I operate, I'll lose $4 million.

If I shut down, I'll take in nothing in sales and I'll pay nothing in variable costs, but I will pay $5 million in fixed cost. So if I shut down, I'll lose $5 million.

So what should I do? I should continue to operate. Remember, you want to minimize your losses. It is a lot better to lose $4 million than to lose $5 million.

Now try another problem: If a firm has fixed costs of $6 million, variable costs of $8 million, and prospective sales of $7 million, what should it do in the short run?

16 If the firm continues to operate, it has sales of $7 million and its total cost is $14 million ($6 million fixed plus $8 million variable). So if it operates, it has a loss of $7 million. If it shuts down, it loses just its fixed costs of $6 million. So it shuts down.

17 Are you ready to make up a general rule? Go back over the last two problems and see if you can derive this general rule: A firm will operate if _____ are greater than _____ .

18 The firm will operate if prospective sales are greater than variable costs.
If you figured out this rule, go on to frame 21, if you got it wrong, go to frame 19.

19 If a firm has fixed costs of $5 million, variable costs of $4 million, and prospective sales of $3 million what does it do in the short run?

20 If the firm operates, it has sales of $3 million, and its total cost is $9 million. Thus, it would lose $6 million. If it shuts down, it loses just its $5 million in fixed cost. Answer: It shuts down.

21 ### The Go-Out-of-Business Decision

A firm has two options in the long run: stay in business or go out of business. It will stay in business if it is at least breaking even (or, preferably, making a profit); if it is losing money, it will go out of business.

22 What will a firm do in the long run if it has fixed costs of $5 billion, variable costs of $8 billion, and prospective sales of $12 billion?

23 In the long run the firm will go out of business because it is losing money. How much money is it losing? If it operates, it will lose $1 billion. If it shuts down, it will lose $5 billion (its fixed costs). So either way, it will lose money in the long run and go out of business.

24 What will a firm do in the long run if it has fixed costs of $8 billion, variable costs of $9 billion, and prospective sales of $18 billion?

25 It will stay in business in the long run because it will be making a profit: prospective sales of $18 billion minus total cost of $17 billion equals $1 billion profit.
Are you ready to make up another general rule? The firm will stay in business in the long run if _____ are greater than _____ . Go back over the last two problems and see if you can derive this general rule.

26 | The firm will stay in business in the long run if *prospective sales* are greater than *total cost*.

Self-Test 1

1. A business firm's costs may be divided into two categories: _____ costs and _____ costs.
2. As output rises
   A. Fixed cost falls.
   B. Variable cost falls.
   C. Total cost falls.
   D. Variable cost rises.
3. A guaranteed salary is an example of a _____ cost.
4. Complete this table:

Output	Fixed Cost	Variable Cost	Total Cost	Average Fixed Cost	Average Variable Cost	Average Total Cost
1	$400	$200				
2		350				
3		550				
4		800				

5. The objective of every business firm is to _____.
6. The dividing line between the short run and the long run is
   _____.
7. In the short run a firm has two options: to _____ or to
   _____.
8. In the long run a firm has two options: to _____ or to
   _____.
9. If a firm has fixed costs of $10 million, variable costs of $12 million, and prospective sales of $20 million, what will it do in the short run? In the long run?
10. If a firm has fixed costs of $8 million, variable costs of $10 million, and prospective sales of $20 million, what will the firm do in the short run? In the long run?
11. In the short run a firm will operate if _____ are greater than
    _____.
12. In the long run a firm will stay in business if _____ are greater than
    _____.

Answers to Self-Test 1

1. Fixed; variable.
2. D.
3. Fixed.

4.

Output	Fixed Cost	Variable Cost	Total Cost	Average Fixed Cost	Average Variable Cost	Average Total Cost
1	$400	$200	$600	$400	$200	$600
2		350	750	200	175	375
3		550	950	133.33	183.33	316.67
4		800	1200	100	200	300

5. Maximize profits.

6. The time it takes for a firm to enter or leave an industry, or the time it takes for all fixed costs to become variable costs.

7. Operate; shut down.

8. Stay in business; go out of business.

9. Operate in the short run; go out of business in the long run.

10. Operate in the short run; stay in business in the long run.

11. Prospective sales; variable costs.

12. Prospective sales; total costs.

27 | **AVERAGE COST**

Average Fixed Cost (AFC)

Are you ready for some easy division? That's all you need to do here.

Average fixed cost = Fixed cost/Output

Using this formula and data from Table 13.3, calculate average fixed cost for outputs 1 through 6.

28 | Check your results with those in Table 13.4. If you had trouble with this, go to frame 29; otherwise, go to frame 30.

29 | Here's how we got the answers. When the output is 1, we divided fixed cost, $1000, by 1. Any number divided by 1 is that number.

When the output is 2, average fixed cost is $1000/2 = $500. Similarly, when output is 3: $1000/3 = $333.33; $1000/4 = $250; $1000/5 = $200; and $1000/6 = $167.67.

Table 13.3.

Output	Fixed Cost	Variable Cost	Total Cost
0	$1000		$1000
1	1000	$500	1500
2	1000	900	1900
3	1000	1300	2300
4	1000	1800	2800
5	1000	2400	3400
6	1000	3200	4200

Table 13.4. Hypothetical Demand and Supply Schedules

Output	Fixed Cost	Average Fixed Cost
1	$1000	$1000
2		500
3		333.33
4		250
5		200
6		167.67

---

30 | ## Average Variable Cost (AVC)

Average variable cost = variable cost/Output

Use the data in Table 13.3 to find average variable cost for outputs 1 through 6.

31 | You'll find the answers in Table 13.5. If your answers came out right, go on to frame 33; otherwise, go to frame 32.

32 | Here are the solutions: When output is 1, average variable cost = $500/1 = $500; when the output is 2, AVC = $900/2 = $450; at output 3, $1300/3 = $433.33; and so forth.

33 | ## Average Total Cost (ATC)

Average total cost = Total cost/Output

Again using the information in Table 13.3, find ATC for outputs 1 through 6.

34 | Your answers should match the figures in Table 13.6. You might have noticed that AFC plus AVC equals ATC. So, instead of finding average total cost by dividing total cost by output, you could add average fixed cost and average variable cost. But I would suggest that you find average total cost the way we did, by dividing total cost by output. Then check your work by adding average

Table 13.5. Hypothetical Demand and Supply Schedules

Output	Variable Cost	Average Variable Cost
1	$ 500	$500
2	900	450
3	1300	433.33
4	1800	450
5	2400	480
6	3200	533.33

Table 13.6.

Output	Average Total Cost
1	$1000
2	1350
3	1733.33
4	2250
5	2880
6	3733.33

fixed cost and average variable cost and seeing if they add up to average total cost. If they don't, check your work for mistakes.

35 | MARGINAL COST (MC)

Marginal cost is the additional cost of producing one more unit of output. Let's figure out the marginal cost of producing a second unit of output in Table 13.3. When output is one, total cost is $1500; when output is two, total cost is $1900. Can you figure out the marginal cost?

36   Marginal cost is $400. How did we get it? We subtracted the total cost of producing one unit of output, $1500, from the total cost of producing two units, $1900.

37   Find the marginal cost for the third, fourth, fifth, and sixth units of output from Table 13.3.

38   Here are the answers: The third unit of output has a marginal cost of $400; the fourth, $500; the fifth, $600; and the sixth, $800.
        If you got these right, go to frame 40; otherwise, go to frame 39.

39   To find the marginal cost of the third unit of output, we subtract total cost of two units ($1900) from the total cost of three units ($2300), which gives us $400. For four units of output: total cost of four units ($2800) minus total cost of three units ($2300) equals $500. For five units of output: $3400 − $2800 = $600. And, finally, for six units of output: $4200 − $3400 = $800.

40   We've saved the best for last. Find the marginal cost of one unit of output. Work out the problem and check your answer against that in frame 41.

41   At an output of one, marginal cost equals $500. How did we get this? The same way we got marginal cost for outputs 2 through 6. We subtracted total cost at an output of zero from total cost at an output of one.
        We know that total cost is $1500 at an output of one. How much is total cost at an output of zero?

42 Remember that when the output is zero, total cost is *not* zero: Total cost = fixed cost. If this gives you difficulty, go back to frame 10, where we explained how to calculate total cost at an output of zero.

So, how much is total cost at an output of zero? It is equal to fixed cost, which happens to be $1000. We now subtract total cost at an output of zero ($1000) from total cost at an output of one ($1500), and we get a marginal cost of $500 at an output of one.

If all of this seems confusing, go to frame 35; if you understand the material, go to frame 45.

43 Given the information in Table 13.7, find the marginal cost for outputs 1, 2, 3, and 4.

44 Here are the answers: at an output of one, marginal cost is $300; at output 2, it is $200; at output 3, it is $300; and at output 4, it is $550.

If you got these right, go to frame 46; otherwise, go to frame 45.

45 At an output of one we take the total cost, which is $700, and subtract the total cost when the output is zero, which is $400 (the fixed cost). We get $300. The other problems are more straightforward:

- At output 2, we subtract total cost at output 1 ($700) from total cost at output 2 ($900), and we get $200.
- At output 3, we subtract total cost at output 2 ($900) from total cost at output 3 ($1200), and we get $300.
- At output 4, we subtract total cost at output 3 ($1200) from total cost at output 4 ($1750), and we get $550.

46 Let's put all of this data in a table. Given the information in Table 13.8, calculate total cost, average fixed cost, average variable cost, average total cost, and marginal cost.

47 Check your results with those in Table 13.9. If your average fixed cost figures were off, go over frames 27 to 29. If your average variable cost figures were off, go over frames 30 to 22. If your average total cost figures were off, go over frames 33 to 34. And if your marginal cost figures were off, go over frames 35 to 45.

Table 13.7.

Output	Fixed Cost	Total Cost
1	$400	$700
2		900
3		1200
4		1750

Table 13.8. Hypothetical Cost Schedule

Output	Variable Cost	Total Cost	AFC	AVC	ATC	Marginal Cost
1	$100					
2	150					
3	210					
4	300					
5	430					
6	600					
7	819					

Note: Fixed cost = $400

48 | GRAPHING THE COST CURVES

Before beginning this frame, you might want to review frames 1 to 4 of Chapter 3. You will need to be comfortable drawing graphs, because that's what you're going to be doing for the rest of this chapter.

49 | Much of microeconomics involves three steps: (1) filling in a table, (2) drawing a graph based on that table, and (3) doing an analysis of the graph. We're ready for the second step—drawing a graph.

We are going to be drawing graphs of the average variable cost, average total cost, and marginal cost curves. We will *not* be graphing the average fixed cost curve, however. Why not? Because we will need the other curves for analytical purposes, but the average fixed cost curve would not be of any analytical use. Later on, we will determine the most profitable output of the firm and decide whether the firm should shut down or stay in business.

Here's an important point to remember: When you draw these curves, always start with the marginal cost curve and *then* draw the average variable cost and average total cost curves. Why? Because you'll need to use the marginal cost curve to help you determine the minimum points of the average variable and average total cost curves. Unless you first draw the marginal cost curve, you will not be able to draw the other two curves accurately. Let's see why this is true.

When the marginal cost curve (MC) is below the average variable cost curve (AVC), the AVC curve will be declining. For instance, when output rises from 2

Table 13.9. Hypothetical Cost Schedule

Output	Variable Cost	Total Cost	AFC	AVC	ATC	Marginal Cost
1	$100	$500	$400	$100	$500	$100
2	150	550	200	75	275	50
3	210	610	133	70	203	60
4	300	700	100	75	175	90
5	430	830	80	86	166	130
6	600	1000	67	100	167	170
7	819	1219	57	117	174	219

to 3 (in Table 13.3), AVC falls from $450 to $433.33 (in Table 13.5). As long as the MC is below the AVC, the AVC will be falling. But once the MC intersects the AVC and rises above it, the AVC will rise. When output goes from 3 to 4, for example, MC rises above AVC: MC goes from $400 to $600, while AVC rises from $433.33 to $450.

The same relationship applies to the MC and average total cost (ATC) curves. This "proof" may not be all that convincing. If you should ever happen to take my microeconomics course, I will put on a whole dog and pony show, which will convince even the most skeptical observer that the MC curve does indeed intersect the AVC and ATC curves at their minimum points.

50 | ## Graphing the Marginal Cost Curve

Before you draw a graph, you should plan it carefully. First, label both axes. Next, figure out how high you'll need to go. Then figure out your scale: Will each box on your graph paper represent $5, $10, or $20.

Using the data from Table 13.9, draw a marginal cost curve on the graph in Figure 13.1. Before you start to draw the curve, set up your graph properly. How low does the graph go? And how high?

51 | The high point on this graph is $500, which is the average total cost at an output of 1. The low point is $50, the marginal cost at an output of 2. These high and low points are already set up in Figure 13.1, but in future graphs, you

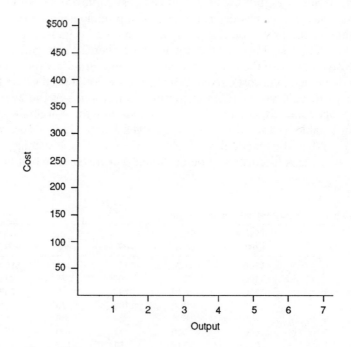

Figure 13.1

will have to figure out your own high and low points before you begin to draw your curves.

Once you've set up your graph, go ahead and plot the MC, AVC, and ATC curves. Remember to plot the MC curve first. Then make sure it intersects the AVC and ATC curves at their minimum points. Draw these curves freehand. Using a ruler is likely to throw you off at those critical low points.

52   Once you've drawn your curves in Figure 13.1, check your results against those in Figure 13.2. Then we'll start our analysis. State the low points of your AVC and ATC curves in dollars and cents.

53   I would estimate the lowest point on the AVC curve at $69. What was your answer? It should definitely be a little below $70. How do I know this? If we go back to Table 13.9, we see that the lowest AVC listed is $70. But this isn't the lowest point of the AVC curve. The lowest point of that curve is the point at which it is intersected by the MC curve. So your answer should be a little below $70—say, $69.90, $69.50, $69.25, $68.90, or thereabouts.

54   By applying the same logic, we would estimate the lowest point of the ATC curve as $165.25 or thereabouts. It should be a little below $166, which is the lowest ATC listed in Table 13.9.

Keep in mind that we are looking for the *lowest* point on the ATC curve, and that is the point at which the MC curve intersects with the ATC curve.

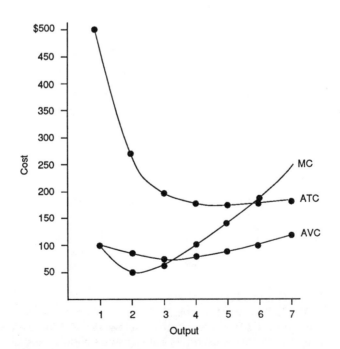

Figure 13.2

55 | Most people have problems with these estimates the first time around. We'll be doing more graphs, however, so you'll have ample opportunity to redeem yourself if you haven't yet caught on.

Self-Test 2

1. As the output rises, what happens to average fixed cost?
2. At an output of 1, variable cost is $100 and fixed cost is $200. How much is marginal cost when the output is 1?
3. At an output of zero, total cost is always equal to _____ .
4. Given the information below and assuming a fixed cost of $100:
   A. Fill in total cost, average fixed cost, average variable cost, average total cost, and marginal cost.
   B. Draw a graph of the MC, AVC, and ATC curves.
   C. State the lowest points on the AVC and ATC curve in dollars and cents.

Output	Variable Cost	Total Cost	AFC	AVC	ATC	Marginal Cost
1	$50					
2	70					
3	100					
4	150					
5	225					
6	340					

Answers to Self-Test 2

1. It falls.
2. Total cost at output 1 ($300) minus total cost at output 0 ($200) equals $100.
3. Fixed cost.
4. A.

Output	Variable Cost	Total Cost	AFC	AVC	ATC	Marginal Cost
1	$50	$150	$100	$50	$150	$50
2	70	170	50	35	85	20
3	100	200	33.33	33.33	66.67	30
4	150	250	25	37.50	62.50	50
5	225	325	20	45	65	75
6	340	440	16.67	56.57	73.33	115

B. See Figure 13.3.
C. The lowest point on the AVC curve is slightly below $33.33, and the lowest point on the ATC curve is slightly below $62.50. (These are not the only acceptable answers to question 4. Your answers should be slightly below $33.33 for AVC and slightly below $62.20 for ATC because we want *minimum* points on the AVC and ATC curves.)

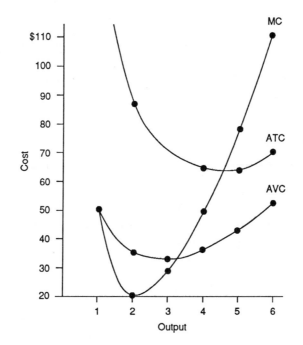

Figure 13.3 Answer to question 4B of Self-Test 2

---

56 | TOTAL REVENUE AND MARGINAL REVENUE

Revenue is the proceeds from the sales of a business firm. As you would expect, as output rises, revenue rises as well.

57 | Total Revenue

We find total revenue by multiplying price times output. For the sake of simplicity, we'll assume that the seller can sell as much output as he or she wants to at a price per unit of $4.

Fill in the total revenue column of Table 13.10. Then check your answer against Table 13.11.

Table 13.10.

Output	Price	Total Revenue	Marginal Revenue
1	$4		
2	4		
3	4		
4	4		

Table 13.11.

Output	Price	Total Revenue
1	$4	$4
2	4	8
3	4	12
4	4	16

58 | Marginal Revenue

Marginal revenue is parallel to marginal cost. It is the additional revenue derived from selling one more unit of output. This is an extremely important tool in economic analysis, as we shall soon see.

Go back to Table 13.10 and fill in the marginal revenue column. Then check your answers by glancing at Table 13.12.

59   Marginal revenue for this seller is a constant—$4. Remember that the seller can sell as much as he or she wants to at that price. Therefore, each unit sold adds another $4 to total revenue.

60 | Graphing the Demand and Marginal Revenue Curves

Do you recall the definition of demand, stated in frame 1 of Chapter 12? Demand is a schedule of quantities that people are willing and able to buy at different prices. We have used that definition on an industry-wide basis and on a market basis. Now we'll apply it to a single business firm.

The demand for an individual firm's product is the schedule of quantities that people are willing and able to buy at different prices. What do we know about the demand schedule for this particular firm's product? We know it can sell an unlimited quantity at $4 a unit. But we know nothing about how much it could sell at other prices. (It doesn't matter how much the firm could sell at *less* than $4, does it? If you could sell your entire output at $4 a unit, would you care how much you could sell at $3.99?

Are you ready to draw the firm's demand curve? Okay, then, given it your best try in Figure 13.4.

61   Compare your graph with the one in Figure 13.5.

Now try another one. Suppose you could sell your entire output at $7 a unit. Draw your demand curve in Figure 13.6. Then check your graph against Figure 13.7. As you can see, this is pretty simple—just a horizontal line at the given price.

Table 13.12.

Output	Marginal Revenue
1	$4
2	4
3	4
4	4

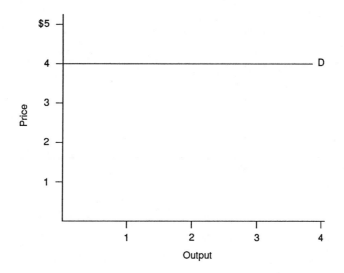

Figure 13.4

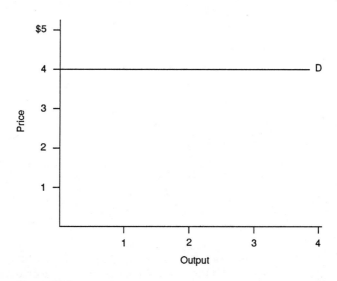

Figure 13.5

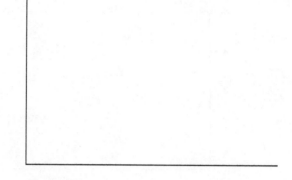

Figure 13.6

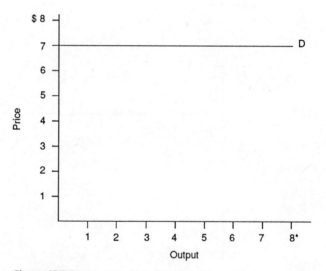

Figure 13.7
Note: Output has been set here at 8. This number has been picked arbitrarily. The only ouput specification was that you can sell as much as you want; so, if you picked an output of 4, or 10, or 100, that's fine, too.

Figure 13.8

62   Are you ready to do some marginal revenue curves? Very well, then, using the data in Table 13.10, draw the marginal revenue curve in Figure 13.8. Then check your work against Figure 13.9.

Do you notice a close resemblance between Figures 13.9 and 13.5? You should; they're identical. The marginal revenue curve is identical to the demand curve when the price is constant; in other words, if you can sell as much as you want to at a constant price, marginal revenue will be equal to price.

63   We'll try one more problem. If the price is $6, fill in the total revenue and marginal revenue columns of Table 13.13 and then draw a graph of the demand curve and the marginal revenue curve in Figure 13.10. When you've done this, compare your work with Table 13.14 and Figure 13.11.

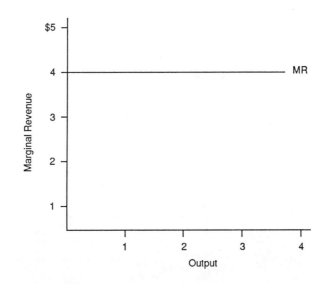

Figure 13.9

Table 13.13.

Output	Total Revenue	Marginal Revenue
1		
2		
3		
4		
5		

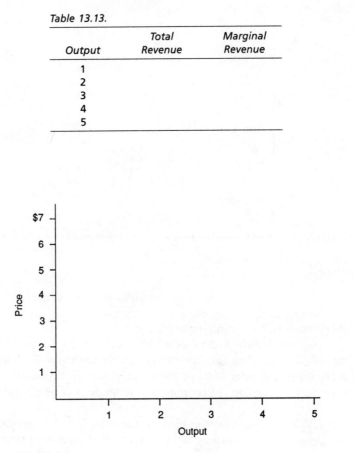

Figure 13.10

Table 13.14.

Output	Total Revenue	Marginal Revenue
1	$6	$6
2	12	6
3	18	6
4	24	6
5	30	6

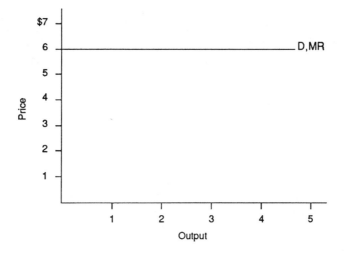

Figure 13.11

64 | MARGINAL ANALYSIS: PROFIT MAXIMIZATION AND LOSS MINIMIZATION

Marginal analysis is central to microeconomics. Economists love to study economic life at the margin. What we'll be looking at here is the point at which marginal cost equals marginal revenue. The output level at which this occurs is our most profitable one. (Or, if a firm is losing money, this output level is the one at which losses are minimal.)

We'll begin by setting up Table 13.15. Fill in the total revenue, marginal revenue, ATC, AVC, and MC columns. Fixed cost is $50, and price is $70. How can you find total profit?

65 |

Total profit = Total cost − Total revenue

Fill in the total profit column as well. Then check your work against Table 13.16.

66 |

According to the total profit column in Table 13.6, we can maximize our profit at an output of 5. But we can do even better than a profit of $20. We'll prove that by means of graphical analysis.

Table 13.15.

Output	Total Revenue	Variable Cost	Total Cost	AVC	ATC	MC	Total Profit
1		$100					
2		150					
3		180					
4		216					
5		280					
6		380					

Table 13.16.

Output	Total Revenue	Variable Cost	Total Cost	AVC	ATC	MC	Total Profit
1	$70	$100	$150	$100	$150	$100	−$80
2	140	150	200	75	100	50	−60
3	210	180	230	60	76.67	30	−20
4	280	216	266	54	66.50	36	14
5	350	280	330	56	66	64	20
6	420	380	430	63.33	71.67	100	−10

I'd like you to draw a graph of these five curves in Figure 13.12, using the data in Table 13.16. Graph the demand and marginal revenue, the marginal cost, the average total cost, and the average variable cost. Of course, you'll draw only four lines, since the demand and marginal revenue curves are identical. Check your graph against Figure 13.13.

67   You need to pay particular attention to two points on the graph: the lowest points of your AVC and ATC curves, where they are intersected by the MC curve. Make sure that that's how you've drawn your graph.

68   Now we're going to prove that the firm maximizes its profits at the point where the marginal cost and marginal revenue curves intersect. We'll start by going back to the definitions of marginal cost and marginal revenue: They are the additional cost and the additional revenue from producing and selling one more unit of output.

If we are producing a certain amount of output, we can ask ourselves if it would be more profitable to produce an additional unit of output. If that

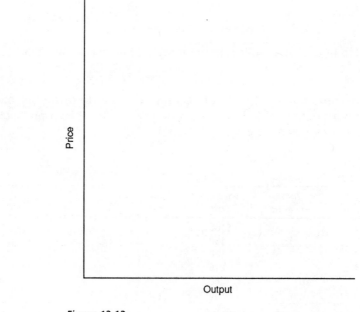

Figure 13.12

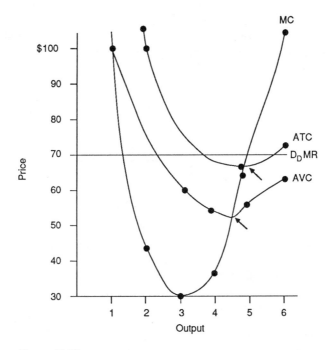

Figure 13.13

additional unit of output would add more to total revenue than to total cost, then it certainly would increase our profits. In other words, when marginal revenue is greater than marginal cost, it would pay to expand output.

In fact, it would pay to keep expanding output until that point where marginal revenue and marginal cost are equal. On the graph that happens at an output of about 5.2. Assuming that we can produce fractions of a unit of output, rather than just whole numbers of output, then we would be maximizing our profits at 5.2 units of output. In Table 13.15, where we are limited to outputs denominated in whole numbers (i.e., 1, 2, 3, 4, 5, and 6), we maximize our profits at an output of 5 with a profit of $20. But at an output of 5.2, we can do somewhat better.

To calculate our total profit at an output of 5.2 we'll start with this general equation:

$$\text{Total revenue} - \text{Total cost} = \text{Total profit}.$$

How do we calculate total revenue at an output of 5.2? See if you can work that out.

69   At an output of 5.2 the price is still $70: $70 × 5.2 = $364. Keep in mind that you find total revenue by multiplying price times output.

Finding total cost at an output of 5.2 is a little trickier. If we multiply price times output to get total revenue, what must we multiply by output to get total revenue?

70   If you haven't been able to figure it out yet, I'll give you a hint. Total cost divided by output equals what?

71   The answer is average total cost.
      Now we should be ready to do business. To find total cost, multiply ATC times output. How much was our output? It was 5.2. Okay, how much is average total cost at an output of 5.2?

72   In Figure 13.13 it looks like $66.00 or $66.05. If we use $66.05, total cost would be $343.46. Given all this information, how much is our total profit?

73   Total profit comes to $20.54: total revenue ($364) − total cost ($343.46) = total profit ($20.54).
      How much would total profit have been if ATC had been exactly $66?

74   Total profit would have been $20.80: total revenue ($364) − total cost ($343.20) = total profit ($20.80).
      We've just shown that the firm will maximize its profits at an output of 5.2 rather than 5.

75   Now we're going to minimize a firm's losses. To do so, we'll use exactly the same type of analysis. Start by filling in the columns of Table 13.17, assuming a price of $120 and a fixed cost of $200. Then check your figures against the ones in Table 13.18.

76   Now, using Figure 13.14, draw a graph of the demand, marginal revenue, marginal cost, average variable cost, and average total cost curves. Be particularly careful when you graph the lowest points of the average variable cost and average total cost curves. Compare your results with those in Figure 13.15.
      After you've checked your graph, state the dollar-and-cents value of these curves at their lowest points.

77   The lowest point of the AVC curve is about $78.90. (It must be below $79, because the MC curve intersects the AVC at an output of slightly more than 4, the output at which AVC is exactly $79.) Similarly, the minimum point of the ATC curve is about $121. (It would have to be below $122, which occurs at an output of 5.)
      Now we're going to estimate total profit. Using the figures from Table 13.17, your total profit reaches a maximum of how much?

78   At an output of 5 there is a total profit of −$10. That means that according to Table 13.17, the best we can do is lose $10. By doing graphical analysis, however, we'll find a way of losing less.
      To do this, we need to find output first. So exactly how much is output?

79   I would say that output is 5.4, which is the point at which MC and MR curves cross. Using 5.4 as output, find total profit.

Table 13.17.

Output	Total Revenue	Variable Cost	Total Cost	AVC	ATC	MC	Total Profit
1		$100					
2		180					
3		240					
4		316					
5		410					
6		600					

Table 13.18.

Output	Total Revenue	Variable Cost	Total Cost	AVC	ATC	MC	Total Profit
1	$120	$100	$300	$100	$300	$100	−$180
2	240	180	380	90	190	80	−140
3	360	240	440	80	146.67	60	−80
4	480	316	516	79	129	76	−36
5	600	410	610	82	122	94	−10
6	720	600	800	100	133.33	190	−80

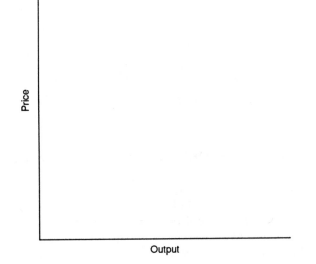

Figure 13.14

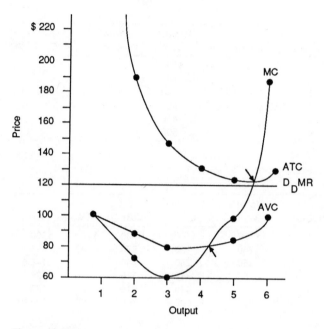

Figure 13.15

80   You should have reached your solution by means of the following formulas:

Total profit = Total revenue − Total cost

Total revenue = Price × Output = $120 × 5.4 = $648

Total cost = ATC × Output = $121.01 × 5.4 = $653.45

Total profit =   − $5.45

Total revenue ($648) − Total cost ($653.45) =   − $5.45

81   ## DERIVATION OF SHORT-RUN AND LONG-RUN SUPPLY CURVES

Don't worry; it's almost over. This is the last topic of the chapter.

In frames 17 and 18 of this chapter we derived this general rule: The firm will continue to operate if prospective sales are greater than variable costs; the firm will shut down if variable costs are greater than prospective sales.

Now we're going to state that general rule in unit, or average, terms rather than in aggregate, or total, terms. We'll do this by dividing prospective sales by output and by dividing variable cost by output. Think of prospective sales as total revenue. Go ahead and divide variable cost by output. Then divide total revenue by output. (Remember that total revenue = something × output).

$$\frac{\text{Variable cost}}{\text{Output}} = ?$$

$$\frac{\text{Total revenue}}{\text{Output}} = ?$$

82

$$\frac{\text{Variable cost}}{\text{Output}} = \text{Average variable cost}$$

$$\frac{\text{Total revenue}}{\text{Output}} = \text{Price}$$

Okay, then, we said that the firm will operate if prospective sales are greater than variable costs, so the firm will also operate if _____ is greater than _____ .

83

The firm will operate if price is greater than average variable cost.

Back in frames 25 and 26 we derived a second general rule: The firm will stay in business in the long run if prospective sales are greater than total cost.

State this rule in unit or average terms.

84

The firm will stay in business in the long run if price is greater than average total cost.

What we're saying is that the firm will not stay in business in the long run unless it is at least breaking even. On the graph this is identified as the break-even point. See if you can find this point in Figure 13.15.

85

The break-even point is the lowest point on the ATC curve (the point at which the ATC curve is intersected by the MC curve—and at which the arrow is pointing). The firm cannot possibly stay in business if the price is below the break-even point.

Next we'll find the shutdown point. The firm will operate as long as price is at least equal to average variable cost. See if you can locate the shutdown point in Figure 13.15.

86

The shutdown point is the lowest point on the AVC curve, where the AVC curve is intersected by the MU curve (and where the arrow is pointing).

Before we go on, we need to recall one last bit of information: The firm always operates where _____ is equal to _____ .

87

The answer? where marginal cost is equal to marginal revenue. That is the output at which the firm maximizes its profits.

Let's look once again at Figure 13.15. Suppose that the price happened to be $190—suppose, in other words, that the demand curve and the marginal revenue curve are depicted by horizontal line at a price of $190. How much would output be?

88

Output would be 6. How do we know this? Because at an output of 6, MC = MR.

How much would output be if the price were $135?

89

It would be about 5.6. How do we know this? Because at an output of 5.6, MC = MR.

How much would output be if the price were $100? There are two answers here: the firm's output in the short run and its output in the long run.

90

In the short run the output is about 5.02. In the long run the output is zero. Why is the output zero in the long run?

91   The long-run output is zero for two reasons: (1) a price of $100 is below the break-even point and (2) the firm can't produce at an ATC of less than $121, so at a price of $100 it would be losing at least $21 a unit. Since it has the option of going out of business in the long run, it will exercise that option and therefore produce nothing. The short run, however, is a different story. Because a price of $100 is above the shutdown point, the firm will operate at that price, even though it will lose money.

    How much will the firm's output be in the short run and in the long run when the price is $70?

92   In both the short run and the long run the output will be zero because the price is below both the shutdown and break-even points.

    We have derived two more general rules: (1) in the short run output will be zero at prices below the shutdown point; (2) in the long run output will be zero at prices below the break-even point.

    If prices are above the shutdown point but below the break-even point, what will the firm do in the short run and the long run?

93   In the short run the firm will operate, producing *some* output. In the long run the output will be zero.

    How much output will the firm produce in the short run? That depends on price. Look back once again at Figure 13.15. Suppose we made up twenty different prices between the shutdown point and the break-even point: $79, $80, $81, $82, and so on. In each instance, we would find the short-run output at the intersection of the MC and MR curves. Therefore, if we happen to have an MC curve like that in Figure 13.15, it is, in effect, the firm's supply curve.

    Remember the definition of supply from frame 4 of Chapter 12: Supply is the schedule of quantities of a good or service that people are willing and able to sell at different prices.

    But we've got to be careful here. The firm's short-run supply curve begins at the shutdown point and moves all the way up the MC curve as far as it goes. It doesn't stop at the break-even point.

    See if you can describe the firm's long-run supply curve.

94   The firm's long-run supply curve begins at the break-even point and runs up the MC curve as far as it goes.

Self-Test 3

1. Fill in the table below.

Output	Total Revenue	Variable Cost	Total Cost	AVC	ATC	MC	Total Profit
1		$100					
2		150					
3		210					
4		284					
5		375					
6		500					

2. On separate paper, draw a graph of the firm's demand, marginal revenue, marginal cost, average variable cost, and average total cost curves. Assuming a fixed cost of $100 and a price of $100, label the firm's shutdown and break-even points on the graph.

3. Using the data from the table in question 1, calculate the firm's total profit.

4. Label the firm's break-even and shutdown points on the graph you drew in answer to question 2.

5. What minimum price would the firm accept in the short run and in the long run?

6. If the price is $125, how much will the firm's output be in the short run and in the long run?

7. If the price is $90, how much will the firm's output be in the short run and in the long run?

8. If the price is $60, how much will the firm's output be in the short run and in the long run?

9. In the short run the firm will operate if price is greater than _____ .

10. In the long run the firm will stay in business if price is greater than _____ .

11. The firm will always produce at that output at which _____ equals _____ .

12. The firm's short-run supply curve starts at the _____ and runs _____ .

13. The firm's long-run supply curve starts at the _____ and runs _____ .

Answers to Self-Test 3

1.

Output	Total Revenue	Variable Cost	Total Cost	AVC	ATC	MC	Total Profit
1	$120	$100	$200	$100	$200	$100	−$100
2	200	150	250	75	125	50	−50
3	300	210	310	70	103.33	60	−10
4	400	284	384	71	96	74	16
5	500	375	475	75	95	91	25
6	600	500	600	83.33	100	125	0

2. See Figure 13.16.

3. Total profit = Total revenue − Total cost

$$\text{Total revenue} = \text{Price} \times \text{Output} = \$100 \times 5.35 = \$535$$

$$\text{Total cost} = \text{ATC} \times \text{Output} = \$95 \times 5.35 = \$508.25$$

$$\text{Total profit} = \text{Total revenue} (\$535) - \text{Total cost} (\$506.25) = \$26.75$$

4. See Figure 13.16.

5. $69.60 in the short run (must be a little less than $70); $94.95 in the long run (must be a little less than $95).

6. 6 in the short run; 6 in the long run.

7. 4.98 in the short run (at a price of $91, output would be 5); zero in the long run.

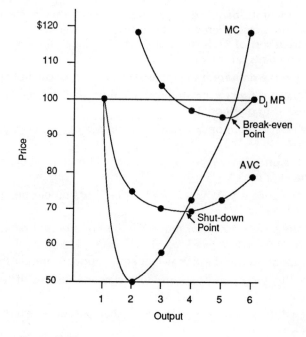

Figure 13.16

8. Zero in both the long and short run.
9. Average variable cost.
10. Average total cost.
11. Marginal cost equals marginal revenue.
12. Shutdown point; all the way up the firm's supply curve.
13. Break-even point; all the way up the firm's supply curve.

PART 5

MICROECONOMICS:

FOUR MODELS

OF COMPETITION

CHAPTER 14

Perfect Competition

and

Monopoly

Perfect competition and monopoly stand at the opposite ends of the economic spectrum. In a perfect competition there are many sellers; in a monopoly there is only one seller. While the monopolist produces the industry's entire output, the perfect competitor produces only an infinitesimal fraction. Still another significant difference between the two is that while the monopolist decides what price to charge, the perfect competitor is a price taker, having virtually no influence on the market price. After you have completed this chapter you will:

- Know the three key characteristics of perfect competition.
- Be able to calculate the profits and losses of the perfect competitor in the short run.
- Understand why the perfect competitor always breaks even in the long run.
- Understand why the perfect competitor is forced to operate at peak efficiency in the long run.
- Know the three bases of monopoly.
- Be able to calculate the monopolist's profit.
- Understand why the monopolist does not operate at peak efficiency.

1 | PERFECT COMPETITION DEFINED

A perfectly competitive industry has three key characteristics: (1) there are many sellers, (2) they all sell the same product, and (3) there is free entry into the industry.

2 | Many Sellers

When we say there are "many" sellers, what do we mean? Fifty sellers? A couple of hundred? A thousand? The answer to the question is: so many that no one firm is large enough to have any appreciable influence over price. So, what we're talking about is many small competing firms.

The most drastic thing a firm can do to influence price is to enter or leave the industry. If a firm enters the industry and puts its entire output on the market, what will happen to industry supply? Obviously it will rise. Will this increased supply affect price? Not significantly.

Even though the supply does increase, that increase is not large enough to push down the price very much. Similarly, if a firm left the perfectly competitive industry, output would decline, but not by enough to raise the industry price appreciably.

3 | The Same Product

All of the firms in a perfectly competitive industry sell an identical product. This doesn't necessarily mean that the product made by one firm is exactly identical to the one produced by another firm. It simply means that the buyers regard the two products as the same thing. The buyers think of them as homogeneous or generic.

Suppose all buyers consider a hamburger a hamburger, whether it's done their way, whether it's delivered in a crispy poppyseed bun or between two pieces of soggy white bread, whether it's called a Big Mac, a Whopper, or a dogburger. If every buyer thinks all burgers are the same, then they *are* identical, even though there may be marked physical differences between the ones produced by company A and those turned out by company B.

4 | Free Entry

In perfectly competitive industries, firms are free to enter or leave the industry. No one will place any obstacles in the way of new firms that wish to enter, nor will any institutional obstacles be placed in the way of existing firms wishing to leave the industry. (Of course, the firm would have to discharge all of its legal obligations such as leases, guaranteed contracts, and so on.)

5 | EXAMPLES OF PERFECTLY COMPETITIVE INDUSTRIES

We would be hard put to think of any real-world examples of perfect competition, but American agriculture probably comes closest. There are certainly many producers of wheat, corn, soybeans, and other crops, and the buyers consider these crops identical regardless of whether they came from farm A, farm B, or farm C. Also, there are no major barriers to entry into farming, or to leaving the industry.

Since we can't think of any other examples of perfect competition, why discuss something that may not even exist. In economics, perfect competition is used as a straw man, which is almost immediately knocked down by reality. Here's the ideal against which real competition—and, of course, monopoly— can be measured. We'll see, for example, that a perfectly competitive industry operates at peak efficiency, allocating resources in an optimal manner, whereas, in reality, American business wastes and misallocates resources. So, we're using the perfectly competitive industry as a model to which real competition can be compared.

6 | THE DEMAND AND MARGINAL REVENUE CURVES OF THE PERFECT COMPETITOR

The perfect competitor's demand curve should be very familiar; you drew several examples of it in Chapter 13. It's a horizontal line, since perfect competitors can sell all they want to sell at the market price.

Where does the market price come from? It comes from the intersection of the demand and supply curves for the entire industry, as illustrated in Figure 14.1.

The perfect competitor's marginal revenue curve is identical to the firm's demand curve. The perfectly competitive firm's demand and marginal revenue curves are illustrated in Figures 14.2, and 14.3.

7 | THE PERFECT COMPETITOR IN THE SHORT RUN

There are three possible short-run profit situations for the perfect competitor: (1) the firm could be making a profit, (2) it could be taking a loss, or (3) it could be breaking even. We'll exclude the last possibility from consideration because its likelihood is about the same as that of tossing a coin and having it land on its side.

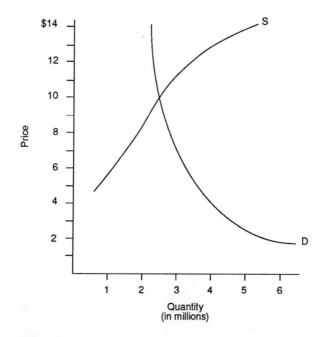

Figure 14.1

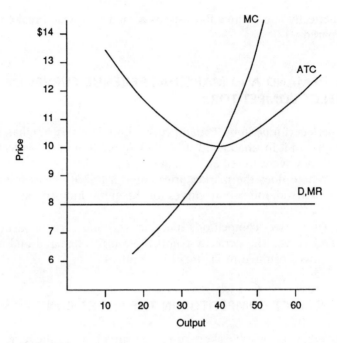

Figure 14.2

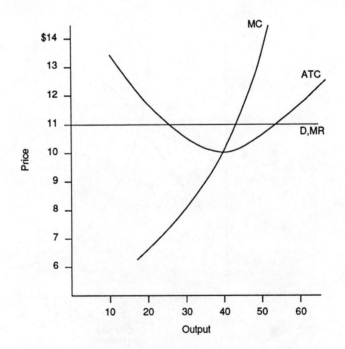

Figure 14.3

Figures 14.2 and 14.3 depict the two most likely short-run possibilities—the firm that is making a profit and the firm that is taking a loss. I'd like you to determine which is which.

8

Figure 14.2 shows the perfect competitor taking a loss in the short run. Figure 14.3 shows the firm making a profit in the short run.

How do we know this? If the ATC curve is above the demand curve for every possible output, the firm has to be losing money. How can you avoid taking a loss if your ATC is greater than your price?

By the same logic, if your price is greater than your ATC at *some* output, you're making a profit.

Here's another question: How much of a loss are you taking in Figure 14.2? To work out the answer, eliminate output (where MC = MR) and ATC. Then calculate your loss. Take your time and see if you can come up with a reasonable estimate.

9

$$\text{Total profit } = \text{Total revenue } - \text{ Total cost}$$

$$\text{Total profit } = \text{Price } \times \text{ Output } = \$8 \times 28.8 = \$230.40$$

$$\text{Total cost } = \text{ATC } \times \text{ Output } = \$10.70 \times 28.8 = \$308.16$$

$$\text{Total profit} = \text{Total revenue } (\$230.40) - \text{ Total cost } (\$308.16)$$
$$= -\$77.76 (\text{i.e., a loss of } \$77.76)$$

Now do the same thing with Figure 14.3. Work out your estimate of total profit.

10

$$\text{Total profit } = \text{Total revenue} - \text{Total cost}$$

$$\text{Total revenue } = \text{Price} \times \text{Output} = \$11 \times 43.2 = \$475.20$$

$$\text{Total cost } = \text{ATC} \times \text{Output} = \$10.12 \times 43.2 = \$437.18$$

$$\text{Total profit } = \text{Total revenue } (\$475.20) - \text{Total cost } (\$437.18) = \$38.02$$

A question may have occurred to you when we first mentioned that we were graphing the perfect competitor making a profit or taking a loss in the short run. How do we know it's the short run?

We've already developed an answer to how we know it's the short run if the firm is losing money. Way back in frames 2 to 26 of Chapter 13, what did we decide a firm would do in the long run if it was losing money?

11

It would go out of business in the long run. So, if we know a firm *is* losing money, it *must* be in the short run. Because no firm would stay in business if it kept losing money.

Now we're going to follow this reasoning to its logical conclusion. If the market price happens to be $8, as it is in Figure 14.2, what will ultimately happen to that market price in the long run if several firms leave the industry?

12

The market price will rise. This happens because market price rises when industry supply declines. We've summarized this process in Figure 14.4 (as supply rises from S_1 to S_2.)

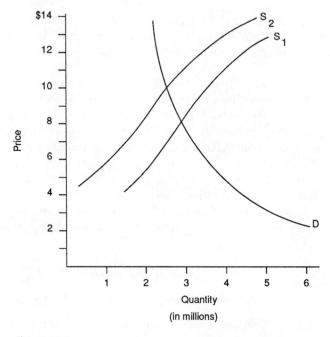

Figure 14.4

Let's do a modified version of the graph in Figure 14.2, using the higher market price. What will happen to the firm's demand curve?

13   It will rise to a level of $10, as shown in Figure 14.5.

Now let's see what happens when a perfect competitor is making a profit in the short run. Since, by definition, there are no barriers to entry into a perfectly competitive industry, new firms will enter this industry. Why? They'll be attracted by the profits being made by the existing firms.

So, industry supply rises. And what happens to the industry's equilibrium price? It declines. You can see all this in Figure 14.6.

How does this affect the individual perfectly competitive firm, which was making a profit in the short run? Just glance again at Figure 14.5. There's the firm in the long run.

Here's one last question for you. Calculate the profit being made by the perfect competitor in the long run (shown in Figure 14.5).

14   The profit is exactly zero. The firm products at an output of 40, at which MC = MR. At that output the demand curve is tangent to—in other words, just touching—the ATC curve: price = ATC = 10. At any other output how much profit would the firm be earning?

15   It wouldn't be earning *any* profit; it would be losing money. How do we know this? Look to the left of the output of 40 units. Notice that the ATC curve is above the demand curve. That means it would cost the firm more to produce

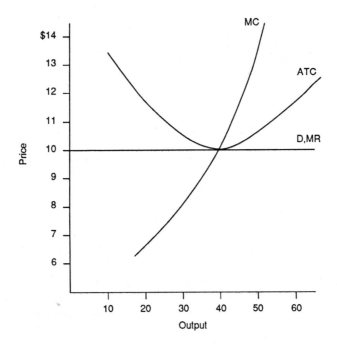

Figure 14.5

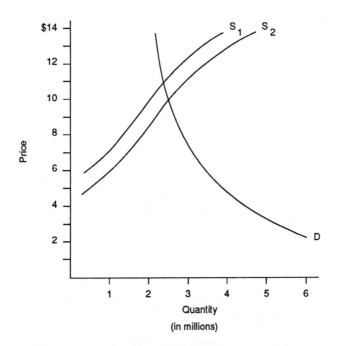

Figure 14.6

each unit than the firm would take in by selling a unit. Now look to the right of 40 units of output. Again, the ATC lies above the demand curve, showing that at these outputs the firm would be losing money.

So, in the long run the perfect competitor really has no choice of outputs whatsoever. If the firm produces at any output other than 40, it will lose money.

16 | PROFITS AND EFFICIENCY UNDER PERFECT COMPETITION

You've noticed that the perfect competitor produces at the lowest point on its ATC curve in the long run. (If this is still not clear to you, reread frame 14 and 15 and study Figure 14.5.) The firm is forced to do this because at any other output it would lose money. So, the firm's owners maximize their profits at zero profits.

This isn't as bad as it first appears. After the firm pays for the resources it uses—the land, labor, and capital—it also gets a fair return on the money that the owners invested in the business. In addition, the owners draw salaries that they could have earned if they had worked for someone else.

By operating at the minimum point of its ATC curve, the firm is operating at peak efficiency. Since economists equate efficiency with low ATC, this firm couldn't be any more efficient.

It is this aspect of perfect competition that has so enchanted economists. The perfect competitor, driven by competitors, is forced to operate at maximum efficiency. As we'll soon see, the same cannot be said of the monopolist, the monopolist competitor, and the oligopolist.

Self-Test 1

1. What are three key characteristics of a perfectly competitive industry?
2. What do we mean by "many," when we say there are "many sellers" in a perfectly competitive industry?
3. Who decides if one firm's product is the same as another's?
4. Describe the perfect competitor's demand curve.
5. How is market price determined?
6. What are the two likely profit situations for the perfect competitor in the short run?
7. What is the profit situation of the perfect competitor in the long run?
8. A. In the graph in Figure 14.7, is the firm making a profit, taking a loss, or breaking even?
   B. Is the firm in the short run or the long run?
   C. How much is the profit or loss?
9. The perfect competitor in the long run always operates at the _____ point of its ATC curve. This represents _____ efficiency.

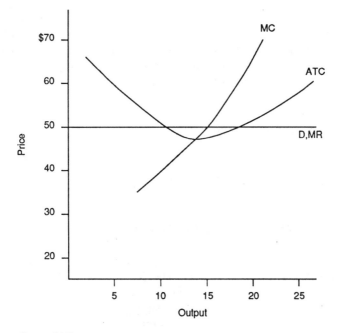

Figure 14.7

Answers to Self-Test 1

1. (1) It has many sellers, (2) they all sell the same product, and (3) there is free entry into the industry.
2. So many that no one firm is large enough to influence price.
3. The buyers.
4. A horizontal line.
5. By industry supply and demand.
6. Making a profit or taking a loss.
7. Breaking even.
8. A. Making a profit.
   B. The short run (in the long run the firm would break even).
   C. Total profit = Total revenue − Total cost.
      Total revenue = Price × Output = $50 × 14.9 = $710.73
      Total revenue ($745) − Total cost ($710.73) = Total profit $34.27
9. Minimum (or break even); peak (or maximum).

17 | MONOPOLY DEFINED

The monopolist is the sole supplier of a good or service for which there are no close substitutes. How close *is* close? Are lollipops close substitutes for cigarettes? If they were, there would be a lot more ex-smokers walking around licking all-day suckers, tootsie pops, and the like.

Once again, it is the buyer who decides if one product can be substituted for another. If you were the sole producer of toothpaste, but buyers were just as happy to brush their teeth with soap, you wouldn't have a true monopoly. If buyers consider soap a close substitute for toothpaste, then it is.

Often there are barriers to entry into a monopoly. After we consider those barriers, we'll talk about the monopolist's demand and marginal revenue curves. Then we will discuss the monopolist's profits and efficiency.

18 | THE BASES OF MONOPOLY

We shall consider, in turn, three bases for monopoly: (1) control of an essential resource, (2) a government franchise, and (3) getting there first.

19 | Control of an Essential Resource

The De Beers Diamond Company of South Africa controls about four-fifths of the world's diamond supply. The Metropolitan Opera Company of New York has under contract most of the world's opera stars. And, of course, the professional sports leagues control the supply of professional athletes. So, one basis of monopoly is the control of an essential resource.

20 | A Government Franchise

A second basis for monopoly is the possession of a government franchise. For many years, the Good Humor company had the exclusive privilege of selling ice cream in the New York City parks. Public Service is the only electric company in central New Jersey. Southern Bell provides all local telephone service in several southern states.

Why do local or state governments grant franchises to just one company to provide the electricity, gas, water, or local telephone service to their jurisdictions? Because it's more efficient than having scores of competing companies. Imagine having eight electric companies running cables under your street and periodically digging them up. Think of the difficulty you would have reaching people by phone if there were fifteen or twenty local telephone companies.

21 | Getting There First

Sometimes a company obtains a monopoly by virtue of getting there before anyone else. After all, someone almost always has to be first. IBM and Xerox are familiar examples of companies that did just that. To this day we say "make a xerox of that," which is a lot easier to say than "make an Addressograph-Multilith of that."

22 | BARRIERS TO ENTRY

Once a monopoly establishes itself, it's often very hard for new firms to enter the industry. Monopolies can take advantage of economies of scale, producing a large output at a relatively low ATC. Smaller firms, just getting started, simply do not have the financial capital to produce such a large output.

The automobile industry is a good case in point. Henry Ford introduced the assembly line back in the 1920s. A company had to be able to produce several hundred thousand cars a year in order to use this process. The number of automobile companies dropped within just a few years from a couple hundred to just eight or ten. In recent years the only new additions to the roster of automobile firms manufacturing cars in the United States have been Volkswagen (which subsequently pulled out) and a few Japanese firms, and these companies were big to start with.

Monopolies also enjoy the economies of being established. A new firm simply does not have the established network of suppliers and retail outlets that the older firms do. Nor does it have the access to capital and the name brand familiarity, as in "Things go better with Coke," or "You can be sure if it's Westinghouse," Nor are you a member of the "Pepsi generation."

23 | THE MONOPOLIST'S DEMAND AND MARGINAL REVENUE CURVES

The monopolist is in the unique position of facing the entire demand curve of the industry. As the only seller of a good or service for which there are no close substitutes, the monopolist can set whatever price he or she wants. But once that price is set, the quantity purchased is determined by how much people are willing and able to buy at that price.

Table 14.1 provides a demand scheduled for a hypothetical monopolist. Fill in the total revenue and marginal revenue columns. Then compare your results with the data in Table 14.2.

24   Now, using the same data, draw a demand and marginal revenue curve in Figure 14.8. Check your work against Figure 14.9.

25   I hope you drew an accurate graph in Figure 14.8 because you've just drawn your last graph—at least in *this* book. And you've filled in your last table. From here on in, you can sit back and watch me do all the work. I'll be applying a lot of the analytic concepts from the last two chapters to monopoly, and to the two remaining concepts—monopolistic competition and oligopoly.

26   Let's put everything together in one graph so we can do some analysis. Figure 14.10 shows our monopolist's demand and marginal revenue curves; it also shows the marginal cost and average total costs curves. These latter two curves are the same for firms in industries, whether they are perfect competitors, monopolists, monopolistic competitors, or oligopolists.

We'll be doing some analysis that's very similar to what we did in Chapter 13 and the first half of this chapter. First, according to Figure 14.10, how much is the monopolist's price and output?

27

$$\text{Total profit} = \text{Total revenue} - \text{Total cost}$$

$$\text{Total revenue} = \text{Price} \times \text{Output} = \$11.50 \times 3.5 = \$42.25$$

$$\text{Total cost} = \text{ATC} \times \text{Output} = \$8 \times 3.5 = \$28$$

$$\text{Total profit} = -\text{Total revenue } (\$42.25) - \text{Total cost } (\$28) = \$14.25$$

Table 14.1.

Price	Demanded	Total Revenue	Marginal Revenue
$14	1		
13	2		
12	3		
11	4		
10	5		
9	6		

Table 14.2.

Price	Demanded	Total Revenue	Marginal Revenue
$14	1	$14	$14
13	2	26	12
12	3	39	10
11	4	44	8
10	5	50	6
9	6	54	4

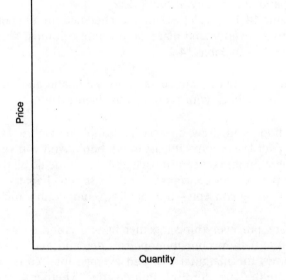

Figure 14.8

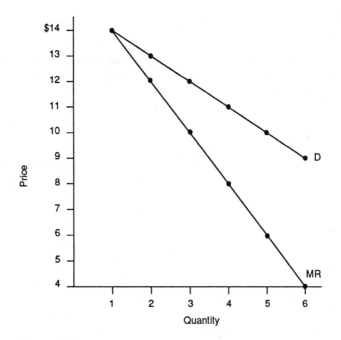

Figure 14.9

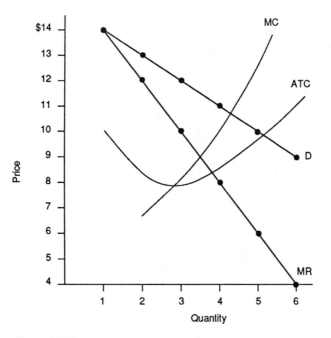

Figure 14.10

If you got this right, go on to frame 30; otherwise, go to frame 28.

28

Figure 14.11 provides us with some more detail from Figure 14.10. Answer this question first: At what output does MC equal MR? The answer is 3.5. This is very important because it sets up our answers for price and ATC.

From which curve on Figure 14.11 do we read price? And how much is it?

Price is always read from the demand curve. How much is price? At an output of 3.5 it is 11.5. How do we know this?

Two ways. First by just looking at the graph we can see that an output of 3.5, the price, read from the demand curve is 11.5. Besides, the line draw from the demand curve to the price axis tells us this.

A second way of determining price is by noting that an output of 3.5 is halfway between prices of $12 and $11 on the demand curve. Since the demand curve is a straight line, the price at the midpoint between $12 and $11 would have to be $11.50.

ATC is read from which curve? The ATC curve, of course. And at what output? At 3.5. How much is ATC at an output of 3.5? It's $8.

Let's try another problem using the same demand and marginal revenue curves, but with a different set of MC and ATC curves. Using the data from Figure 14.12, calculate total profit. Remember to find output first, then price and ATC.

29

$$\text{Total profit} = \text{Total revenue} - \text{Total cost}$$

$$\text{Total revenue} = \text{Price} \times \text{Output} = \$10.50 \times 4.5 = \$47.50$$

$$\text{Total cost} = \text{ATC} \times \text{Output} = \$9 \times 4.5 = 40.50$$

$$\text{Total profit} = \text{Total revenue}(\$47.50) - \text{Total cost}(\$40.50) = \$7.00$$

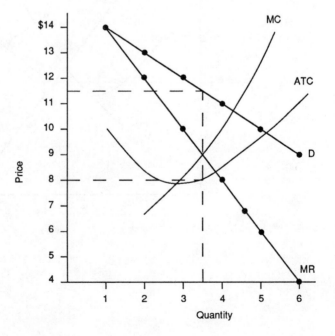

Figure 14.11

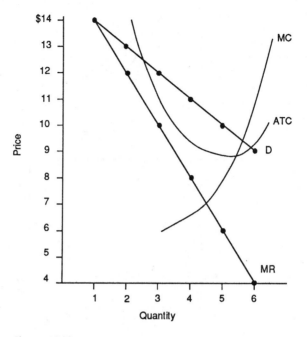

Figure 14.12

30 | THE MONOPOLIST'S EFFICIENCY

As I said in frame 16, the perfect competitor is forced to operate at peak efficiency. We can see this in Figure 14.5, where we have a perfect competitor producing at the break-even point, which is the minimum point on the firm's ATC curve.

If the monopoly shown in Figure 14.13 produces at the minimum point of its ATC curve, what would its output be?

31 |

Its output would be 5.3 or so. Clearly, then, the monopolist, unlike the perfect competitor in the long run, operates at lower efficiency.

But as I noted in frame 20, the government sometimes grants one firm exclusive rights to sell its product within its jurisdiction. This is often done in order to reduce the price paid by the consumer. Examples of this practice are the franchises granted to public utilities such as local phone, water, gas, and electric companies. So, we would best suspend judgment with respect to a monopoly's economic efficiency.

32 | ARE MONOPOLIES ALWAYS LARGE?

Obviously, the answer must be no, or we never would have raised the question. Did you realize that even you could easily form a monopoly? And you wouldn't need to be all that large. For example, you could set up the only pie-throwing service in your town. That's right. You could hire yourself out to throw coconut custard or lemon meringue pies at the faces of the enemies of those who pay you for your services.

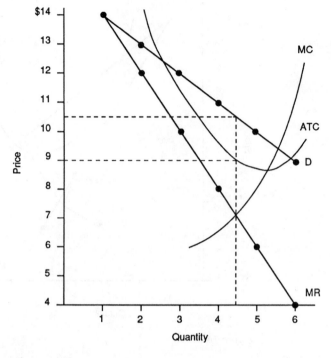

Figure 14.13

Another monopoly that might be feasible would be a dog psychotherapy clinic. Dogs, like other household pets, not to mention humans, have personality problems, neuroses, and other mental disorders, and they would do well to avail themselves of the services your clinic would provide. As your business expanded, you could branch out by providing psychotherapy to cats, rabbits, birds, goldfish, and other pets.

Although monopolies can be large or small, very few business firms in the United States would fall into this category. Those firms that seem to be monopolies are, in most instances, oligopolies. An oligopoly is an industry with a few firms rather than just one. The largest firms in the United States—Exxon, General Motors, Mobil Oil, and Ford—are oligopolies. Monopolies are generally local, like the public utilities firms.

We have now covered the two extremes on the economic spectrum—perfect competition and monopoly. In Chapter 15 we'll discuss the two remaining types of competition and oligopoly.

Self-Test 2

1. A monopolist is the only supplier of a good or service for which there are no _____ .

2. Who decides if one product may be substituted for another?

3. What are the three bases for monopoly?

4. What are some of the economies of becoming established?

5. Given the information in Figure 14.14, what are the monopolist's profits?

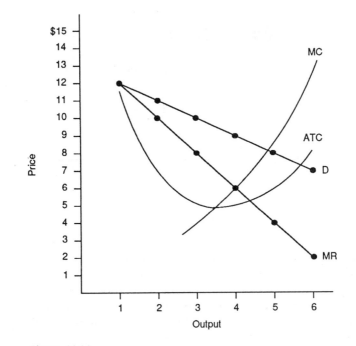

Figure 14.14

6. Using the data from Figure 14.14, how much would the perfect competitor's output be in the long run? Does this monopolist produce at peak efficiency?

7. Which statement is true?
   A. All large firms are monopolies.
   B. All monopolies are large.
   C. The largest firms in the United States are generally not monopolies.
   D. The only reason monopolies exist is because there are barriers to entry into monopolized industries.

8. Which statement is true?
   A. The monopolist always produces at peak efficiency.
   B. The monopolist never produces at peak efficiency.
   C. Monopolies are inherently evil.
   D. Monopolies generally break even in the long run.

Answers to Self-Test 2

1. Close substitutes.

2. The buyers.

3. (1) Control of an essential resource, (2) a government franchise, and (3) getting there first.

4. Network of suppliers, retail outlets, access to capital, and brand name familiarity.

5. Total profit = Total revenue − Total cost
   Total revenue = Price × Output = $9 × 4 = $36
   Total cost = ATC × Output = $5 × 4 = $20
   Total profit = Total revenue ($36) − Total cost ($20) = $16

6. 3.5; no.

7. C.

8. B.

CHAPTER 15

Monopolistic Competition

and

Oligopoly

Welcome to the "real world" of competition. In this real world nearly all business firms are either oligopolies or monopolistic competitors. A few thousand oligopolists produce most of the goods and services in the United States. But over 99 percent of all firms are monopolistic competitors. In short, our big firms are oligolopolists and our smaller firms are monopolistic competitors. After you have completed this chapter you will:

- Know the main characteristics of monopolistic competition.
- Understand why product differentiation is so important to the quality of our lives.
- Be able to distinguish between monopolistic competition in the short run and the long run.
- Be able to calculate concentration ratios.
- Understand how oligopolies range from cartels to cutthroat competitors.

1 | MONOPOLISTIC COMPETITION DEFINED

A monopolistically competitive industry is one in which many sellers produce differentiated products and to which there is free entry into the industry.

How, then, does monopolistic competition differ from perfect competition? Only in one respect: product differentiation.

In Chapter 14, frame 3, we noted that in a perfectly competitive industry, the products of various companies are identical in the minds of the buyers. By contrast, under monopolistic competition, the buyers regard the products of various sellers as different from one another. How different? Different enough so that each buyer prefers one seller over the others in the market.

But monopolistic competition comes closer to perfect competition than do the two other forms of competition—monopoly and oligopoly. Why? Because there are many sellers in a monopolistically competitive market. How many? Enough so that no one seller in large enough to have any appreciable influence over the price of the product.

Typical monopolistic competitors are beauty parlors and barber shops, grocery stores, drug stores, restaurants and fast food emporiums, gas stations, dry cleaners and laundries, (small) accounting and law firms, doctors, dentists, electricians, plumbers, and all the other small businesses you'd see along any Main Street, U.S.A. And each has many competitors, and each produces a differentiated product.

2 | PRODUCT DIFFERENTIATION UNDER MONOPOLISTIC COMPETITION

The most crucial feature of monopolistic competition is product differentiation. Keep in mind that, as a monopolistic competitor, you must somehow convince the buyer that your product is in some way superior to those of your competitors. Even if there are no physical differences among the products in the market, you will have to work hard at creating the impression that there *are* differences and that your product is best.

Monopolistic competitors compete with one another on several levels. They may sell physically different products, or at least create the *illusion* of physical differences. But they may also compete on the basis of convenience, ambience, service, or even status.

What are you really buying when you go to a fancy restaurant? Surely not just a meal. Undoubtedly, you'll order something on a somewhat higher culinary plane than a Big Mac, a large fries, and a Coke, but is that meal worth $80? It is when it is served by a waiter with a phony French accent, there are flowers on your table, a nice linen table cloth, candlelight, soft music, a solicitous maitre d', and the restaurant is a restored seventeenth century carriage house.

Monopolistic competition with its attendant product differentiation may be viewed as wasteful and inefficient, and a case can easily be made that it is. Think of all the money spent on advertising, packaging, marketing, sales promotion, fancy interiors, elaborate facades, and window displays. All of these expenses add maybe 10 or 20 percent to the prices of most of the things we buy. So, we may well ask: It is worth it?

You decide.

Now I'll bet you're saying to yourself; there he goes again, copping out and passing the buck. And you're right. You see, the buck stops with you because it's *your* buck and it's *your* decision how to spend it.

Do you want to spend it on advertising, ambience, service, and convenience, or are you basically a no-frills person? Do you buy no-frills products in the supermarket, fly coach rather than first class, drive an economy car, and consider a dinner in a fast food emporium "eating out"? If you have answered yes to each of these questions, then you are indeed a "no-frills" person who knows the value of a dollar.

On the other hand, if you answered no to all of the above, you are clearly a person of refined taste, high style, and very au courant (that's French for "up to date"). Whether we like it or not, product differentiation is the way monopolistic competitors compete. And whether we're aware of it or not, our entire environment is flavored by product differentiation. Imagine, for instance, walking along a commercial street in December and seeing every window stocked with no-frills products—Christmas in black and white boxes, jars, and cans.

Imagine what our supermarkets would look like in black and white. And imagine what people would look like if they all wore the same styles and colors. In a word, product differentiation adds flavor, texture, and variety to our lives. But whether you want to pay the price is a matter of individual taste.

3 THE GRAPHS OF THE MONOPOLISTIC COMPETITOR

Don't worry, I'm not going back on my word. I won't make you draw more graphs or even do more calculations. I just want to make a couple of observations.

Figure 15.1 shows the graph of a monopolistic competitor in the short run. Why the short run? (That's a two-part question.)

4   The firm depicted in Figure 15.1 is making a profit, so it must be in the short run. Here our analysis is identical to that of perfect competition. What happens in the long run? New firms, attracted by the profits, enter the industry. This increases industry supply and pushes prices down so that profits are squeezed down to zero. If this doesn't sound familiar, you would do well to reread frames 7 to 15 of Chapter 14.

Now take a look at Figure 15.2. Is the firm making a profit, breaking even, or taking a loss? Is it in the short run or the long run?

5   The firm depicted in Figure 15.2 is taking a loss, and it is in the short run. How do we know this? Because in the long run, no firm would stay in business if it was losing money.

What happens in the long run? In the long run enough firms leave the industry so that supply falls sufficiently to raise price to the degree that the remaining firms break even.

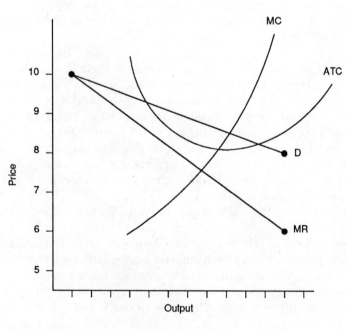

Figure 15.1

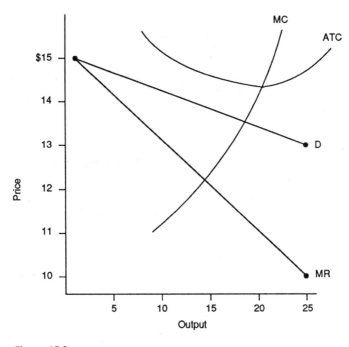

Figure 15.2

Just two more questions. Does Figure 15.3 represent a monopolistic competitor in the short run or the long run? Is the firm making a profit, taking a loss, or just breaking even?

6   Figure 15.3 shows a monopolistic competitor in the long run, and this firm is just breaking even. How do we know it's the long run? It *could* be the short run, but it would be extremely unlikely that a firm would exactly break even in the short run. Theoretically, if it made a dollar of profits, it would be making a profit, while if it took a loss of one dollar, it would be losing money. There are an infinite number of possible profits and losses: $2, $3, $1000, $4,000,000, and so on. Just breaking even, however, is a purely *mathematical* possibility, and the chances of its happening are infinitesimal.

How do we know this firm is just breaking even? Look again at the graph in Figure 15.3. Notice the dotted lines. Look first at the vertical dotted line crossing through the intersection of the MC and MR curves. This line rises to the point where the demand curve is tangent to the ATC curve. Then we have a horizontal line going across to the price axis, indicating the price. Notice also that at that output, price is equal to ATC. In other words, the firm is just breaking even.

7   You've probably noticed that the demand and marginal revenue curves of the monopolistic competitor bear a striking resemblance to those of the monopolist. This is no coincidence. The monopolistic competitor *does* have a partial monopoly—a very partial one—in that the firm's product is unique. No one has quite the same location, ambience, service, or perhaps even the same particular product.

Take, for example, Marcello's Pizza. It's a class place. New Formica tables. Fast service. And Marcello delivers. Is his pizza any different from the pizza made

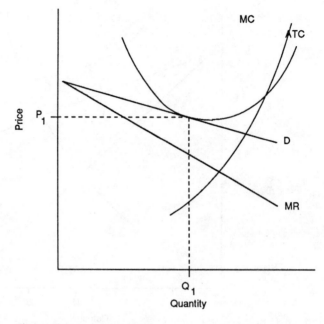

Figure 15.3

by the scores of other pizza parlors in the area? It *is*, according to Marcello. And what exactly *is* it that makes Marcello's pizza different from everybody else's? A secret ingredient. And what *is* that secret ingredient? "If I told you," said Marcello, "it wouldn't be a secret."

Self-Test 1

1. A monopolistically competitive industry has _____ firms producing a _____ product.

2. The most crucial feature of monopolistic competition is
   _____ .

3. How does the monopolistic competitor get the buyer to purchase his or her firm's product rather than that of rival firms?
   _____ .

4. In the short run the monopolistic competitor will:
   A. Definitely make a profit.
   B. Definitely take a loss.
   C. Definitely break even.
   D. Either take a loss or make a profit.

5. In the long run the monopolistic competitor will:
   A. Make a profit.
   B. Take a loss.
   C. Break even.

6. The demand curver of a monopolistic competitor is:
   A. Identical to that of the perfect competitor.
   B. Identical to that of the monopolist.
   C. Unlike either the perfect competitor's demand curve or the monopolist's demand curve.

Answers to Self-Test 1

1. Many; differentiated.
2. Product differentiation.
3. By advertising and by trying to provide better service and convenience, better ambience, and possibly a better product.
4. D.
5. C.
6. B.

8 | OLIGOPOLY DEFINED

An oligopoly is an industry with only a few firms. How few? So few that at least one is large enough to influence price.

In an oligopoly, is the product identical or differentiated? It doesn't matter. In the steel, copper, and aluminum industries, the product happens to be identical. But in most other cases, the product is differentiated.

The crucial factor under oligopoly is that there are only a few firms in the industry. Because there are so few firms, every competitor must think continually about the actions of rival firms, since what each does could make or break the business. So, there is a kind of mutual interdependence among oligopolists.

9 | CONCENTRATION RATIOS

One way we measure the degree of oligopolization is by means of concentration ratios. A concentration ratio gives us the percentage of output or sales that is accounted for by the four largest firms in an industry. For example, if the four largest firms produced, respectively, 10 percent, 8 percent, 7 percent, and 5 percent of the industry's output, how much would that industry's concentration ratio be?

10

It would be 30: 10 + 8 + 7 + 5 = 30
One of the hallmarks of oligopoly, then, is a high concentration ratio. How high is high? Eighty percent is pretty high. In Table 15.1, we have rounded up a few of the usual suspects.

11

Have you noticed that we haven't done any graphs since we left monopolistic competition? Figure 15.4 is simply a diagram. It doesn't qualify as a graph because it has only one line and no numbers.

The oligopoly section has no graphs because there are so many types of oligopoly that we couldn't possibly draw graphs for all of them. Just for starters,

Table 15.1. American Manufacturing
Industries with Concentration Ratios
of over 80*

Industry
Motor vehicles
Chewing gum
Electric light bulbs
Cigarettes
Typewriters
Photocopiers
Copper
Detergents
Sewing machines

*This is only domestic production; imports
are excluded

there are cutthroat oligopolists, cooperating oligopolists, competing oligopolists, and even duopolists (a term that some people think was derived from the 1950s rock 'n' roll style known as doo-ops). A duopoly is an industry composed of only two firms.

Now let's look at Figure 15.4. At the left end of the oligopoly spectrum is the cartel, which is a formal association of oligopolists (which is illegal in the United States). A good example, on an international basis, is OPEC—the Organization of Petroleum Exporting Countries. Anchored by the world's leading oil producer, Saudi Arabia, OPEC is made up of most of the world's leading oil exporters, including Iran, Iraq, Libya, Kuwait, and Nigeria.

At the opposite end of the oligopoly spectrum we have the cutthroat competitor—the firm that will stop at nothing to beat out its rivals. Industrial espionage and sabotage, underselling, disparaging of rival products, and other normally questionable competitive practices are the trademarks of such firms.

Near the middle of the oligopoly scale are the mildly competing oligopolies and the occasionally cooperating oligopolists. Sometimes their leaders are called corporate statesmen.

Where on this spectrum is U.S. industry? Where do we place the industries listed in Table 15.1? Near the middle? Toward the cutthroat end of the spectrum? Or toward the cartel end?

The answer is that there *is* no answer. You won't pin *me* down on that one. There are two reasons why there is no answer to this question. First, U.S. industry is not located in any one place because different industries are competitive to different degrees. Some oligopolized industries, in other words, are more competitive than others. So to say that *all* U.S. industries are located at any given point on the spectrum has got to be wrong. Second, there is very widespread disagreement as to the degree of competition in any given U.S. industry. Take banking, for example.

Cartels	Cooperation	Mild Competition	Cutthroat Competition

Figure 15.4

Suppose that we decide to judge the degree of competitiveness among banks by their newspaper ads. We would probably conclude that banking is a very competitive industry, wouldn't we? Now suppose, instead, that we base our judgment of the competitiveness of banks on the fact that when one or two major banks change their prime rate of interest (which is charged to major corporate borrowers), within a day or so, all the other major banks do the same thing. This time we would probably conclude that banking is a very cooperative industry.

Bankers, of course, would tell us that they're not oligopolists to begin with, and that, in any event, their concentration ratio is no more than about fifteen. However, there is no question that the twenty largest banks in the country do over one-third of all the banking business. Furthermore, just five banks have issued nearly three-quarters of all bank credit cards.

12 | A FINAL COMMENT

In Chapter 14 we noted that there were very few, if any, cases of perfect competition and that monopolies were not very numerous. While major segments of the U.S. economy are oligopolized—indeed, the oligopoly is the prevalent form of economic organization in U.S. manufacturing—most firms in the United States are monopolistic competitors.

Self-Test 2

1. An oligopoly is an industry with _____ .
2. What is the crucial factor under oligopoly?
3. Given the information below, what is the concentration ratio in this industry?

Firm	Percent of Industry Sales
A	10%
B	8
C	4
D	7
E	20
F	35
G	16

4. A high concentration ratio would be _____ percent.
5. What two things are wrong with this statement: U.S. oligopolies are located at the cutthroat competitive side of the oligopoly spectrum.
6. Most firms in the United States are:
   A. Perfect competitors.
   B. Monopolists.
   C. Oligopolists.
   D. Monopolistic competitors.

7. Ford Motor Company is a(n):
   A. Perfect competitor.
   B. Monopolist.
   C. Oligopolist
   D. Monopolistic competitor.

Answers to Self-Test 2

1. Few firms.

2. Fewness.

3. 10 + 20 + 35 + 16 = 81

4. About 80.

5. (1) All U.S. oligopolies cannot be located at one point on the spectrum; industries have varying degrees of competitiveness. (2) There is widespread disagreement about the degree of competitiveness of any oligopolized industry.

6. D.

7. C.

Index